Dietrich Fischer-Dieskau

Dietrich Fischer-Dieskau
A Biography

by Hans A. Neunzig

Translated and annotated by
Kenneth S. Whitton

Amadeus Press
Reinhard G. Pauly, General Editor
Portland, Oregon

ISBN 1-57467-035-2

Printed in Hong Kong

AMADEUS PRESS
The Haseltine Building
133 S.W. Second Avenue, Suite 450
Portland, Oregon 97204, U.S.A.

Library of Congress Cataloging-in-Publication Data

Neunzig, Hans A. (Hans Adolf), 1932–
  [Dietrich Fischer-Dieskau. English]
  Dietrich Fischer-Dieskau : a biography / by Hans A. Neunzig ;
translated and annotated by Kenneth S. Whitton.
     p. cm.
  Translation of: Dietrich Fischer-Dieskau : eine Biographie.
  Includes bibliographical references (p.), discography (p.),
and index.
  ISBN 1-57467-035-2
  1. Fischer-Dieskau, Dietrich, 1925– 2. Baritones (Singers)–
Germany–Biography.   I. Title.
ML420.F51N4813 1997
782.1'092–dc21
[B]   97-27573
                                                                              CIP
                                                                              MN

Contents

Translator's Foreword

In my book, *Dietrich Fischer-Dieskau: Mastersinger, A Documented Study* (London: Wolff, 1981), I wrote that "a definitive biography is, I trust, a task for a far distant day." After a career on concert platform and operatic stage stretching from his debut in Verdi's opera *Don Carlos* on 18 November 1948 to his decision to retire from singing after a concert performance on the stage of the Bavarian State Opera on 31 December 1992, Dietrich Fischer-Dieskau, at seventy-three still active as author, teacher, raconteur, painter, and orchestral conductor, deserves the biography that Hans A. Neunzig has written and which it has been my great pleasure to translate.

The book is indeed the "definitive biography" of this great German musician and provides a full and frank account of Fischer-Dieskau's rise to his undisputed position as the leading Lieder singer of his generation, and is supported by generous quotations from his private correspondence and from reviews of his art.

—Kenneth S. Whitton

The Singer

Background and Early Life

When did it all begin? The beginnings must, of course, lie far back beyond the birth of this one individual. Talent flows from known as well as from hidden sources, some near at hand, some far back in the past—here, they combine to produce one unique individual.

No sudden escape from a bourgeois way of life to an artistic one had to be made; no well-meant warnings about the uncertainties of the artistic profession stemmed the flow of events. Dietrich Fischer-Dieskau's spectacular career as a singer began with a surprising inevitability.

His father, who had studied Classics and was an educational reformer and headmaster of a Berlin secondary school, had more to do with this unhindered development than might have been suspected from his paternal role, especially since only twelve years were allotted to him to play that part before he died. He had gone through a similar transitional phase himself, but unsuccessfully, for when he told *his* father of his wish to become a musician, the father banned him from playing the harmonium and effectively forbade any further discussion of the "unprofitable art" becoming his future profession. In those circumstances, there was certainly no talk of violin lessons either, yet music became an integral part of his father's own work as a Protestant clergyman. The chorale, the very core of the Protestant church service, had so attracted him that he became one of the most distinguished hymnologists of his day. Concrete proofs of this attraction included a lexicon of church hymns and a doctorate from the Faculty of Theology of the University of Jena in Thuringia. It is therefore probable that the clergyman, who, as Fischer-Dieskau's father recalled, liked to gather his family round the harmonium in the evening to sing chorales, had definitely decided *his* answer to the old musicological question: *Prima la musica, pòi le parole, o prima le parole, pòi la musica?* (First the music, then the words, or first the words and then the music?) His answer: the words. One day, his grandson was to give a very different answer to the same question.[1]

The grandfather, a church superintendent, is said to have been very musical, as was not infrequently the case among whole generations in Protestant clergymen's families, particularly in Saxony and Thuringia in the east of Germany, where the Fischer family originated. Their forebears were noted as peasant farmers from the middle of the sixteenth century in the village of Etzdorf, although a much more distinguished ancestry could be claimed by the Fischers who were soon to form a chain of Protestant clergymen. Albert Fischer (-Dieskau), the singer's father, discovered a sheet of paper among the possessions of his great-grandfather, who had been a church superintendent in Ziesar near Magdeburg from 1749 to 1824, and he revealed its contents in a hand-written family history:

> Fischer, an ennobled family from Bavaria: this family received in the year 1164 an escutcheon and the patent of nobility. Jakob Eduard Fischer was raised to the Silesian nobility with the epithet of von Seidlitz.

This same ancestor wrote several "freedom songs" in essence not far removed from the enthusiasm and the anger of the German Romantic movement of the early nineteenth century; for example, the opening lines of a poem entitled "Napoleon's Monument":

> First of all, you must build a fine mausoleum from the 100,000 skulls of the patriotic noblemen whom he strangled.

The patriotic feelings, rather than the literary effusions of his ancestor, are of more importance for Fischer-Dieskau's family history, for these continued to influence his early life.

The Protestant manse, as the germ cell of future cultural development, is a very German phenomenon, and it preserved a natural sense of patriotism that had its origins in the Wars of Liberation, which ended in Napoleon's defeat at the Battle of the Nations near Leipzig in 1813. To be German took on a powerful yet rather limited meaning. Little Germany—always to be preferred, of course, to the later, perverted Greater Germany of the Nazis—also had its source in Protestantism, which by its very origins seemed provincial beside the internationalism of Rome. That infamous "German soul," which eventually would have needed rehabilitation anyway, even had not too much been asked of it, experienced an exuberant overvaluation, without having had first to prove itself.

In retrospect, one could say that the marriage of Superintendent Albert Fischer to Emma von Dieskau in 1860 added a patriotic, Prussian element to the family history, and a photograph of the young wife does show an extraordinary likeness to her grandson, Dietrich. Today's most famous bearer of the name Dieskau can see his famous ancestor on the monument to Frederick of Prussia (Frederick the Great) in Berlin. Fischer-Dieskau wrote:

> I could never pass it without looking for my ancestor, Artillery General von Dieskau, who can be seen among the other soldiers. I presume that he is there because he helped his royal friend win his

battles with his ballistic inventions. As a token of his thanks, the king, bare-headed, followed his coffin into the old Garrison Church. The light cannon that my ancestor had had constructed were known as "Dieskausche."[2]

None of the Prussian general's warlike spirit seems to have been inherited by his descendant; as for the indisputably aristocratic inheritance, one would think rather of the "aristocracy of the mind." What the singer likes about the figure on the monument is probably the proximity to the great king, rather than his rank.

The Dieskaus are an old family and are mentioned as the oldest family in a book on the Saale district in the sixteenth century. One of the first documentarily testified von Dieskaus, a Friedrich, took part in a tournament in Brunswick in 996 A.D. To be able to participate, he had to prove four generations of "noble blood."[3]

The Dieskaus, like the Fischers, hail from Thuringia in east Germany. Their coat of arms depicts a silver swan ready for flight—and in this context, can one help adding, "like Lohengrin"? It is a bird that the Dieskaus in the Saale district still keep in their seal. The name Dieskau comes from the Wendish dialect; *Dis* in Wendish means *yew tree*, so Dieskau means *a property under yew trees*. A few yews still stand in the park of Castle Dieskau, a Renaissance building in the style of a country house.

One other place occupied by a succession of Dieskaus as "lords of the manor" from 1372 to the middle of the seventeenth century must be mentioned: Burg Giebichenstein near Halle. The present descendant of the Dieskaus came across this castle again as an author when writing the history of the musician Johann Friedrich Reichardt (1752–1814).[4] Reichardt chose Giebichenstein as his home, where, a composer of Lieder himself, he entertained the celebrated German poet Johann Wolfgang von Goethe (1749–1832) and the young poets of Germany's Romantic movement. Thus, another thread connects Fischer-Dieskau with Giebichenstein.

The last Dieskau at the family castle was the Royal Prussian Councilor and Court Chamberlain Karl von Dieskau, who died childless in 1744. Like other families, the Dieskaus, too, found themselves at the mercy of the winds of change. They went to live all over the world. Of those who remained in Germany, Emma von Dieskau (1835–1908), daughter of the Royal Prussian Colonel of Gendarmerie, August von Dieskau, married Superintendent Dr. Albert Fischer, and thus the Fischers were joined to the Dieskaus. Emma Fischer (von Dieskau) had nine children: five sons and four daughters. All five sons found their professions in the same stratum of bourgeois society as their parents: as a clergyman, a doctor, an officer, and two teachers—one of them rather special, and not just because he was Dietrich Fischer-Dieskau's father. Two of the daughters married: one, following family tradition, married a clergyman, and the other, a merchant. Two remained unmarried, of whom only one took a job; this daughter, the youngest, worked in the German Sanitarium in Davos in Switzerland. Thus, we have a family picture of an almost model, educated bourgeois family of the second half of the nineteenth century. It was a bourgeoisie that believed its world to be secure because of its standing and position in society and because of its culture, in whose civilizing influence all had confidence.

Albert Fischer (1865–1937), a musician *manqué*, took his substitute profession of teaching to heart, but music remained his great passion. Like most great passions, it brought him both joy and sadness. The joy of many happy hours improvising on the piano, so many hopeful hours of composing music, were undermined by the secret knowledge that his talents scarcely reached the level of a praiseworthy dilettantism. Nevertheless, there were performances of his compositions. In November 1917, and again in June 1918, his *volkstümliches Musikstück* (popular piece of music) bearing the title *1914* was produced in the Berlin suburbs of Zehlendorf and Friedenau. "Intending to influence the mood of the moment, I wrote and composed the music for a musical play *1914*," he wrote in a summary of the family history.[5] The Berlin press gave the nationalistic text and its music a friendly reception.

> In the details, as well as in the whole conception, it was far superior to the normal combination of pretty little individual touches and familiar melodies such as we are accustomed to hearing in such occasional works. On the contrary, here is a musical ability of remarkable individuality and creative originality, whose sure and steady development we followed most willingly. The celebrated orchestra of Berlin's Orchestral Union, conducted by Herr Grünberg, had been engaged and had found itself a most worthwhile task.[6]

According to the composer, the work was meant to reawaken the patriotic sentiments of 1914, but in a joyful rather than a heroic form of presentation. This was understood by one of the reviewers:

> The charming arrangement of the scenes, three from the days of mobilization and a celebration of the Victory of Tannenberg [the 1914 victory over the Russians], is very pleasing because of a sequence of lively, tuneful, and well-instrumented marches, dances, choruses, and solo items, which all have the great benefit of tasteful popularity. In particular, a new version of "Heil dir im Siegerkranz" (All Hail to You with the Victor's Laurels) and a

catchy Hindenburg March with a witty text, both of these for chorus and orchestra, promise to enjoy an enduring popularity.

At that time, 1917, Albert Fischer might have realized that his work had a "keep your chin up" character (a rather odious description nowadays). In 1918, he displayed his sense of realism by announcing at the last of his "Communal War Evenings" the certainty of a coming military defeat, which earned him the reproof of being an incorrigible pessimist—and this just three weeks before the end of World War I!

Later, however, it was not feelings of patriotism that made Albert Fischer go on composing but the sheer joy in the work—and he wanted success, too. Thus, in the 1920s he wrote a Singspiel cautiously subtitled *A Musical Idyll* after the main title *Sesenheim* [a depiction of the love affair between Germany's greatest poet, Johann Wolfgang von Goethe, and young Friederike Brion (1752–1813) in Sesenheim near Strasbourg from 1770 to 1771]. The work was premiered in Berlin's Wallner Theater in September 1927 and received a good deal of praise. One critic wrote: "The musical joys that Albert Fischer has produced here cannot be expressed in words—one must experience them with heart and ears." There was talk of "a symphony of Sunday tranquillity, of the scent of flowers, of the song of birds, of moon- and sunshine." The work had fifteen performances but then disappeared from the repertoire: "A month after my *Sesenheim*, Franz Lehár produced his *Friederike* [on the same theme] to enormous publicity, and conquered the world with it."

Albert Fischer did not give up his work on his opera, however; he just resigned himself that there would be no more public performances of it. He continued to try to improve it for the rest of his life, as his youngest son Dietrich well remembers. It was with some pleasure, too, and not a little melancholy, that the son heard his friend Sviatoslav Richter call his father's "rival," Lehár, "a really great composer."

Albert Fischer's enthusiasm for music also had its effect on his professional work as a school teacher and later as a headmaster who not only wrote about a cultured upbringing or on "The Principle of Artistic Appreciation in Education" but who actually introduced a concert season in his Zehlendorf secondary school:

> From 1906 on, I presented four subscription concerts every winter in the main hall of the school. We had first-class artists (Richard Strauss, Hugo Rüdel, Fritz Kreisler, Ernö Dohnányi, and the most famous singers of the day). The hall was always filled, and, after the concerts, the artists used to be our guests, often a very large gathering indeed. But the Great War forced me to give up these concerts.

Albert Fischer had got on well, and that was also reflected in the respect that he enjoyed from his social peers—enjoyed in both senses of the word. His view of life corresponded to that of the ruling classes, yet it is clear from a study of his biography that he never succumbed to a facile opportunism. He was a reformer in educational matters, one who looked far ahead and was therefore subject to the criticism of reactionaries. In his book on the old secondary school and the new age, one can read his views (perhaps not liberal, but certainly devoid of dogma) on a pedagogy that included, above all, a cultural element—and this in a book published in 1900.[7] In that, the former classical scholar Albert Fischer shows himself as an independent and original-minded participant in the much-debated subject of school reform. He demanded a "fruitful educational system that would warm hearts and minds"; his vision was one of a cultural education, which in his eyes and "in the broadest sense" was "the prerequisite for a superior education for heart and mind." Who would not agree with him, when he added ironically: "In no art form have we achieved so much as in school-teaching," or, when, very topically, he set "imagination" against "materialism"? The classical scholar's candor was also surprising, as when he opposed Greek as a compulsory subject because it did not help pupils in later life. The fresh air of life is missing in our schools, he claimed, and he opposed a secondary school that was not really "humanistic" but "grammatical."

How was this humanism to be put into practice?

Germany could not stay anchored in the "philosophical climate of earlier centuries." Christianity, whose teachings the author accepted "with all my heart," was to a great extent, however, "borrowing" rather than "living." Life—and this was the essential point—was to be found in the German nation itself. "What can enthuse us, what can enthuse our young people above all, is the German character, life in and for our German nation." So, there it is: the German nation and its character in its unsullied state, as it were. From today's standpoint, this naive expression of a patriotism that could slip so easily over into nationalism is hard to stomach. "The author must declare himself guilty of one prejudice: his love of all things German."

Here we have, no more and no less, the feelings, more accurately, the elation of the great majority of the educated and, one must add, the well-off German bourgeoisie. So it went on, through the Great War, surviving the catastrophe of 1918—a little less secure, it is true, yet still in the belief that the old ideals could not have been false gods.

The Weimar Republic (1919–1933) gave opportunities to few. When the prophets of a false Germanness appeared in 1933, most of the nation did not recognize their true enemy. Alas, the dam of humanistic ideals did not

The father, Albert Fischer-Dieskau. This picture, painted in 1930, hung for years in the staff room of "his" school, after the founder and first headmaster of the Zehlendorf secondary school had retired.

hold; it proved to be porous and thus ready to be swamped by the forces of inhumanity.

This familiar prehistory has relevance, of course, for an artist of our own times who has to find his own answer to the intellectual challenge it poses. Albert Fischer, a man of truly good intentions and of a goodness of heart confirmed by his pupils, colleagues, and particularly by his own family, seems to have had little or nothing to do with these developments, yet he is nevertheless a good example of a prejudice—as he calls it himself, albeit with pride— that can also, alas, make one blind. He soon gave up the one political-party activity of his life. He was not made for it.

Soon after 1918, I worked for the foundation of a nationalist-oriented party. I was elected to the committee, which was preparing the agenda, and then I founded Der deutsch-nationale Lehrerbund (the German-National League of Teachers), and was then elected to the committee of the newly founded deutsch-nationale Volkspartei (German-National People's Party). But party political life was not for me, and so I soon left it again.

Here again, a recurrent pattern: The best, or more accurately perhaps, the most sensitive people prefer to refuse to take on the daily political grind. Today's question is also yesterday's: Who is left to do it? Albert Fischer, who with his pedagogic zeal marked by tolerance and cultural *engagement*, could have given such a positive impulse to the formation of the political landscape in Germany, remained faithful to his customary, seemingly unpolitical, work in the service of the common weal.

It had indeed been no small achievement to extend the Zehlendorf school, with its original three elementary classes and a middle school, to a fully fledged secondary school. In addition to the cultural activities, such as the concerts already mentioned, were sporting activities: a rowing and tennis club, Die Zehlendorfer Wespen (The Zehlendorf Wasps), and other sports facilities for his pupils. He would not have been able to interest his youngest son Dietrich in sport, however, even had he tried. Instead, Dietrich profited from the erection of a theater, the Theater der Jugend (Theater for the Young), which gave the young boy his first theatrical experiences. The performances seen by the young Fischer-Dieskau deeply impressed him and fired his imagination and his already strongly developed flair for imitation. Theater in those days meant the old-fashioned theater of make-believe. In *Wilhelm Tell* (1804) by Friedrich Schiller (1759–1805), the actor Heinrich George appeared on stage on a horse; young Dietrich felt sorry for the poor horse groaning under George's considerable weight. Eugen Klöpfer, playing Tell, struck terror into the young audience with his fearsome, "You know who the bowman is, look not for another" [as he shoots the tyrant Gessler dead with his crossbow]. George as Gessler fell from his horse and had to be half-carried off stage by the other actors.

Heinrich George, first as an actor under the direction of Jürgen Fehling, Erwin Piscator, and Leopold Jessner, then from 1936 as director of the Schiller Theater, was among the most important figures in Berlin's theatrical life. In the role of Götz von Berlichingen in Goethe's 1773 play of that name or as the Mayor of Zalamea in the translation of Calderon's play, he remained unforgettable to Fischer-Dieskau, not least for his breath control, which enabled him to speak long phrases like no other actor. Apart from George and Klöpfer, there were Paul Wegener (who played Beethoven in a contemporary piece, *The Tenth Symphony*) and the young stars Horst Caspar and Will Quadflieg, who were still playing after World War II but who were representatives of a vocal culture that has either disappeared or been denounced. Nor was opera forgotten in the afternoon programs for the young people of Berlin. Fischer-Dieskau saw, as Lohengrin, a singer with whom he was one day to share the stage of Berlin's Städtische Oper: Ludwig Suthaus, who played Don Carlos when Fischer-Dieskau made his debut as Rodrigo, Marquis of Posa in Verdi's opera on 18 November 1948.

The initiative behind this cultural education of the young—available only to pupils of the secondary schools, it is true—was none other than Albert Fischer, along with a few other like-minded teachers. His energy and drive were part and parcel of that inner sense of absolute security. Edith Schmidt (*née* Fischer), later a close confidante of her cousin Dietrich, who was younger by some years, was certainly right when she wrote to him: "Your father lived in a wonderful world; he represented a generation that still had so much strength, which we of 1914 no longer possessed." There follows a passage that throws a revealing light on the son, so much more insecure because of the times and his own cast of mind: "for, in addition, as a real Fischer, he kept his own private life inside him, into which not even those closest to him could ever enter." Thus, Fischer-Dieskau's energy and his tendency to introversion are part of his parental inheritance. How much the singer has drawn on both traits is marked, for taciturnity can also indicate a wish to be private, something that was first noticeable in his singing, in music-making generally, then later in his painting and his writings. His father had also tried to be an author and a composer—nothing at all like the old-fashioned, hectoring headmaster. In public meetings he spoke in a quiet but determined voice, thus avoiding any impression of histrionics but also making himself very difficult to understand. His son wrote later:

> I can still see him, the lectern deliberately placed to his left, stand-
> ing beside it as he spoke so informally, only leaning on the edge now
> and then. Then he used to pull a bunch of keys out of his pocket and
> play silently with them, as he considered what to say.[8]

At that time, his father had already retired and was visiting his old school for a graduation. How often he had stood on that platform welcoming important visitors! Fischer-Dieskau remembers vividly the visit of the Hohenzollern Prince Eitel-Friedrich, son of Emperor William II, who never deigned to turn to the headmaster as the latter introduced him. So the headmaster had to move in front of the distinguished guests and address them with his back to the auditorium. He then spoke in his usual quiet voice—and no one in the huge hall understood a word. He was not one to raise his voice.

In 1917, during World War I, the father's first wife, Elisabeth (Elli) Puder (1874–1917) had died; she had been a doctor's daughter from Ziesar. Following her husband's precepts, she had founded the Kaiser-Wilhelm-Spende deutscher Frauen (the Emperor William Fund of German Women) in 1915, and had collected four and one-half million marks for war welfare. Albert Fischer himself took on war work for the Red Cross, which he continued until 1919. That was also the year in which he met his second wife Theodora (Dora) Klingelhöffer (1884–1966), at that time a teacher in the girls' secondary school in Mariendorf in Berlin. The young wife, twenty years younger than her husband, came into a house that had been built to his own design as the headmaster's house, with a connecting corridor to the school, and here the three children of his second marriage were born. The house, unfortunately, is gone, but the school building still stands, and its towers, which rather frightened the children, give some idea of how splendid the house must have looked.

An upper middle-class family, the Klingelhöffers hailed from the south of the state of Hesse. There were clergymen among their ancestors as well, for their family crest on Pastor Klingelhöffer's gravestone at the church at Michelbach shows two crossed alms bags with bells on long poles. The next generation replaced the alms bags with a single bell. But there were other instruments, apart from these alms-bags' bells, in the Klingelhöffer's house. Young Fischer-Dieskau was delighted when he came across the name Klingelhöffer in one of the novels of Friedrich Gerstäcker (1816–1872). What a chance for him to identify and fantasize!

Fischer-Dieskau's maternal grandfather, a municipal architect, married a pianist and was an enthusiastic amateur singer. (In the Brandenburg district, one can still see yellow-brick barracks and office buildings as examples of his work.) One of the Klingelhöffer family composed the Christmas carol "Kling, Glöckchen, klingelingeling" (Ring Little Bells, Ringalingaling) as a joking play on the family name. Dora (Klingelhöffer) Fischer-Dieskau played the piano well into her old age and loved to sing, even though she did not have a particularly powerful voice. Thus, musicality is found in all of the singer's ancestors, although one could not speak of "one of those old, inbred, highly talented families," which, according to the German author Gottfried Benn (1886–1956), "is one of the most common requisites for the creation of genius."[9] There must be other prerequisites, and Fischer-Dieskau's ironic remark, "So, I'm rather the result of suppressed complexes," may not be so far off the mark.[10]

Nevertheless, it is remarkable and worthy of mention that two outstanding musical talents had arisen in the same generation. Fischer-Dieskau's older brother Klaus, born in 1921, displayed considerable musical talent

The mother, Dora Fischer-Dieskau (née Klingelhöffer).

early on, composing a piano concerto when he was eighteen. At the end of the 1940s and the beginning of the 1950s, the younger brother, upon returning from POW camp, sang many of Klaus's compositions. In a letter to her parents on 15 December 1949, the cellist Irmgard Fischer-Dieskau (*née* Poppen), then recently married to the singer, quoted a few sentences from the review of a church concert:

This baritone's intense presentation and his rapidly growing artistry, along with the expressive and technically accomplished cello playing of the very talented Irmgard Poppen, gained the new work warm applause.

She added, "These were Klaus's Lieder."

When in 1989 Klaus Fischer-Dieskau took leave of the Hugo Distler choir, which he had founded and had directed for decades, the Berlin *Tagesspiegel* wrote of "a piece of Berlin church music history." At the farewell concert, they performed the *Loblied in musicam* (Song in Praise of Music) for soprano and baritone solo, with which (according to the *Tagesspiegel*) "the choirmaster Klaus Fischer-Dieskau had, in 1951, first brought the composer Klaus Fischer-Dieskau to the attention of the public." It was the composer's first choral work.

What the father contributed to the development of his sons' talents was probably the general atmosphere that he created in the family home. Until his retirement in 1930, that home was the rather fine headmaster's house in Zehlendorf in southwest Berlin, a somewhat forbidding neo-Renaissance building with high gables; then came the apartment in the Holbeinstrasse, in the Lichterfelde district of Berlin, which, although roomy enough, had to accommodate the furniture of their former large house and is therefore remembered by the sons as rather crowded. The heavy dining-room furniture in the Old German style, all designed by the father himself, made it all seem rather gloomy.

At the end of the family history that Dr. Fischer compiled is a page on which the names Fischer and Dieskau finally come together. Above the signature, "Dr. Albert Ludwig Fischer-Dieskau, Geheimer Studienrat" (headmaster honored by the Government), it states:

> I am the founder of a new branch of the family, since I have brought the two families together by adding to our old family name Fischer that of my mother, von Dieskau. My taking this compound name was approved by the Prussian Minister of the Interior on 26 March 1934. Whoever in the future bears the name Fischer-Dieskau will certainly be a member of my family. May God's rich blessing rest on it for all time![11]

The Voice of an Angel

Dietrich Fischer-Dieskau was born on 28 May 1925. The events of the year of his birth contain the future history of Germany in a nutshell, albeit in retrospect. The first president of the German Reich, Friedrich Ebert, had died on 28 February. On 27 March, the NSDAP (The National Socialist German Workers' Party, i.e. the Nazi Party) was reconstituted in a Munich tavern, the Bürgerbräukeller, and on 26 April, Field Marshal Hindenburg was elected president of the Reich. On 14 June in Mannheim in south Germany, the art exhibition Neue Sachlichkeit (a new matter-of-factness) was opened, and, a little earlier, on 21 May, Ferruccio Busoni's last opera *Doktor Faust* had its premiere in Dresden. On 13 December, Berlin staged Alban Berg's opera *Wozzeck* for the first time.

Of course, similar dates from any other year could be assembled that point to future events, but rarely have there been so many that actually affected a future life. These events of 1925 were selected to cast a light on the world into which Fischer-Dieskau was born. The death knell of the Weimar Republic (1919–1933) had already been sounded.

Fischer-Dieskau already had two brothers from his father's second marriage when he was born in 1925, Klaus and Martin. Martin was born mentally and physically challenged. "I shared a room with Martin during all those years and grew up with his suffering," wrote the singer, remembering his childhood and early adolescence: "His disability betrayed his whole psyche by a look or a sigh, and his lack of mobility affected me, too."[1] How often was he wakened at night by his brother's epileptic fits, how often did he experience the alternating moods of silent lethargy and excitable recognition? His close relationship with his brother clearly had its effect, and the physical surroundings of this companionship were also anything but cheerful. Over the youngest boy's bed hung a huge reproduction of the painting of the *Entombment of Christ*; the parents seemed to be unaware of the effect that such paintings have on children. Despite all that, Fischer-Dieskau, looking back, thinks of his childhood as a happy one. His father was well-known in his profession as a mild and undoctrinaire teacher, and he had no time for indoctrination at home. The father found receptive ears in his son and a precocious sense of beauty, and that seemed to him to be of most importance. The son could be as poor a scholar as he wished, so long as he developed the correct feelings for beauty, truth, and goodness. And that he did.

Disagreements between father and son, which often seem to be *de rigueur* in families, did not happen here, and for two reasons: first, since the father was already sixty years old when the youngest son was born, the difference in years turned their relationship into more of a grandfather-grandson one; second, because the son was only twelve when the father died, there was little chance of friction between his ways and his father's. Did he miss his father later—either as a model or as a spur? It is sad to read a passage in the singer's memoirs in which, reminiscing about a childish love affair, he states that "this was one of the very few instances that I had a 'real conversation' with him."[2] Dora Fischer-Dieskau, like all mothers and housewives of that time, had her hands full looking after her husband and their three children, whom she "served," to put it bluntly. She was their companion in all their activities but never a partner in their quarrels. Thus, a vacuum arose and, strange though it may seem in the house of a well-known headmaster, a tangle of personal developments as well—all, of course, within that cultured musical ambience:

> To lie like a little animal under the grand piano, listening to those eerily near, loud notes coaxed out of it by my father, was my greatest joy. When I was four, I heard bits of *Lohengrin* on the radio (so my father told me later) and fell completely under the spell of this, my first experience of an excerpt from opera. For days afterwards, I ran around as if in a fever."[3]

The schoolboy sang, recited, and played for himself everything that he had heard or seen—and that was plenty, for his father had founded the Theater for Secondary Schools (later the Theater for the Young), which allowed his son to see really good productions of the German classics, one right after another.

Poetry also attracted him; he learned poems by heart and recited them so grandiloquently that he drove a maid out of the house. (They had maids in those days in retired headmasters' houses!) It is difficult to picture him reciting, in his high childish voice, Goethe's ballad "Prometheus," Friedrich Schiller's "Die Bürgschaft" (The Hostage), or Conrad Ferdinand Meyer's "Die Füsse im Feuer" (Feet in the Fire).

Then someone came along who was to take note of the spindly young lad's voice: Herr Tapper, his elementary school teacher. He took the mother aside and uttered the magic words: "Your son has got the voice of an angel."[4] Was it he who discovered the singer? He was most certainly the first to realize that what came from this voice was out of this world.

Fischer-Dieskau's primary school class with his teacher, Herr Tapper. The
singer, with his "Titus crop," is in the middle row on the extreme right.

When asked: "Did you discover him?" Ernst Rittel, in 1948 the first
recording producer in the studio of station RIAS, *Radio im amerikanischen
Sektor* (the radio station in the American sector of divided Berlin after the
war), where Fischer-Dieskau, straight from American POW camp in Italy,
broadcast his very first *Winterreise*, hit the nail on the head: "Whoever
heard him, discovered him immediately."[5] Nonetheless, Herr Tapper has the
honor of having been the first. He must have heard something that was quite
out of the ordinary, for most boys' voices sound like the voices of angels, or
at least what some people think sound like angels' voices.

There was no aura of the *Wunderkind* about the young singer, who, after
all, was not a singer yet, nor had he yet decided to become one. If he did
imagine a career in music, it was as a conductor—a dream that many young
(and some older!) children often have, one of those common masculine
fantasies that often go hand in hand with a desire for power. In this case,
however, it was later shown that this wish had little to do with a desire for
power—and everything to do with a desire to make music. As for the "voice
of an angel," the break in the voice had yet to come. The time after puberty,
when the vocal chords lengthen with the growth of the larynx, is remembered by Fischer-Dieskau in one pregnant, self-confident remark, strange in
a schoolboy otherwise inclined to self-doubt: "I sensed that my voice was now
beginning to produce a beautiful sound."[6]

By then he was sixteen, and had long since decided on a career as a singer, although other possibilities of self-expression also appeared attractive. Finding ways and means of expressing his artistic emotions and their innate spirituality was to remain the driving force for the rest of his life. Music had become his natural element. To immerse himself in this world of sound corresponded to his early love for poetry. His love of declaiming poems might well be seen as a love of speech-melody and its rhythmical components, to which his parents' love of music had opened the doors. The puppet theater, which the five-year-old had received as a present from a generous uncle, came with a recording of Carl Maria von Weber's opera *Der Freischütz* (1821) (The Free-shooter, i.e. one who fires magic bullets), and the décor for another opera was already set up on the stage: "What could have moved the good fairies to present me with Act II of Wagner's *Tannhäuser*, the Song Contest on the Wartburg?" asked Fischer-Dieskau in *Nachklang* (Resonance).[7] The wonderful invention of the little Reclam paperbacks allowed the "director" of the puppet theater to present countless productions of the classics, ranging from the eighteenth-century classicist Friedrich Schiller to Ernst von Wildenbruch (1845–1909). "I drew on almost every classical author to give me the great pleasure of declaiming the various characters in various voices,"[8] a remark very similar to that made in Goethe's autobiography, *Dichtung und Wahrheit* (Poetry and Truth): "It [the puppet theater] had a great effect on the young lad, which was to last for a very long time."[9] Yet not only the puppet theater, but the whole world around him became a stage for the growing boy. Looking back, it is strange to think of how the nine-year-old used the window blinds of their apartment as stage curtains — on the one hand regarding the street as the set, and on the other, regarding himself as both actor and impresario. He even thought of the passers-by as his "audience." The record was an audience of eighty in ten minutes!

There were moments in the life of the nine- to ten-year-old that had an electrifying effect but that only now seem significant; for example, when Herr Forck, his music teacher, let him stand on a chair and conduct a piece of music. Fischer-Dieskau vividly remembers the feeling that shot through him then — the feeling that he was creating music with his own hands.

His first attempt at conducting in public was in the garden of the radium baths at the Silesian spa, Bad Flinsberg, not far from the home of the German dramatist Gerhart Hauptmann (1862–1946) in Agnetendorf. Fischer-Dieskau's father was "taking the waters" there, and the eleven-year-old was very eager to enter the conducting competition that was open to guests. It ended in catastrophe for the young conductor, although no one else seemed to mind. Strauss's *Blue Danube* waltz did not seem to be too difficult.

> Stupidly, I didn't think that I needed the score and conducted "by heart," that is, as I liked to do! I didn't know that there is a very awkward rest in the music just near the end. I conducted straight through the silence—and the gaffe seemed huge to me.[10]

It was not just any old spa orchestra that day in Bad Flinsberg, but the orchestra of the Görlitz Municipal Theater, and the good-natured conductor who had refused to allow the lad in the sailor suit to conduct the "Freischütz" Overture was Walter Schartner.

Music from records (and for the 1930s there were already a remarkable number of these in the house), his games with the puppet theater and its silent figures for whom the theater-mad young man supplied all the voices, visits to the theater and the opera, wide and undirected reading from classical authors to sentimental plays and novels—all this was the life of a growing boy of unusual seriousness who had hardly any contact with children of his own age. Among his few close friends was one who went to the same elementary school. When they eventually were sent to different secondary schools, they kept in touch through mutual visits and games of cowboys and Indians in the garden of the house in Lichterfelde, where they were always a little afraid of the caretaker, Herr Kallert, who found their games a little too noisy; or they would read aloud to each other in friend "Hansi's" house (Hans Wolfgang Wunschel), and Dieter, who never came without a book under his arm, would, of course, organize that too. All sorts of plays were performed on invented topics and without much action, often in the cozy surroundings below the table with the light filtering through the ends of the tablecloth. Hans Wunschel, who later became one of Fischer-Dieskau's closest friends and is so again now, remembers that the future actor with a flair for producing always wanted the plays to have a tragic ending.

What did he look like, the ten- to twelve-year-old Dietrich Fischer-Dieskau? Tall and spindly like all the Fischer-Dieskaus, with a rather thoughtful, but not sad, childish expression and a rounded face, which became like his father's only in later years. The haircut that crowned this picture was the so-called "Titus crop," much loved by his mother, but which made him rather the laughing-stock of his classmates until a kindly teacher consoled him. Imaginative, with an inclination to self-doubt, he made himself a world of his own, a fantasy world of constructive dreaming that did produce quite definite results: a profound, if rather heterogeneous knowledge of literature and music that he would present to an audience of his closest friends—initially with the borrowed voice of the gramophone. It is not surprising if this private world clashed with the world outside. School was always a source of friction, an evil, the necessity of which became less and less obvious to the owner of a private, and much more important, world. Later, this neglect of his school work did worry him, but quite unnecessarily. Nor could he gain much from the practice he had in school for his own very particular talents. He blundered his way (as he describes it today) through his early piano lessons, something that horrifies him now when he looks back. Much more exciting were the experiments in painting by the father of his second piano teacher, Friedrich Seyer, which he was allowed to observe. It would not be going too far to suggest that there was a general interest here already, an unconscious identification with the creative process—a theme that was to accompany the singer's entire career. Yet his piano-playing, which he remembers as pretty terrible, cannot have been all that bad, for he did play in school concerts. He especially remembers playing Handel's Organ Concerto in B-flat Major, when his performance earned him the praise of his musical mathematics teacher—an achievement otherwise rarely gained in his least favorite school subject! It was as a schoolboy, too, that he first appeared in opera in Michael Haydn's *Der Bassgeiger zu Wörgl* (The Bass Fiddler in Wörgl), yet it was not anything musical that was so memorable about this performance: the young star remembers the fiddler's jump into the stream. The pupils had invented a genuine sound effect to imitate the water splashing: they let an open book fall on the floor. After many rehearsals, it sounded just like the real thing.

Fischer-Dieskau then began to play chamber music with a friend that he had made in his very first class in the secondary school. Max B. played the clarinet. The pair became inseparable and had endless conversations about life and the world but mostly, as befitted their age, about themselves. A certain discrepancy between their shared feelings of self-importance and superiority and external reality, where their own feelings became insignificant, mainly because of their inborn and acquired shyness, did not prejudice the next intellectual step forward:

> I agreed with this gentle friend Max, during our long conversations, that it was our task to strive for moral perfection. Each of us, in his own modest sphere, has the duty of discouraging vice by the example of virtue.[11]

Max and he took confirmation and dancing classes together. Visits to concerts in the Berlin Philharmonie concert hall and the State Opera—but also to Café Delphi and the jazz music that was soon to be forbidden—shaped their young minds. In 1939, Max B. was one of the war's first victims.

Fischer-Dieskau's father's death in 1937 took the twelve-year-old by surprise, so much so that he at first refused to accept the fact:

> At any moment, I expected to see him among the passers-by in the street. Whenever I saw a stocky man with a reddish face going past with little steps, my heart took a jump. I loved my father, but not until he died did I realize how strong that love was.[12]

Little was altered in the young schoolboy's daily life. The importance of his two worlds, fantasy and reality, remained constant. Did he become much more aware of his mother's role in the life of the small family to which, after all, his sick brother Martin still belonged? His mother felt Martin's sufferings more than anyone. Fischer-Dieskau's cousin Edith, in whom the young boy had complete confidence, called Dora Fischer-Dieskau a "Löwenmutter" (a lioness). It is much more difficult to form a picture of the mother than of the father, who acted and ruled, of course, like a patriarch, albeit a mild one. If the father was perhaps personified by his profession, the mother—also a teacher, for she still tutored—was not so characterized. As a housewife and mother, she almost disappears behind the husband's superior position in public and private life. In that way, the Fischer Dieskaus were a fairly perfect mirror-image of a German family of the educated middle-class—but only sociologically speaking, for the strong cultural ambiance, a certain *laissez-faire* in the internal running of their domestic life, made them the exception already described. One might say that there was a humus here in which a yet undetected talent was being nurtured.

Dora Fischer-Dieskau belonged to that group of women who uncomplainingly did what they were told was their duty, which they accepted. Hers was the life of most mothers. They try to understand their children throughout their lives—and so never really have to argue about the things that worry the children most: the normal situation, indeed. Frau Fischer-Dieskau wanted to see her sons get along completely harmoniously with one another, and so she easily nipped any disagreements in the bud. An immediate way to achieve a close and companionable relationship with her youngest son Dietrich was to take him to the cinema, but through these visits, the growing boy found reality overlaid by yet another dream world. The danger was obvious: so much avoidance of reality can have serious effects on what is usually termed "the ability to cope with life." Could it be that the proverbial discipline of the adult musician, the almost pedantic division of each day's activities without which he never could have achieved what he has achieved, is the result of those years of seemingly wasted time?

One person did point out reality to him, in a friendly way: his stepbrother Joachim (Achim), twenty years older, from his father's first marriage.

He opened a window here and there for the much younger lad—even onto the world at its coarsest. Even in later life, Fischer-Dieskau would still confide in the older man. He would never forget how Achim, the realist, had tried to open his eyes when Germany was led into the dark of night:

> I am just reading Jochen Klepper's diaries and am reminded of the days before 1939 when unrest was growing, and you, with your usual far-sightedness, could see what was coming. I, an innocent, was not so aware of the threat to our lives, but when you were with us, or I with you, your worries always made the little, silent listener think. And how terribly it rained down on us, from outside and from inside![13]

How did a child of seven experience the beginning of the Third Reich? 1933 did have several highlights (if one could call them that) that would have excited the mind of a child. He remembered above all the so-called "Day of Potsdam"—30 January 1933—when President Hindenburg appointed the "Bohemian lance-corporal" Adolf Hitler to be chancellor of the German Reich. It was one of the great days of the early radio, which was later to be so misused by the Nazis as their most effective propaganda machine. Fischer-Dieskau still remembers the seven-year-old's feelings of elation. He loved the march music most of all! He arranged his rubber toy soldiers in front of the radio and imagined that the wonderful martial music was coming out of their instruments. The Reichstag fire of 27 February 1933 has vanished from his memory, however, and memory of the burning of the books in May has been replaced by the recollection that everything remained as it had been on his father's bookshelves, that is, Thomas Mann's novel *Buddenbrooks* (1901) stood beside Adolf Hitler's *Mein Kampf* (1924), the latter unread, as in millions of German homes.

How could political arguments mean anything to the eight-, ten-, or twelve-year-old boy when very few were heard at home, really only when that generous uncle who had given him the puppet theater poured out his anger about Hitler and his cronies to a disconcerted father? The first signs of annoyance were caused by what young Dietrich saw with his own eyes, and what older people turned their eyes away from:

> My way to school took me to the railway station at the Botanical Gardens every day, where I used to wait a long time on the bridge just breathing in that wonderful steam that the puffing trains used to give out as they passed. One day in 1938, I was walking innocently up the street to the bridge with a friend when I was taken aback by the sight of glaring white-painted signs, arrows pointing to a group of shops, swear words, obscene insults on the pavement—and first my

Summer vacation with friends, 1938. The thirteen-year-old Fischer-Dieskau is unmistakable as the tallest on the extreme right.

feet stopped, then my heart. The door to Friedländer's, the men's tailors, stood wide open, the furniture shop beside it was half-empty, the shop windows all around were smeared over with signs. The crowds passed by with frozen expressions.[14]

Those personal experiences reinforced his instinctive dislike of the regime. "Street games," so called by the Jungvolk (young people), those on the first step to the HJ, or Hitlerjugend (Hitler Youth), led to legalized brutalities. The sensitive boy's intelligence and feelings revolted against the pathetically banal "social evenings" with their lying slogans. War, Fischer-Dieskau recalls, lay like a mildew over everyone's life and work and also over the growing boy's spirits; yet the world that he had created for himself still existed, and not only was he able to immerse himself in it, but it was strong enough for him to hold onto, like a weir in a fast-flowing stream. There were poems, of course, but also music that he had learned by heart. Reconstructing these helped him through the bombing of Berlin and, later, through the horrors of the front line.

While still at school, his vocal talents were maturing under the eyes and ears of Herr Forck, the music teacher at his Zehlendorf secondary school, and later at the new school, the Drei-Linden-Schule (Three Limetrees School) in Wannsee, near the famous lake, but there, it was mainly by study on his own. His mother was responsible for his taking up regular studies in singing at the age of sixteen (although "regular" may be too grand a word for them). Georg A. Walter, a superlative Bach singer and music enthusiast, did not spend much time on the basic technicalities of singing, but went on directly to study Bach's cantatas with his pupil. Yet he did abide by the old rules and made the precepts of the Spaniard Manuel Garcia's school of singing the basis of his own instruction, while incidentally making way for the Spaniard to play an important role in Fischer-Dieskau's career later as an author.[15] Herr Walter followed the comet-like rise to fame of his former pupil not many years later with just as much enthusiasm as he had evinced in his teaching, even though his pupil had left him quite quickly to continue his studies with Professor Hermann Weissenborn at the Hochschule für Musik (Academy of Music) in Berlin. A few years later, Herr Walter wrote to Frau Fischer-Dieskau about his "dear former pupil," and of the "enormous pleasure" he had received from a private performance by the young Fischer-Dieskau of Johann Sebastian Bach's *Kreuzstab* cantata (BWV56 of 1726). It seemed to him that "his whole performance had been inspired directly from on high." Walter recalled:

> Everything that I had gone through and discussed with him in our lessons, everything was still there, the correct support of the diaphragm, the wonderfully round resonance, the aesthetically beautiful sound in *forte* as well as in *piano*, the fine blend from the top of his head for the high notes, the tension of the palate to project the sound forward, the feel for vocal coloration, so esthetically and precisely chosen, and then the musicality! Oh yes, he is a real musician — that sums it all up.

Indeed, the old teacher had summed up in a nutshell all the possible explanations of the phenomenon Dietrich Fischer-Dieskau. To this character sketch by his first teacher, one could add that when that letter was written, Fischer-Dieskau sang Bach's solo tenor cantata *Ich armer Mensch, ich Sündenknecht* (BWV55), which, as Herr Walter wrote, "I have never heard from another singer, but which at seventy-four and one-quarter, I am now beginning to master."[16] That was in 1950! Before then, however, came Fischer-Dieskau's last school classes with his teachers, some of whom had been brought out of retirement, and a final examination (Abitur) with only two other pupils, since the rest of the class, who were all a year older than

Fischer-Dieskau and had gone to school earlier, had already been called up to the armed forces! Examinations for music were conducted then by a substitute examiner, the (albeit musical) biology teacher, who had devised something rather original to accommodate this examinee, although it was presented in such an obscure fashion that the examinee only realized what was happening after a first moment of panic. The biology teacher had asked for parallels to Bach's *Phoebus and Pan.* These were to be found note for note in Bach's *Bauernkantate* (Peasant Cantata) (BWV212), "Mer hahn en neue Oberkeet" (We have a new master), which the composer had written for the court chamberlain Karl Heinrich von Dieskau in 1742. The *Bauernkantate* ends with a jubilant chorus that includes the line, "Es lebe Dieskau und sein Haus" (Long live Dieskau and his heirs). The descendant of that court chamberlain to whom this wish had been sung in 1742, sailed past his music examination and so received his diploma.

War, War Service, POW Camp, and His "Apprenticeship"

Dietrich Fischer-Dieskau's studies at the Academy of Music began in Berlin in 1943, followed quickly in the same year by his call-up to Germany's Wehrmacht, a painful period of training in Fürstenwalde and Perleberg. In Perleberg, Fischer-Dieskau, the city boy, received training in veterinary work, and found himself looking after horses. With another young soldier, it was his duty to look after 120 horses, whom he calmed by singing to them! These experiences provided remarkable memories that stayed with him for years. The horses were led in long columns to drink. The lead-horse would break the ice of the frozen pond with its front hoof, and the other horses would follow patiently to drink from the hole. Every day, horses would die from lack of fodder, collapsing exhausted, pulling their harness-mates down with them. The Russian winter landscape also remains an unforgettable memory for the singer. Everywhere there was singing—again and again he would hear mixed choruses of deep Russian voices coming from he knew not where.

Then came a short leave in bombed-out Berlin. Their house in Lichterfelde was burned out:

> We have only managed to save a little. Most of the music has been burned, as well as both instruments. I saw the grand piano lying in the cellar, without legs. It had fallen through the floors above.[1]

His next posting was to the front line in Italy, where he was captured by the Americans in the Po Valley on 5 May 1945, three days before VE Day, followed by two years of imprisonment in US POW camps. Then, at last, came his return home in 1947, the resumption of his singing studies—and, hand in hand with that, the rapid and unstoppable rise to stardom.

Hermann Weissenborn had been a concert singer himself and had been teaching at the Academy in Berlin since 1920. Now, at age seventy, he had his pupil back, but a pupil who had been through a practical school of music in war and prisoner-of-war camps. Throughout these four long years, Fischer-Dieskau had had to work out a strategy for survival: how to manage

1943: Immediately after his graduation (Abitur), he was drafted into the army.

to study by himself, how to obtain music scores with the help of some comrades, and how to learn the secrets of artistic expression. "I want to, I must, draw out what is in me though I do not yet know what it is that inspires me,"[2] he wrote in his diary, but in POW camp he had simply been ordered to sing! He had to leave his filthy surroundings and appear before the general in a smart new uniform. The singer's art did not move the general enough for him to dismiss Fischer-Dieskau from his menial chores — he still had to go back to his foxhole — yet he and his pianist Bruno Penzien considered this "order" a brief leave, for it did give them two days of relative freedom. In his heart, however, Fischer-Dieskau did not really enjoy these appearances — not only because the nineteen-year-old disagreed with the state-ordered lie and the war, although these were the most oppressive elements of his world. As late as 1982, to a question about his experience of the Nazi period, he answered: "When I was a child, my first experiences of all the horrors came as a shock, and this was then repeated in the war until it became a frightening crescendo."[3] This struggle with the world outside became an inner struggle with himself. His cousin, Edith, who was also taken into his confidence at this time, wrote, with some justification:

> I wish you all the best and am thinking of you in the hope that friendship and understanding will bring you some sort of consolation. Life is always at its most difficult when one is twenty — how could that be any different right now?[4]

The letters from "your old cousin Edith," as she liked to sign herself, contain just a hint of the contradictions pulsing through this nineteen-year-old then, who was separated by his particular talents, as well as by his sensitivity, from his surroundings. His married cousin (who, incidentally, was confined to a wheelchair) seems to have sensed very well how mature this young man had already become, and how difficult he found coming to terms with that. Writing of his early life, she tells him:

> Much too early the curtain was torn away from the facts of life—how will you manage in this unveiled world? For there is no way back for your type of mind into happy-go-lucky pastures! If, in spite of everything [she was writing this letter in March 1944!] the miracle of surviving the war (I mean peace) were to happen, and everything were to return to its normal way of life, it would not make any difference to your awareness of things. All beautiful things will still hurt, all happiness will be sadness, and you will stand apart from people of your own age.[5]

Edith Schmidt took her correspondent's crises very seriously, crises in which, of course, were also mirrored the tribulations of the times. She carefully tried to combat them. She wrote that even if madness seemed to be getting the upper hand at the moment, the world was still shaped by the gentle, irresistibly powerful forces of the world of ideas. When the Nazis forced Martin, Fischer-Dieskau's disabled brother, into a so-called "nursing home" and then, in accordance with their euthanasia program, let him starve to death, she tried to soften this fresh blow: "You write, too, about how differently people judge life and death in the world outside." One wonders how the twenty-year-old felt when he read the next remark: "Now the poor little martyr will become a sad memory for you all—that is the only way that it will be bearable."[6]

Perhaps these were the right words at the right time, in the sense of a life-preserving resignation in the face of the inevitable. Or did they just strengthen the feeling of despair vis-à-vis the prevailing sense of helplessness? Or did they perhaps awaken feelings of protest? None of these three emotions was apparent, but all together have left their marks.

Nevertheless, despite his worries, cousin Edith regarded the young man as a "Sunday child," born under a lucky star. A person who had such a divine talent must also have a guardian angel. If "divine talent" meant, of course, his voice, then she soon began to talk about a second present from heaven, in the form of the dark-haired girl that Fischer-Dieskau had gotten to know in his early days at the Academy of Music.

Irmgard ("Irmel") Poppen, a young cellist, and the young singer soon found that they were soulmates, but not much time remained before he was to be called up to the army. Cousin Edith wrote something unusual:

> By the way, I saw Irmel's handwriting at your mother's—now, I know I'm a bit silly about these things, but I "feel" something here too much—much too much, I don't like it at all. Now I know your Irmel a little because of this, and I am amazed at the almost comical similarity in your ways of thinking—I've seldom seen anything quite like it.[7]

The picture of Irmgard Poppen that she gives here is certainly biased by her love for her "Dieter," but it does perhaps hit the nail on the head because of that. His cousin wrote once:

> She is what they would have called a "beautiful soul" (eine schöne Seele) a hundred years ago. I'm very fond of her; she is one of those people who live by a genuine inner law, completely natural and free, unworried by others' standards, and so, every action, every look, every word, is true, pure, natural—and a joy. There is a gentle happiness that seems to radiate from within, not strident, but constant. That is how I see Irmel, and I can only wish you happiness—but her too . . . . Just recently, I dreamed that you were a famous singer and were standing on the Riviera showing her the countryside where you had been "in the past," quite a long time ago "in the past," during the war. I wonder if that will ever come about?[8]

(To look ahead for a moment: It did come about. In 1950, six years after that anxious question, the Fischer-Dieskaus were in Italy for a concert. Fischer-Dieskau related how they "allowed" themselves a "journey into the past, to Pisa where I had had my longest stay as a prisoner-of-war").[9]

Still during the war, and before he was called up to the Wehrmacht, Fischer-Dieskau had given his first public recital on 31 January 1942: Schubert's song cycle *Winterreise* (Winter Journey). Two of the twenty-four songs were omitted, Nos. 8 and 9, "Rückblick" (A Look Back) and "Irrlicht" (Will o' the Wisp), because he was not absolutely certain of remembering the words. This remarkable event, which was interrupted by an air-raid warning, took place in the town hall in Zehlendorf. He had already given recitals at student concerts, of course, and the six months spent at the Academy of Music, prior to the involuntary interruptions caused by the war and POW camps, had offered the possibility of recitals there, as had the short leaves from the army.

Perhaps this is the place for a true anecdote about a class on "The Art of the Lied." Professor Arthur Kusterer, who was later (in 1958) to direct the opera studio at the Komische Oper in Berlin, was lecturing on song cycles, and he asked the audience whether Johannes Brahms had also written a cycle. The answer came from a tall, thin student in army uniform: yes, he knew *Die schöne Magelone* (The Fair Maid of the Mill). Could he sing something from it? One can imagine what happened then. The young man sang song after song, and the listeners were "overwhelmed." Then came the standard end to all fairy stories, the recognition scene, with the question: "And what is your name, young man?" "Dietrich Fischer-Dieskau."[10]

When the war was over in 1945, this same young man developed in his American POW camps an urge to do things that no one who had known the dreamy high-school senior could have imagined. At his own behest, and with great élan, he began to counter the apathy of camp life. In the very first camp, he stood on a platform made of sand-filled boxes and sang, on his own and without an accompanist—and slowly all fell quiet. He wrote in his diary at the time:

> Very lonely among lots of people . . . . My present job in the orderly room means that I can type up all sorts of poems from memory into an anthology, which then goes the rounds after it has been mimeographed. This helps to prevent one from becoming a complete zombie.[11]

The prisoner in his camp in Livorno in northwest Italy returned to his secret world, reconstructed it, and found it habitable. He began to arrange Lieder recitals as well as recitations and piano recitals. The prisoners read Goethe's *Faust* and Schiller's *Don Carlos*, with the parts divided among them. Fischer-Dieskau took the parts of Gretchen in *Faust* and Princess Eboli in *Don Carlos* as well! Not all the prisoners liked the classical music, however. In the military hospital in Pisa, he sang Schubert's *Winterreise* for the second or third time in front of a large audience. (Did he guess how many performances were to follow these? Hardly!) He also sang all the solo parts in Heinrich Schütz's *Christmas Oratorio* (SWV435 of 1664); soon afterward, the camp theater Capitol Dora was founded at Foggia in southeast Italy. It opened with a comedy, *Die Feuerzangenbowle* (The Rum-punch Bowl) by Heinrich Spoerle (1887–1955). The high-school senior cheat, Hans Pfeiffer, was played by none other than the hopeful singer-to-be. *Der Vetter aus Dingsda* (The Cousin from What-d'ye-call-it) gave him some musical stage experience. ("A musical comedy in four acts, freely adapted by Dietrich Fischer-Dieskau from the operetta by Eduard Künnecke," said the program. The "adaptation" referred, incidentally, to the production sets.)

The cast members (including Fischer-Dieskau) sang, whistled, or played what they could remember of the music to the conductor Paul Fischer, and he in turn arranged it for the Capitol Dora orchestra. The cast list had "Peter Braun, tramp and composer . . . . Dietrich Fischer-Dieskau"—the baritone as tenor. (It is perhaps almost unnecessary to mention that all the women's parts in a POW camp were played by men.) Airplane parts were used to make an almost perfect stage setting. The *pièce de résistance* of the sets was a waterfall made from huge stones with an ingenious construction for letting the water splash in and out.

Capitol Dora offered also "variety programs": the Prologue to *Pagliacci*, "You Are My Heart's Delight," etc., performed by Dietrich Fischer-Dieskau (baritone), Fritz Meyer (violin), Guenther Vutk (trumpet), and Ernst Probs (trombone). Fischer-Dieskau regards all these performances as substitutes for what Germans call the Provinzzeit (whereby young singers learning their craft have to travel around to small towns). These performances were among his very few forays into the field of light music.

There are two LPs of Fischer-Dieskau in operetta: Johann Strauss's *Die Fledermaus* (1874) conducted by Willi Boskovsky in December 1971 and *Der Zigeunerbaron* (The Gypsy Baron) (1885), recorded on LP in 1971 and on CD in 1983. *Die Fledermaus* does have the status of an opera, of course, and can hardly be surpassed as an example of its genre, particularly when recorded by first-class singers, as on that occasion. Vienna and Munich give such performances from time to time. Nonetheless, Fischer-Dieskau has never wanted to sing even in this superlative example of this type of music on stage. "No," he used to say when invited, "I'm not really the man for it." His demands on himself were the same as his demands on the music.

At that time, however, it was almost impossible not to appear in such performances of popular music in American soldiers' clubs. It must have been very difficult for him to force himself to do this, just when he was discovering Ravel and Debussy. This was with the pianist Detlev Jürges, whom he had gotten to know in POW camp, along with the musicologist Gustav-Adolf Trumpff. Trumpff, who later became one of his longest-lasting friends, once managed to obtain the music of Hugo Wolf's *Italienisches Liederbuch* (The Italian Song Book) (1891) for two packets of cigarettes—a small fortune in those days. Its real worth, however, was as indispensable study material for the young singer, and for new Lieder recitals. (Here a legend has to be destroyed, namely, that Dietrich Fischer-Dieskau first became aware of his vocation as a singer in the POW camps. His study with Georg A. Walter lay far behind him, and he had begun his study with Professor Weissenborn at

1946: "Capitol Dora," the theater of the German POWs in Italy, presents *Der Vetter aus Dingsda* (The Cousin from What-d'ye-call-it) by Eduard Künnecke. In the title role, Dietrich Fischer-Dieskau (*top*, in the middle; *bottom*, second from left).

the Academy of Music before he was called up to the Wehrmacht.) Detlev Jürges reawakened his practical interest in the piano, too. They played Brahms's Variations on a Theme by Haydn (Op. 56b) in the arrangement for two pianos, and Fischer-Dieskau recorded it with Ravel's 1905 solo Sonatine.

Then a new sort of dissatisfaction occurred. While he was working with the young composer Werner Hübschmann on the theory of harmony and counterpoint, a thought occurred to him that was never to leave him. He wrote in his diary: "How can I combine my loves of acting, singing, conducting, and painting? No one will believe me when I say how much I love each of these possibilities."[12] His faithful echo, Edith Schmidt, gave him the answer, albeit some time later, when his career as a singer was firmly established. Even when he had attained stardom, the question had not vanished but had become ever more persistent. She wrote:

> And so you want more time for all your extra talents? That is the curse of the Fischers—they have too many irons in the fire. As your dear father used to say so nicely: We can do a bit of everything, and we want to do too much.

That was probably an understatement in this particular case of a man of so many talents, but she had to add:

> But I cannot imagine any different life for you than the one that drives you on from within; and you want to achieve, oh, so much! I am certain that you will become a professional actor, and your painting and writing will be the joys of your leisure hours.[13]

Is there any doubt that, even in his youth, Fischer-Dieskau had wished for more than that? He had been a POW up until 1947 and had become almost too useful as an "all-round" musician and provider of culture for his fellow prisoners. "At any rate, I am very sad that they are keeping me here, and that after two years of longing and waiting, I shall only be able to make it homewards in June," he wrote to Hans ("Hansi") Wunschel, the friend of his younger days, on 18 May 1947. "All the unpleasant and bitter sides of life in Germany will be counterbalanced by the love and the music that is waiting for me there." How closely he bound love and music together—there was never to be a difference. After he had told his friend about life in the POW camp, how he had managed to fashion a bearable life as "singer, actor, producer, and reciter," he mentioned his other "love," not to be so different from his love of music:

> You'll want to know about the "little Swabian girl"? Yes, she is already much more than I am, musically speaking, and has "quite a reputation" (!) down there in south Germany, but she has remained wonderfully faithful to me despite the extraordinary patience that she had to—and still has to—show. We shall certainly have to get to know each other again after such a long break.

Then he shows just a little concern when he adds: "I've avoided asking for anything—including being released directly to Freiburg." This letter to his friend, the first after many years of being apart, had clearly one major *raison d'être*: this is a letter from someone who is about to shape his new life. His demands on himself had been enormous from the very beginning. That serious cast of mind already mentioned is still the unchanged and dominating feature of his nature: "Because I now have a deeper and firmer awareness of Christianity, my judgment damns . . .," and the twenty-two-year-old's lack of compromise now shows, ". . . damns all past as well as present systems of government." But then his intelligence makes him add:

> but how relative any judgment is when you are stuck behind your own blinkers. What really matters is the awareness of one's own sense of responsibility—the moral, ethical awareness of all people in power.

The Fischer-Dieskau of today could well have written that final sentence. Even his response to his art shows how faithful he has remained to that belief. One arbitrary review might serve as an example: it is the review of the premiere of Luigi Dallapiccola's *Preghiere* (Prayers) on 24 March 1965, almost twenty years after the letter above. Gerhard R. Koch, the music critic of the *Frankfurter Allgemeine Zeitung*, one of Germany's leading newspapers, wrote: "Dietrich Fischer-Dieskau sang the extensive baritone part with all the strength and delicacy of which his voice is capable. It has always been at its best in works that express human concern."

Fischer-Dieskau came back to Germany with, literally, the last hospital train from Pisa in June 1947, not directly to Freiburg, although he did manage to be demobilized in south Germany. There he stood in Göppingen (not far from Stuttgart in Baden-Württemberg) in his hospital outfit with a wooden case in his hand: "a bit embarrassed about how I looked in front of Irmel, who picked me up from the railway station to go to Freiburg," he noted in his diary.[14] In that wooden case, incidentally, were mainly gramophone records, a well-guarded treasure.

Freedom then became rather complicated. Göppingen was then in the American Zone in the south, Freiburg in the French Zone to the west. The ex-POW had his demobilization pass but no interzonal permit; so the engaged couple sneaked along from carriage to carriage to avoid the guards, and so reached the French Zone.

The First Postwar Years:
Love and Music

Love and music were the themes of that three-month stay in Freiburg. If the joy of being with his fiancée again was complicated by the admixture of nearness and distance, of getting to know each other again in all ways, the world of music opened itself up to the young singer without any resistance. Nothing seemed too difficult, nothing too risky. The first test was ready and waiting: Theodor Egel, founder and director of the Freiburg Bach choir, was delighted to be able to replace the indisposed baritone soloist in Brahms's *German Requiem* (Op. 45) in Badenweiler with the young Fischer-Dieskau —the first steps to future cooperation. Hermann Meinhard Poppen, the brother of Fischer-Dieskau's future father-in-law and a former junior col- league of the German composer Max Reger (1873–1916), was conductor of the Heidelberg Bach Society, and he took under his wing the enormously talented young singer who had become such an all-round musician as a soldier and then as a POW, albeit involuntarily. The Bach *Passions*, Brahms's *Four Serious Songs* (Op. 121), Schoenberg's *Gurrelieder* (Songs of Gurra) (1911), in which the orchestral interludes were shortened with the energetic help of the young singer, since the orchestra could not learn them quickly enough—all these and more were in his schedule for these three months. Dietrich Fischer-Dieskau relates all this in *Nachklang*, looking back with a smile, with a gentle irony mingled with a little sentimentality. In a letter to his in-laws, the Poppens, of 1 August 1984, he wrote with reference to a publication planned on Hermann Meinhard Poppen:

> You should not forget to mention, by the way, that Hermann Meinhard Poppen was the very first conductor with the courage to engage me as a soloist—me, a complete beginner. And my singing of the soprano part in the *German Requiem* in Ludwigsburg could add a nice little bit of spice to it—and, of course, the natural hospitality shown by your parents, when they took me into their home at that time.[1]

The return journey to Berlin was an adventure in those early postwar years—and a dangerous one at that. To use the interzonal train with only a demobilization pass was risky enough, but the train did not go all the way to Berlin. Some miles before the frontier at Helmstedt, Fischer-Dieskau had to get out with the now-familiar wooden case in his hand and cross the zonal border on foot, once again to the sound of shooting. After an uncertain train journey, he reached his "hometown," bombed-out Berlin.

On 30 September 1947, he wrote from Berlin—again to his friend, Hans Wolfgang Wunschel, who was by now studying law in Munich:

> Yes, I stayed for some time in Freiburg, and my mother had to wait a long time after my first attempt to come up here had failed. But I've made amends now, for I have changed my original idea of just paying a visit to staying here for good. It's true, I had to give up the most attractive career opportunities in Freiburg—a lectureship in singing at the Academy of Music, among others [this mirrors those wild postwar years in which disorganized careers almost became the order of the day], and being with Irmel—but what does that matter when I had already made up my mind that a temporary separation (we'll have to wait now to get married!) cannot be all that tragic.

All the doors to the world of music in Berlin were opening quickly as well:

> Professor Weissenborn is teaching me here *gratis*, and I am soon going to start a well-paid job in the studio of the State Opera (the place of my earliest pipe dreams!). And there will be radio broadcasts and concerts too. So!

The young singer was seeing the heavens open—but he then added a very down-to-earth remark that so accurately described the living conditions in the occupied zones of Germany at that time: "But something else—not unimportant. The food situation here is much better than in the French zone, here with Mother, above all!"

His career began with the first Lieder recitals and the now legendary *Winterreise* for RIAS against the background of a bombed-out Berlin and coincided with the development of that peculiar "island culture" of that city, which was then called "an island in the Red Sea," isolated in the Soviet-occupied zone. Fischer-Dieskau became one of its most important representatives, despite the many concert tours and his regular operatic performances all over the world.

Elsa Schiller, a Jewess who had had to emigrate from Germany but at the end of the war was immediately willing to help to rebuild Berlin's cultural life, earns a thankful and respectful acknowledgment in Fischer-Dieskau's memoirs. As soon as she had heard his voice, she felt that she must immediately invite this unknown young man to record *Winterreise*—and so she, too, was a person who discovered him immediately!

The situation in Berlin at that time was well described by Hans-Heinz Stuckenschmidt, a pupil of Alban Berg and Arnold Schoenberg, and one of the great names of German music criticism: "Nowadays, Berlin is joined to the West by only one railway line, two bus routes, and two weekly flights." It was going to get worse. Stuckenschmidt wrote his article on "Berlin's Music Problems" as part of a discussion about Berlin's situation as an "island," in the *Neue Zeitung*, the American newspaper for the German population that was published by the American military government from 1945 in Munich in the American Zone, and then from 1947 in Berlin. The paper quickly became famous for its excellent cultural pages edited by the well-known novelist Erich Kästner (of *Emil and the Detectives* fame) in Munich. He invited the journalists who had returned from abroad to work with those who had stayed in Germany throughout the war (the so-called "inner emigration"). They were among the best journalists there were. The newspaper, and, in particular, the edition of 28 March 1948, is not mentioned here just by chance, for in that article on music in Berlin, Stuckenschmidt "discovered" a young singer. He described all the famous people who had come to Berlin: the Amsterdam String Quartet ("convincing") and the Quartetto di Roma ("disappointing"), and, from "the other direction," Andrzej Panufnik, a Pole who conducted the Staatskapelle and the Berlin Philharmonic. The critic also wrote about Wilhelm Furtwängler and the Romanian conductor Sergiu Celibidache and a few soloists, and then: "There were not many newcomers: only one young baritone, Dietrich Fischer-Dieskau, who made us all sit up with his Wolf and Schumann Lieder."

Stuckenschmidt's ears had not deceived him at the young baritone's first Lieder recital. In conversation some forty years later, he said:

> I shall never forget how in 1948—I think it was in January—a young man, fresh from POW camp, came to Dahlem [a suburb of Berlin] with a group called the Dahlem Music Society and sang in the hall of a girls' school. We were all absolutely fascinated."[2]

Another witness of Fischer-Dieskau's first Berlin concerts was the music journalist (now Professor) Karla Höcker, who was later to become a collaborator in his work as a writer. This resolute, musically cultured woman not only remembered everything accurately but was also able to recount how his interpretations differed from traditional ideas. Even after she had heard his *Winterreise* of 1947 for the first time, she also spoke of this "very, very young man" who reminded her at first of Schubert's friends, Moritz von Schwind

(1804–1871) and Eduard Bauernfeld (1802–1890). Then all that suddenly vanished: "He began to sing—and that was the curious thing: the voice, the man, the music, all became one. I had the feeling that he was developing the whole wonderful cycle out of his own being." Karla Höcker was describing what the singer was doing even then, and what he later perfected, namely, "allowing the emotion to continue between the songs, in the intervals," and she added: "Only Furtwängler had been able to do that before."

What was new, in part, in Fischer-Dieskau's approach to a Lieder recital cannot be deduced from these early recitals, since it is the momentum of his development that has such a particular significance. On the singer's sixtieth birthday in 1985, Karla Höcker spoke not only of the singer's debuts—one has to use the plural, since the sum of the debuts was greater than the parts—but also of what grew out of them:

> The Lieder recitals before the war were quite different from those of today. There were very beautiful voices then, too, and very subtle renderings and interpretations that moved us deeply. The great difference from today was that the famous singers succeeded by never altering their style. That was it. When we went to a recital and Emmi Leisner or Heinrich Schlusnus sang Brahms or Schubert, then people met afterwards during the intermission and said: "It's amazing, I heard her (or him) sing just like that three years ago." It was a sort of ideal version. So Lieder recitals became a sort of comfort, something refreshing. They didn't demand discussion afterwards . . . . With Fischer-Dieskau we had quite a different development right from the beginning. He knows that works of genius, above all, make new demands on each generation, and these must be met.

In truth, this author, much experienced in reporting on concert performances, expressed one of the rules that Fischer-Dieskau has always applied to all of his artistic activities: every song, every role, no matter how often it was sung or played, was regarded as a challenge, unknown territory to be conquered. The learning of each individual work was never "concluded," thus, every work was really seen as "work in progress." The listener who understood that would then feel the immediate tension that the singer imparted to every song-cycle, every group of songs, every operatic role. One could not expect, nor did one receive, a spectacularly different interpretation each time, for the point was not change for change's sake, but rather an unconventional approach to the work—or, better perhaps, a lack of convention in the approach—in order to allow a new, independent understanding and interpretation to emerge. A work of art can only remain alive for the interpreter and his audience as long as the one or the other is still living with it. If Fischer-Dieskau always has an hour-long final rehearsal immediately before each recital, this proves that his study of the work is not yet concluded, but is to be continued during and beyond the recital.

The recording of *Winterreise*, made under such difficult circumstances in the RIAS studio in Berlin in December 1947, is still heard from time to time. The accompanist had to be changed (Klaus Billing took over), and one part of the recording that was spoiled by noise on the tapes had to be re-recorded. The performance, very gentle, a little sentimental, but sung with plenty of voice, immediately set a high vocal standard. The reactions of the first listeners are easy to understand. Some listeners, and many a critic, may well have been pleased at the time that the twenty-two-year-old was not yet so aware of the ice-cold atmosphere of loneliness that surrounds the wanderer in Schubert's "cycle of gruesome songs" (as he called them to his friend Josef von Spaun in 1828). Yet this interpretation had really nothing at all in common with the sweet, restful picture of earlier Schubert convention (or with the more bitter Schubert of modern interpretations). From his very first recitals, Fischer-Dieskau has contributed a great deal to the new, fair, one might almost say, adult picture of Franz Schubert. He sings of a Schubert who well knew what he was writing about, even when his God (his genius, that is) was dictating it to him.

This is the singer's concern, even now. Decades after those early years of his career, he wrote:

> I believe that the work of art is much more important than all the interpreters, that it forces them to be watchful, to want to know the work more thoroughly, to rediscover what has already been discovered . . . . But does that mean that the role of the interpreter is to be rather unfairly diminished, since he or she must not only illuminate or explain the work, but also throw a new, unforeseen, unexpected light on it? . . . On the contrary: for me it means putting our task into sharper focus and maintaining that the best interpreter is the one who retreats behind the work.[3]

Fischer-Dieskau claims that those who insist on forcing their own, falsifying views on a work of art can have no idea of how wide is the "bull's-eye" that they might have hit had they adopted a more sensible interpretation.

That 1947 recording of *Winterreise* with Klaus Billing points to another phenomenon in relation to Fischer-Dieskau: it already has in a nutshell everything that made him incomparable. With all the work that he had already put into the cycle, there was no long, hard road to maturity. In Wagner's *Die Meistersinger* (The Mastersingers), Hans Sachs sings about

Walther von Stolzing's rise to artistic maturity. (Sachs was a role that Fischer-Dieskau did not sing until much later, when he himself was fifty.) Sachs sings that "Spring's command" has laid a song in his breast that sounds like "birdsong in May": "now he sang as he had to! And as he had to sing, he could!" It was much the same for Fischer-Dieskau, and yet a little different. It was not "Spring's command" that spurred him on, but the desire for a knowledge of artistic expression and a mature will to express himself. So, to paraphrase Hans Sachs, one should say: "And because he sang, he could do it." An exceptional talent is not fashioned, it is just there. It is often shaped in silence, and is sometimes growing even when it seems to be dormant.

Martha Musial, who sang Elisabeth in Fischer-Dieskau's first *Tannhäuser* at the Berlin Städtische Oper (Municipal Opera) in 1949, remembers her young partner very well. In a telephone interview with Helmut Kühn, she said, quite extemporarily, what she had felt at the time:

> Everything about him was so natural. His range of emotions was so enormous—and that was there from the very beginning—so that we all sat up and listened. You really got goose pimples. He looked like a boy, yet when he opened his mouth, there was an artist who seemed to have thirty years experience behind him.

She meant thirty professional years, of course, for Fischer-Dieskau was only twenty-four at the time.

The singer's operatic debut had taken place the year before, in 1948. Instead of in the studio of the State Opera (as he had prophesied in the letter to Hans Wunschel), the twenty-three-year-old had been engaged by the Städtische Oper (later the Deutsche Oper Berlin). He had also sung an audition with the intendant of the State Opera: the Count's aria from Act III of Mozart's *The Marriage of Figaro*. When he had finished, the intendant, Ernst Segal, said, delighted, "Oh, sing it again!" Segel was surprised when the young man disagreed with his comment: "You're engaged for the studio." Fischer-Dieskau wanted more than that: it had to be the regular operatic stage. Walter Felsenstein, the celebrated producer and theater director, also saw him, but neither his comment ("If you want to learn, come here to us!") nor his offer to let the beginner sing Mozart's *Don Giovanni* quite convinced Fischer-Dieskau. Clearly, it was Heinz Tietjen who gave him most confidence. What had made the critic Stuckenschmidt sit up had opened Tietjen's ears as well. Tietjen, then sixty-seven, a pupil of the conductor Arthur Nikisch, had been intendant of the Städtische Oper from 1925 to 1927, and then intendant of the Prussian State Theater through 1945. His work with the stage designer Emil Preetorius is seen as particularly significant in their development of new ways of staging Wagnerian operas. Since

1933, Tietjen had been the artistic director at Bayreuth and was producing Wagner there as early as 1931. Although his steadfast loyalty to Bayreuth, and later his position as intendant in Berlin during the Nazi period, had been controversial, his abilities as a theater director were not.

It was a stroke of luck for Fischer-Dieskau when he was engaged by the Städtische Oper in 1948. When asked about the past, Fischer-Dieskau replies that he is engulfed by a "wave of forgetfulness." The Allies found the machinations of the Cold War much more important than an examination of Germany's past, and the conquered Germans were looking above all for food, that is, survival, but also for the food of culture.

That *Winterreise* at the RIAS station had been preceded by a general audition with a long queue of applicants; it was then followed by a recording of several Bach cantatas. Afterwards, Heinz Tietjen, like the other opera chiefs, invited the young singer to a private audition. The result is well known: "You'll sing Posa [the role of Rodrigo, the Marquis of Posa in Verdi's *Don Carlos*] for me in four weeks!" Fischer-Dieskau wrote later about Tietjen: "I wished there had been more intendants who cared so much about young beginners."[4]

Tietjen was thinking, of course, about the advantages to his theater as much as about sparing the young singer's voice when it came to allowing him to accept guest appearances. When there was the offer of a guest appearance at La Scala, Milan, in 1950, Tietjen, in refusing permission, wrote of "his measures to protect his highly gifted young singer who is not yet ready to appear in operas abroad." It was different with recitals—he could manage these anywhere, he wrote. In short, this caring intendant wanted to keep "the young man" (whom he had introduced to opera) from guest appearances for "at least a whole season." "Herr Fischer-Dieskau will understand." But "Herr Fischer-Dieskau" was very disappointed indeed.

The young singer's career was getting underway and he was beginning to move from concert hall to recording studio, and from there to the theater to get a feeling for the stage from all these rehearsals. He was giving his all every time and hardly knowing where the strength to do it came from, for the situation in Berlin had become a "crisis of nerves."

The Berlin blockade was begun on 24 June 1948 by the Soviet Occupation Power; on 26 June the Western Allies started the airlift (the Germans called it the "air bridge") to feed the Western sectors of Berlin. The new currency, the Deutschmark, had been introduced on 20 June, thus setting in motion uncontrolled trading in the two currencies. That was the atmosphere surrounding Fischer-Dieskau's beginnings as a singer.

From May 1945, there were four occupying powers, fifteen daily papers, countless weekly journals, daily political announcements,

five radio stations, theaters, countless nightclubs, important visitors
from all over the world, and three million ambitious people with
strong nerves,

reported *Die Neue Zeitung* on 1 July 1948. Then, from a report on the
beleaguered city in the *Neue Zeitung* for 11 July 1948:

> The children are shouting on the balcony next door; they've got a
> new game: "Listen to the aeroplane, it's bringing raisins—no,
> they're all twisty, they're noodles!" We're living under a droning
> bridge, the "air bridge."
>
> The siege is now obvious to all. The little black market in
> Mommsen Street, mainly housewives. Everyone is asking for bread.
> Four to seven marks per loaf. Butter thirty marks.

Meanwhile Dietrich Fischer-Dieskau was studying the role of Posa in
Don Carlos, broadcasting for RIAS, and singing in Lieder recitals, ambitious
to contribute something new to old traditions. It was a nerve- and energy-
consuming time.

Two important elements of the success of Fischer-Dieskau's debut as an
operatic baritone were the conductor Ferenc Fricsay and the bass Josef
Greindl, who, as King Philip II, helped the beginner with his early stage
problems: "After all, I can't upstage you, can I, lad?" he laughed. Fricsay's
remark—"An Italian baritone here in Berlin?"—did not excite critical opinion right away, when everyone was still speechless at the musicality and the
natural stage presence of the singer, but it did later.[5] But what did it mean,
anyway? Was Dietrich Fischer-Dieskau not a German singer, a well-nigh
perfect example of a German artist? The remark had nothing to do with
italianatà, but rather with the Italianate flow of the legato, which Fischer-
Dieskau does indeed produce. The Italian singing teacher and music critic
Elio Battaglia said, in another context, when talking about the stage roles of
Italian grand opera generally, that no Italian could sing them in a more
Italian manner than Fischer-Dieskau. How could he make such a claim?—
not because Fischer-Dieskau had mastered the finest nuances of the Italian
language but because he understands the language through the spirit of the
music. At the same time, there has to be a vocal readjustment, demanded by
the Italian language. The Italian way of "attacking the intonation" is the
decisive, differentiating factor. The timbre changes, and if a singer does it
properly, the voice changes with it.

Yet the most important element remains the composer's coloring of his
work. In an Italian radio program on Dietrich Fischer-Dieskau, Elio
Battaglia discussed the question of the singer's penetration of a text in a

As Rodrigo, Marquis of Posa, in Verdi's *Don Carlos*. Debut on 18 November 1948 at Berlin's Städtische Oper.

foreign language. He played examples, beginning with a Purcell duet sung by Fischer-Dieskau and Victoria de los Angeles, a Petrarch sonnet set by Johann Friedrich Reichardt, a Venetian *canzonetta* by Giacomo Meyerbeer, a song by Tchaikovsky, a Debussy *ballade*, a simple song by the American Charles Ives, and, finally—the climax of the selection—the *Five Popular Greek Melodies* by Ravel. Common to all the excerpts was the authenticity of the music and the language and, to quote Elio Battaglia, "the endless possibilities of expression and the sheer technique of this voice."

This takes us far beyond the beginning of Dietrich Fischer-Dieskau's career as a Lieder singer and operatic baritone with a characteristic tendency to reach beyond present interests. Fischer-Dieskau saw an expressly prophetic meaning in his Verdi debut: "Verdi's masculinity and purity, represented so clearly in Posa, left a mark on my future life; it affected me *as a man*, not just my wish to be creative."[6]

The first masculine role he had to take on was, of course, that of a husband. It was not easy to set up a home in those days, especially when his fiancée was living far away in Freiburg in south Germany in the French zone of occupation, quite apart from the difficulties of furnishing the much sought-after living quarters and from Berlin's peculiar situation. A complaining letter to friend Hansi of 1 April 1948 throws some light on living conditions in Berlin at that time:

> Our appalling conditions here exclude almost any plans for the immediate future. I would love to have gotten away for Christmas from my much too large family here (you have to do that if you want to make anything of your life!!) and move into a nice two-room flat in Charlottenburg [a district of Berlin] with Irmel. But how can I expect her to leave her home and sever all connections with her parents for a long time when the border is completely closed?

But then he plucked up a little courage: "Yet even in all this loneliness and discontent of the moment, I never lose my faith in our future life together."

He writes that he has heard from Irmel that she has been invited by her cello teacher Enrico Mainardi to take part in a private course in Salzburg and may also have the chance to go with him to Switzerland for a few weeks after that. "I haven't managed to do much yet, but let's hope that next year might bring something." His debut as Posa was due in the same year too. And marriage?

> With a bit of good fortune and not a little cheek, Irmel managed to cross the border illegally one day and cheered me up out of my lethargy. So we went (or flew, more correctly), with the help of a

generous American friend, to Frankfurt, though not without suffering all the nervous tension of an AOA passenger first. Everything in Freiburg was like paradise—they gave us a wonderful celebration, just like in peacetime—and so those happy days, where we also managed to find room for three concerts, seem to me now like one huge dream.

The "wonderful celebration" was, of course, his marriage to Irmgard Poppen. The "happy days" were having been able to get away from the Berlin blockade introduced by the Soviets on 24 June 1948. The blockade was finally lifted on 12 May 1949—a day of celebration for Berlin. The young couple now began to settle in to the town, and their togetherness was clearly shown by the letters to Irmel's parents in Freiburg—letters written, by the way, by either one yet scarcely distinguishable one from the other: "Dieter wrote that" or "this is from Irmel" is often the only clue. They had found their home in an aunt's house—at first, two rooms at the end of a long suite of rooms. As time went by, they slowly worked their way forward when another room became free because the tenants could no longer put up with the constant music! This was the house in Berlin's Charlottenburg district, in the Lindenallee, still Fischer-Dieskau's Berlin home, which the singer now shares with Julia Varady, whom he married in 1977.

It says much for Dietrich and Irmel Fischer-Dieskau, who occasionally gave recitals together in the early years of their marriage, that one of the two rooms they possessed was immediately declared the music room. It was quite a room! As early as December 1949, a complete set of Biedermeier furniture, packed in wooden cases, arrived by truck in Charlottenburg: "Two grateful and happy children thank you from the bottom of their hearts," they wrote in a letter dated 15 December 1949 to Irmel's grandmother in Baden-Württemberg, who had seen the furniture in an antique shop and had persuaded the grandfather to buy it.

The mutual letters to Freiburg also shed light on the pleasant, and not so pleasant, aspects of a singer's professional work. Those who later noticed that Fischer-Dieskau, after a recital or even after a premiere, would vanish quickly and rarely if ever take part in the so-called Nachsitzungen (post-recital discussions), might understand the reason after reading these accounts of the singer's early career. His young wife wrote once—quite without embarrassment:

We just don't feel at home among those turnip-heads and art philistines, i.e. the singers and some of the local worthies. Besides their obscene jokes, they just talk about the Toto [the German football lottery] and the rate of the dollar! Only the Lord Mayor of

With Irmgard Fischer-Dieskau (née Poppen). The two musicians married in February 1949.

Berlin, Herr [Ernst] Reuter, expressed his thanks for the evening's concert. He (Dieter) picked me out, however, which was a little embarrassing in front of the others. Dieter gave so much of himself during the performance that I was always moved to tears. But the reviewers, apart from a very few, never noticed that at all.[7]

Nothing could describe the young couple's way of life better than that short extract. Fischer-Dieskau still lived, it seems, in that other world of fantasy and music-making that he had fashioned for himself from the very beginning, and the secret of his relationship with his young wife was simply that she came from a similar world of make-believe.

He was not exaggerating in his description of the importance of his stage debut for himself, for he really did believe in the optimistic Schiller-Posa creed that "one should respect the dreams of his youth when one becomes a man."[8] He realized even then that not attending those post-event discussions would be taken as arrogance, as would his shrinking from fraternizing with his colleagues: "For when I was young and people told me the truth now and then, they called me either an eccentric—or arrogant."[9]

In Thomas Mann's novella *Death in Venice* (1912), there is a description of the main character, a writer, Gustav von Aschenbach (a thinly veiled portrait of the Austrian composer Gustav Mahler) that fits the high-tensile life of this type of artist:

> "You see, Aschenbach lived like this from the very beginning," the speaker made a fist of the fingers of his left hand, "never like this," and he let the open hand hang down from the arm of his chair. And he was right; and the brave moral of it all was that he had only been called to this constant tension in his career—he had not been born to it.

The similarities should not be over-interpreted, however; the extraordinary, and speaking purely quantitatively, enormous achievements of Fischer-Dieskau as a musician could not have been achieved without such tensions. The price is isolation: "For in spite of all the musical life of this town and all the many people that we know, we do not have any real friends."[10]

His concentration increased immediately before every appearance, for Fischer-Dieskau is not one of those artists who can let nervous tension be warded off by distractions before going onto the platform. That is one side of the coin; the other side is his gift for admiring other artists. You only have to hear him enthuse over Daniel Barenboim's Mozart-like musicality, which would have made him in other, "shall we say, more musical, times?" a composer as well, or hear how he speaks of his younger accompanists Hartmut Höll and András Schiff with such loving admiration. Their art, like that of many of their predecessors, presented him with new challenges and joy in making music together; and then there is Sviatoslav Richter, to whom he felt bound by a perfect understanding. These are only a few examples among many.[11]

Fischer-Dieskau wrote later about Ferenc Fricsay: "To have met this great musician, to have accompanied him a little way on his journey, was a

With the conductor Ferenc Fricsay before the premiere of Mozart's *Don Giovanni*, which opened the new Deutsche Oper Berlin in September 1961.

gift for which one can only be thankful."[12] This ability to admire like-minded experts as enthusiastic about music as himself, restores the balance between closeness to some and distance from others. Such admiration was, and is, naturally felt for other singers, conductors, and stage directors. Actors are counted among his friends, and writers have an almost exaggerated respect for his nature (which tends to praise rather than criticize), perhaps because of their, and his own, high standards.

Among conductors, it was Wilhelm Furtwängler (1886–1954) who impressed him first of all. How highly, and yet how precisely, he can rate him can be seen from a letter to the music critic Professor Karla Höcker, which also suggests the impetus that he received from him:

Perhaps I should say the following about Furtwängler: unfortunately, I only got to know him in the last years of his career, at a time when he was having hearing difficulties after his journeys by air. He also told me again and again that conducting was giving him less and less pleasure and that he longed to have more peace to compose. He kept asking me when we were rehearsing Mahler's *Kindertotenlieder* (Songs on the Death of Children) (1901–1904) in Berlin, whether this or that section of the orchestra was actually playing, whether the winds were in tune, and so on.[13]

H. H. Stuckenschmidt wrote very positively about Furtwängler's compositions, but reading between the lines, one could see how problematic the creative achievements of any artist could appear when, as an interpreter, he was so bound to tradition. Furtwängler, who held fast to the belief that music was bound to its place of origin, and that that was given by its tonality, was quite able to interpret the spirit of Romanticism for contemporary audiences. Stuckenschmidt's article on the conductor's Second Symphony (1944–1945) (in the *Neue Zeitung* of 26 February 1948) illuminates both Furtwängler's own compositions and the musico-cultural background of Fischer-Dieskau's beginnings as a singer:

> Wilhelm Furtwängler's Second Symphony in E minor, a fruit of the years 1944–1945, continues his series of colossal works. It lasts eighty minutes, and its four movements, which demand great respect from the initiated, develop a compendium of the arts of constructing symphonic movements. In its mighty developments, massive, many-voiced, and powerful outpourings from the orchestra, one finds Romantic ideas reworked, then reappearing in a multiplicity of themes . . . . The Berlin Philharmonic Orchestra under Furtwängler gave a performance that illuminated every detail of this enormously difficult score. It would be difficult to say whether the generous applause was meant for the great conductor or for his work, which was certainly unusual and which gave proof of a high level of culture.

Fischer-Dieskau occasionally pleaded for modern conductors and orchestras to play Furtwängler's compositions more often. When put to the test, however, such as by listening to a recording of Furtwängler's Second Symphony, the singer was disturbed by its epigonality.

Might this have encouraged Fischer-Dieskau—who, after all, has been active in several artistic spheres—to compose himself? Furtwängler's example had nothing to do with his own decision, either negatively or positively. He traces his lack of desire to compose back to his basic convictions. He claims that art must always have something new and fresh to say, and when it is pointed out to him that he has been able to achieve this goal through his own interpretations, he answers that the interpreter has really very little room in which to do this. He can make works live, and he can keep works alive, but the composer has to say something new. He feels that as an interpreter, he cannot say anything new, nothing that would cause a shock. Then again, he wonders whether everything has not been said already.

Dietrich Fischer-Dieskau continued his memories of Furtwängler's later years:

> Then Furtwängler tried to evoke more than ever before an imagined sound, which he could never evoke in rehearsals, since he never spoke much during the preparatory work. Having previously hugely enjoyed going into detail in rehearsal, he now sought creativity more and more in the performance. Indeed, there, through his very presence and the aura of complete involvement in the work being played, he was able to achieve sheer miracles of transformation in both musicians and audience.

Fischer-Dieskau did not restrict his description to the mere effect that Furtwängler had on his contemporaries, but went on to discuss his working method in detail:

> His own (very personal) conducting technique had a great deal to do with achieving this act of transformation; he gave only the minimum of metrical beat and was much more concerned with the overall structure, giving time for breathing and preparation, and, above all, a lead-in to those hugely impressive crescendi and decrescendi. He kept insisting on "naturalness," by which he meant a technical loosening of tension, which could then be applied to the internal development of the music.

Fischer-Dieskau's own experience confirmed this:

> When, much too early, I recorded the role of Kurwenal in *Tristan and Isolde* with him [in 1952] at his insistent request, I tried to get an "older" vocal timbre and a heroic tone by darkening my voice. He turned that down with the remark that I should just listen to the sound of my own voice—and let it remain "natural." And the beginner never forgot that piece of advice.

(Later music critics—or at least some music critics—have had a field day with terms like *naturalness, artistic consciousness,* and *artificiality.*) Here is one example of the cooperation between conductor and singer:

> When I was singing the recitatives of Jesus for him in Vienna [in 1954], I conceitedly tried to start right on the written note after the strings had begun. Furtwängler waggled his baton in his inimitable

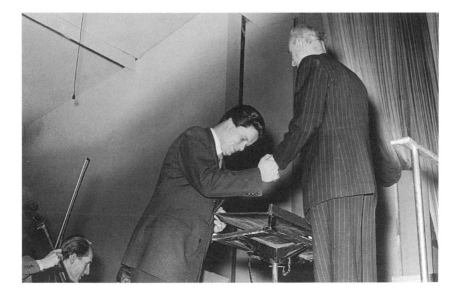

With the conductor Wilhelm Furtwängler in 1953 at the end of a concert in Berlin's Titania Palast. Fischer-Dieskau sang Gustav Mahler's *Kindertotenlieder* (Songs on the Death of Children).

way and said: "Now, just let the accompaniment get underway first!" And, true enough, the recitative sounds much more effective if, by letting the voice hold back, there is "space" made for the Christ figure.

His meeting with Furtwängler was arranged by Enrico Mainardi, with whom the future Frau Fischer-Dieskau, Irmgard Poppen, was attending the summer course in Salzburg, as has already been mentioned. Fischer-Dieskau has described how he had to sing Brahms's *Four Serious Songs* for the great man. After shaking hands, the conductor mumbled (quite unnecessarily!) "Furtwängler," and then sat down at the piano and began to play the music on the music stand, which had, of course, already been agreed on: Brahms's *Four Serious Songs*.

Elisabeth Furtwängler later recalled the remark of her astonished husband,

> that such a young man should already know exactly how that should be sung . . . and then he added thoughtfully: "Of course, I knew that, too, when I was quite young." It sounded almost like surprise— I had a good laugh and so did he.[14]

The discrepancy between doing real justice to a work of art, on the one hand, and of having to present it to an absolutely heterogeneous audience, on the other, was felt equally by the young artist and the aging conductor.

Fischer-Dieskau has never quite lost a certain shyness with people, and he still does not find this unusual. "Concentration on your work forces you to be lonely," he said during a conversation at the 1993 Berlin Festival. From the very beginning of his career, quite practical circumstances played the most important role: "You had to reckon with being in the studio all day, working on your own or with colleagues, so, you were always on the job," he said. On the other hand, he looks at his profession very pragmatically: "As an artist, I help people to pass the time — and so it has to be. You must just put up with it."

In the early stages of his becoming famous, he was not able to be so casual about it, and his inborn shyness, coupled with a constant awareness of the crucial importance of art, led now and then to the fear of not being able to measure up to others', and his own, high standards. His young wife Irmel was always there to encourage him, however.

Yet not even a couple of musicians such as this pair could live solely in the isolated world of art. Living conditions in the beleaguered city affected everyday life. The cardboard-thin walls between the provisionally separated flats in the house in Berlin's Charlottenburg district (and the regular journeys for coal) kept them both in touch with cold reality, not to mention the daily question of what there might be to eat.

Fischer-Dieskau lived in Berlin, but he soon became one who came and went; he left the town for Lieder tours, and always saw it in a new light on his return. That was yet another obstacle to creating and maintaining friendships, something that he really wanted to do, and why he felt it important to travel whenever possible, not alone, but with his wife. Thus developed a quite conscious need for union with Irmel, which could only be strengthened with the passing of the years. This was the typical paradoxical situation of the artist, who seeks, simultaneously, freedom and a bond. Examples are legion. The practicing musician, the soloist above all, is an exception, an outcast, if you will, who needs a bond with an intimate confidante.

The singer's unique career, with its impressive beginnings in Berlin in 1947–1948, took off under such exceptional circumstances that Herr Stuckenschmidt's remark that "there were not many newcomers" (see above) was, in fact, accurate. The war had destroyed many promising young talents and had also ruined the careers of many established singers. Yet there was also a fairly large group of experienced singers against which the debutant was immediately measured. Heinrich Schlusnus (1888–1952), the idol

of at least two generations of concert-goers, had even twice alternated with
Fischer-Dieskau as Posa in Verdi's *Don Carlos* at the Städtische Oper in
Berlin—the twenty-three-year-old with the sixty-year-old! Fischer-Dieskau
had heard him sing in a recital when he was a schoolboy and had admired
the beauty of the voice and the "easy, high notes," but without ever having
wanted to model himself on him. Indeed, he felt himself to be, artistically
speaking, closer to Hans Hotter, the bass, born in 1909 and thus sixteen years
older than Fischer-Dieskau. A younger artist who challenged him in many
ways was the baritone Hermann Prey (born 1929), who, although not
singing in public quite as early as this, nevertheless had a crucial experience
vis-à-vis the young Fischer-Dieskau. Prey wrote:

> Despite all my enthusiasm for music and for my studies, there were
> also moments of self-doubt, the feeling of not being able to achieve
> what I wanted and of having to give it all up. In short, I had my
> crises; for example, in 1948, after I had heard the baritone Dietrich
> Fischer-Dieskau, four years older than myself, in the Berlin Titania
> Palast. Hertha Klust accompanied him in Schubert's *Winterreise*.
> The way Fischer-Dieskau sang, the way the pair made music
> together . . . made an enormous impression on me. When I left the
> hall, I asked myself if there was any point in my going on singing.
> Here was someone doing everything that I myself had imagined
> as perfection. I think that Fischer-Dieskau was setting new standards
> at that time—if he had not set them, perhaps I would not have got
> so far.

(Fischer-Dieskau recalls that his first recital with Hertha Klust was not until
1949, and then it was *Die schöne Müllerin*—but that does not detract from
the reality of Prey's experience.) Prey went on:

> Later we appeared together on the stage in Salzburg and Munich,
> or in radio programs, and I look back with pleasure at that coopera-
> tion with the great singer.[15]

They sang together as Figaro and Count Almaviva in *The Marriage of Figaro*
and as Alfonso and Guglielmo in Mozart's *Così fan tutte*—and the appreciation is truly mutual.

It is no coincidence that most of Fischer-Dieskau's early memories are
of his Schubert recitals, for indeed his interpretations of the great Schubert
song cycles *Die schöne Müllerin* and *Winterreise* demonstrated most clearly
his new vocal timbre and his new style of interpretation. At the same time,
later impressions throw some light on the earlier ones.[16] How often has he
sung both these cycles in his forty-five-year career as a singer, taking 1948 as

his starting-point? One should not forget either that not just in the course of his career, but from his very first recitals and concerts, the older music as well as the "modern" formed a goodly part of his repertoire.

Immediately after his return from POW camps he sang the role of Jesus in J. S. Bach's *St. Matthew Passion* in Freiburg and surrounding towns. In 1992, he sang, for the last time, the role of Jesus in Bach's *St. John Passion.* In between these, there stretches a seemingly endless list of interpretations of sacred music, centered around Johann Sebastian Bach: "There is no music that is at the same time more expressive, more technically demanding, and more rewarding for the voice than Bach's," he said later in an interview.[17]

Bach cantatas were among his first broadcasts from the RIAS station in 1947; the most convincing example of the early maturity of his Bach interpretations might be the 1951 LP recording (APM 14004) of the *Kreuzstab* (BWV 56) with the Berlin Chamber Orchestra, conducted by Karl Ristenpart. Those who know the later recordings—with the Festival Strings, Lucerne, and Rudolf Baumgartner from 1963; with the Munich Bach Choir and Karl Richter from 1969; and with the Gächinger Kantorei and Helmuth Rilling from 1983—will agree that the singer had already understood and mastered this technically very difficult work on the first recording, but also that although none of the interpretations is exactly the same, the spontaneity of that first recording is to be found in all the others. The *Kreuzstab* cantata is only one, albeit a particularly significant, example of this feature of his art. If one follows his recordings chronologically, be they of classical, Romantic, or modern music, this phenomenon recurs continually, namely, that there are no mere repetitions, no conservation of a once worked-out formula, and yet all the recordings encompass the musical shape of the work completely. Many of Fischer-Dieskau's interpretations have evoked sharp criticism (whether these were valid or not will not be discussed for the moment) and aroused the antipathy that new and unusual things always do. But, to repeat: quite independently of what might have been "right" or "wrong" (by which criteria is that measured anyway?), they were indicative of an unceasing absorption in the works, with each single work, over several decades. That was true for music of every genre and from widely differing epochs.

During the first Berlin Festival of 1951, the young Fischer-Dieskau partnered the tenor Helmut Krebs in Béla Bartók's *Cantata profana* (1930) for double chorus, soloists, and orchestra as naturally as he had a few days before in Igor Stravinsky's *Oedipus Rex* (1927); then, some days later, he sang Schubert's *Die schöne Müllerin*, again with Hertha Klust as accompanist. (He describes Hertha Klust in his memoirs as one of the few great "originals" in the theater, which is otherwise usually a place for "commercial normality.")[18]

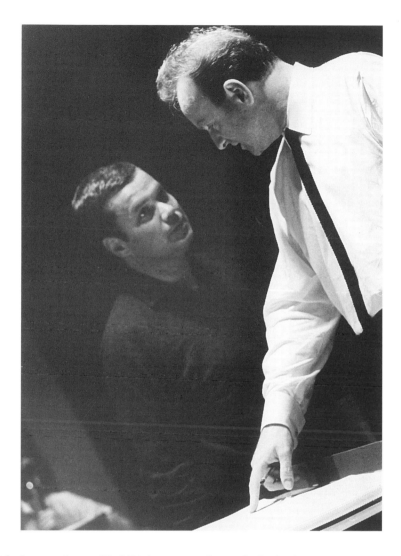

With the conductor Karl Richter at a rehearsal of Gluck's opera *Orpheus and Eurydice* in the Hercules Hall in Munich, 1967.

There was no question of specialization for Fischer-Dieskau from his earliest days as a singer, mainly, of course, because of the wide and varied repertoire of the Städtische Oper but also because of the singer's own musical and intellectual curiosity. He did not become totally absorbed in the albeit beloved sphere of the German Lied, because he was the last person to be totally absorbed in any one thing. Those who have seen and heard him in a recital will remember their impression of a very alert interpreter. He regards the Romantic art song as a challenge as much to the listener as to the singer. The voice evokes no sad memories of an age long past, unless it is a longing for the lost past itself. Yet this has nothing to do with the distance in time between epochs. The young musician did not want to be a "keeper of the past" but rather an "awakener," although, once again, that would really be too grand a word for him today. Just the same, there are remarkable witnesses to his attitude toward the music of his own times (which he did not just discover later on in his career), as, for example, when the younger (and the older) composers came to him in the hope of winning recognition of their music through him. Frank Martin, the Swiss composer (1890–1974) expressed this very plainly when he invited Fischer-Dieskau to sing the role of Prospero in his opera based on Shakespeare's *The Tempest:* "J'ose penser que ce rôle chanté et incarné sur la scène par vous, c'est déjà partie gagnée" (I dare to think that this role, when sung and incarnated on stage by you, is certain to be a success). That was in 1955, and there is a 1963 DGG recording with excerpts from the opera, conducted by the composer. Yet Fischer-Dieskau has never sung this part on stage. Scheduled to sing in the premiere in Vienna in 1956, he had to withdraw because of food poisoning, which, in fact, nearly cost him his life.

In 1953 Fischer-Dieskau called to the composer Paul Hindemith for help. Fischer-Dieskau wrote:

> Dear revered Maestro,
>
> It is not so easy nowadays for a poor uncreative interpreter of the German Lied. *Winterreise,* [*Die schöne*] *Müllerin, Dichterliebe,* [*Die schöne*] *Magelone* are dear companions, and I should miss them. But, again and again, I am accused of treading the same, old "well-worn paths"—for Lieder programs are based mainly on the cyles, after all.
>
> Aren't the women lucky? They can sing your *Marienleben* (The Life of Mary) cycle [1922, rev. 1948], but we male voices have to be content with the choice of those songs of our contemporaries that are timeless.
>
> Only you can compose a really "classical" counterpart to the *Marienleben*—and you really should do it."[19]

Nothing came of it. He did sing Hindemith's Lieder later—there is a 1984 recording with Aribert Reimann at the piano—and, of course, he regularly sang the title role in Hindemith's opera *Mathis der Maler* (Mathis the Painter) (1935), often claiming it to be his favorite role, then the eponymous

Cardillac (1926) and *Requiem für die, die wir lieben* (A Requiem for Those We Love) (1946). When the composer invited him, in 1960, to sing his new work (Latin psalms), however, Fischer-Dieskau had to decline:

> I have at last managed to study the motets more closely . . . and, after some hesitation, I came to the conclusion that you would do better with a tenor for so specifically a tenor role. I should have to put the whole work down a minor third and that would mean that the piano would be just growling away in the bass. But, even then, in its whole thrust and character, it really is a work for a tenor.

All the same, Hindemith signaled his intention of dedicating the work to Fischer-Dieskau, but the tenor Ernst Haefliger, who sang the work at its premiere, was the right person, both for the work and the dedication.

At the beginning of the 1950s, Fischer-Dieskau was deeply involved, both willingly and unwillingly, with new, modern music. Winfried Zillig's opera *Troilus and Cressida* was premiered in 1951, and Fischer-Dieskau, now twenty-six, shared the stage of the Städtische Oper in Berlin (as Troilus) with Elisabeth Grümmer as Cressida. His short Grecian "skirt" caused him just as much trouble as the epigonal music of this first operatic attempt by a pupil of Schoenberg. Later, when he was able to choose his operatic roles as he chose his Lieder programs, he always looked for modern music that would suit his voice. Twenty years later, he wrote:

> As a man of and for my own times, I feel a duty to help talented young people, and not just to work exclusively in the service of the great names of the past.

He sharply rebutted injudicious criticisms of contemporary settings of poetry: "Intolerant young people like you have always criticized anything unusual or frightening."[20] These words were clearly not just meant to protect the talented composer Friedhelm Döhl and his attempt to set fragmentary notes of the mentally ill German poet Friedrich Hölderlin suitably to music; beyond that, they underlined his own existential problem. He refused to be seen as the keeper of an inviolate and inviolable classical heritage. He did not simply refuse, he justified his refusal:

> The task of not allowing the tattered remnants of a sunken culture to be buried, but rather to guide them toward the possible reestablishment of a link with the present, is always uppermost in my mind. But to bring this about, you must also come to terms with all the serious experiments of our own times.

He took this view most earnestly and was not amused when someone tried to offer him "old wine in new bottles." His honesty did not allow a polite sparing of feelings. One writer received these answers:

> After all the creative richnesses that have succored the Lied during the past two centuries, pretty, rather trivial tunes are really not good enough. . . . [or] We are not helped by the eclectic plagiarism of so many others now that the source of previously available material has dried up. . . . [or] You should take an accredited course in composition so that you actually learn the basics, and then you might avoid all the offenses committed in the search for that simplicity which seems to be your goal. . . . [or] We have seen numerous attempts in past decades to reach a new naiveté. We have to realize that it can no longer be found, for we have been through a process of awareness that cannot be reversed. To try to write with the innocence of a Neefe or a Zumsteeg seems to me to be almost blasphemous vis-à-vis poems that, for the great part, have received perfectly valid treatment by the great masters.[21]

Such quotations are, of course, somewhat anticipatory, because they are taken from the correspondence of later years, but the 1950s are nowadays already seen so much as a historical epoch (particularly in Germany) that people have long since begun to collect its signs and symbols, and, no less, its slogans and catchwords.

It was in the 1950s that Dietrich Fischer-Dieskau's career began to take wing—and that was also the time of the burgeoning West German Wirtschaftswunder (the economic miracle) set in motion by the West German Christian Democrat politician and later Federal Chancellor (1963–1966) Ludwig Erhard (1897–1977). Looking back, it is that economic boom, the lust for food, cars, travel, and houses with kidney-shaped tables, swinging garden-seats, and abstract-patterned wallpaper, that one remembers. This second "postwar" period can hardly be thought of as a "Restoration"; indeed, anyone who had imagined that the Stunde Null (the zero hour, i.e. 1945) was a chance for a new beginning must have been very disappointed. But that first postwar period was itself artificial—it never really existed in a historical sense—and defeated Germany did not stand alone in the world; hardly had it reawakened after the catastrophe of defeat in 1945 than it found itself tied into a network of interest groups in which it tried to orientate itself. Much goodwill was invested then, and much of the awkward past was swept under the carpet. The Allies, with their partly naive, partly half-hearted de-Nazification policies, helped Germany back on her feet. That meant a return to a normal, essential way of life. The premises for life in a democracy (first of all, prescribed, then quickly accepted) and for extensive personal freedom (in the West) were created in May 1949 by the approval of the Grundgesetz (the Basic Law) by the Parliamentary Council for the Federal Republic of Germany. Before this, a market economy and the 1948 currency reform had opened the door to affluence. Yet this important date has to be seen as part of the interests of the two great power-blocs. The years of West Germany's, and West Berlin's, economic booms were also the years of the Cold War. Berlin became the arena of the power struggle between West and East. After the 1948–1949 blockade, Berlin suffered crisis after crisis, and it was seen more clearly in that city than anywhere else that it was all indeed about power, but also about a struggle between systems and about the relative freedom of the individual. Through his attitude to the arts, and even more through his way of singing, Fischer-Dieskau was one of those who sang about freedom without having to underlay it with tendentious words. His art said implicitly what the Marquis of Posa in Schiller's *Don Carlos* said explicitly to the Spanish King Philip: "Geben Sie Gedankenfreiheit!" (Give freedom of thought!).[22]

When the 1950s and early 1960s were over, the Germans learned to turn a blind eye to the political element in every aspect of art and everyday life, and because of this, the 1950s now appear to have been quite apolitical. Ivan Nagel, the German author and critic, referred to this period, with which he identified himself, when he wrote:

> I think that the incomparable effect on all of us of Dietrich Fischer-Dieskau's debut had something political in it—certainly in our peculiarly apolitical political consciousness of those first years of peace. His new style of singing was the negation, not only of political violence and power, especially of the cursed sort just past, but it was also the rejection of all ideologies, with their sacred beliefs, of which German singers of the past had regarded themselves as the guardians: rejection of the Sublime, of that woolly fervor and profundity whose true name was—once again—power.

The sentimentality of the late nineteenth century had also settled on the vocal tradition of the early twentieth. Yet Fischer-Dieskau's "new style of singing" was rightly seen as a rejection of all ideologies, of all prejudices. Rejection was not what he had in mind, however, but rather the courage to express his personal feelings. A human voice sang what a human being can feel. Therefore, the truth lies in an additional sentence in Ivan Nagel's complimentary remarks: "The singularly personal element in the voice of that twenty-six-year-old was our guarantee of credibility: for us, you see, it came from a knowledgeable contemporary, and not from a know-it-all."[23] Thus, the artistic effect was closely bound to the personality—perhaps another justification for this genre of biography.

On the world's stage, the 1950s had begun with the outbreak of the Korean War in June 1950. Europe's population, just recovering from the ravages of World War II, feared an escalation of the conflict, since it marked the first military confrontation in the festering East-West crisis. In German domestic politics, it was the beginning of the debate about German rearmament. The thesis of Alleinvertretung [sole representation, i.e., that the Federal Republic, and *not* the German Democratic Republic (GDR), was the legitimate successor to pre-Nazi German] was born in the Federal Republic. The East Berlin Superior Court of Justice ordered the destruction of the Stadtschloss (town castle), and in far-off Indochina, the guerrilla war between the Vietminh and the French colonial power took on new dimensions. During the decade, and far beyond it, Berlin was the center of that political and ideological struggle. Both sides, East and West, regarded the city as a security in the Cold War.

Nor did the rebuilding, or the cementing, of social structures proceed as quickly in Berlin as in West Germany. The pacifying effect of the economic boom was not felt as quickly in Berlin because of the immediacy of the threat from the new totalitarian power bloc, the German Democratic Republic, which had been founded on 7 October 1949, a month after the inauguration of the Federal Republic under the chancellorship of Dr. Konrad Adenauer. Nonetheless, as everywhere else, so also in Berlin, there was not only the desire to eat as much as possible, to have a roof over one's head and, perhaps, a bath in the house—the term coined was the *Wohnwelle* (a wave, or a rush for accommodation)—but also a *Reisewelle* (rush to travel), the wish to see other countries after years of self-incarceration. There was also the need to catch up on developments in the arts, which had not yet been satisfied, beyond what the writer Ursula von Kardorff had called "the comfortable reliance on art-without-risk" or on the familiar. World literature, particularly American, British, and French trivia, flowed into the almost parched literary landscape of West Germany. *Rowohlts Rotations-Romane* ("rotation novels" from the firm of Rowohlt) were, to begin with, actually printed in the format of newspapers and popularized books and readings, or, at least, were intended so. Underground and forbidden plays and authors were produced once again, and the Existentialist philosophy of the French writer Jean-Paul Sartre (1905–1980) influenced Germany's literary fashions. The churches could recall the fortunate existence during the Nazi period of the Bekennende Kirche (literally "confessing church," an organization of churches that had bravely opposed the Nazi régime). Bertolt Brecht's (1896–1956) left-wing plays were produced (or, at any rate, attacked, overpraised, or damned); then again, diametrically opposed to any ideology was Samuel Beckett's (1906–1989) "Theater of the Absurd"; and, in Germany, the plays of Eugene Ionesco (1912–1994) particularly amazed the audiences. We read in the magazine *Der Spiegel* for 8 March 1961: "Beckett, whose musical tastes are well developed, has a particular penchant for the art of the German baritone Dietrich Fischer-Dieskau and has offered Mihalovici three one-acters in English," for setting to music, it was clear. Marcel Mihalovici (1898–1985) chose *Krapp's Last Tape*; Fischer-Dieskau never sang the work, but he did attend the German Sprechtheater (Speech Theater, where only spoken drama is performed) performance in 1959 with his friend Walter Franck, the actor.

The singer has never lost his love for the German Sprechtheater. He had lived through and much enjoyed the great era in Berlin of the director and producer Oskar Fritz Schuh. An unforgettable discovery for Fischer-Dieskau was the Wiener Ensemble, directed by Leopold Rudolf and Aglaja Schmid, who created memorable theatrical evenings with *Der Schwierige* (The Difficult Man) (1921) by the Austrian dramatist Hugo von Hofmannsthal (1874–1929). Eric Ode was then living in the top floor of the Fischer-Dieskau house in Charlottenburg, and when his theatrical colleagues came to visit him, they often found their way down to the Fischer-Dieskau flat. Aglaja Schmid and Leopold Rudolf became good friends of the Fischer-Dieskaus; Ernst Stankowski used to love to sing there with his guitar; the actor Gustav Knuth dropped by now and then, as did Walter Gross, the comedian Theo Lingen, and the Meisel-Lingens.

The singer first worked with Oskar Fritz Schuh as director as early as 1956 in Salzburg. A dozen or so years later, Schuh recalled that for the first time in his experience of opera, he had found a singer with whom he could make real contact: "This mixture of true vocal genius and an understanding for art—we never had this before you came along."[24]

The 1950s in West Germany were, however, not all of a piece. The popularization and commercialization of culture certainly went hand in hand. Art (and this was of course nothing new) came after bread and all those other needs that had to be satisfied. Art became part of the Marktwirtschaft (the market economy) and yet also escaped from it at the same time—through subventions. The freedom of the arts was guaranteed in the West, and it became difficult to speak about the limitations that nevertheless clearly existed, particularly when they could not be laid at the door of the State, and especially when the Berliners could observe the totalitarian system right in front of their eyes on the other side of the Iron Curtain in the Soviet sector of Berlin. It was also in the 1950s that the first wave of commuters began coming over from East to West; in 1953, 42,000 West Berliners still worked in the eastern half of the city, and 33,000 East Berliners in the western half; 1953 was also the year when, on 17 June, the population of the East rose up against the regime in the GDR. By 19 June, the revolt was stifled. In the young Federal Republic, Konrad Adenauer and his Christian Democratic Union (CDU) party won an absolute majority in the Bundestag elections on 6 September, so this was "Adenauer Time"! But it was also the great time of the so-called Gruppe 47. [Group 47 was a group of new young writers that included the future Nobel Prize winner, Heinrich Böll (1917–1985).] In 1953, the prize of this group, founded by Hans Werner Richter (1908–1990), went to the Austrian poet Ingeborg Bachmann (1926–1973), whom Fischer-Dieskau met with Hans Werner Henze in Naples and who later visited him regularly in Berlin.

All this formed part of the contemporary background to Fischer-Dieskau's career as a musician, and influenced him, too, of course. It would not be too far-fetched either to claim that he helped to shape that part of cultural life in Berlin and the Federal Republic that could be defined as "high culture" and that was connected with the famous (or infamous) "restoration" of those years. As an operatic singer, he was also involved in the reclaiming of what had been the rather uncertain terrain of bourgeois high culture, which could be observed in the building of new opera houses and the rebuilding of those which had been bombed. And what about the Lieder singer? There he stood in evening dress, like all the others before him; he profited, too, of course, from the general need and longing for Kultur. What he had to offer corresponded to the hopes of a duped and disappointed bourgeoisie, which the old, neglected values, dragged through the mud with the rise and fall of a barbaric regime, had revived. In the Lieder of Schubert, Schumann, and Brahms, they would surely find something of their old cultural heritage, of that unassailable tradition. They were proved right: what they heard from him had remained viable, had remained valid, because they accepted it intuitively and, what was really the same side of the coin, they looked at it with a new consciousness.

Fischer-Dieskau's operatic debut in Verdi's *Don Carlos* on 18 November 1948 was described by Walter Hardt, at that time editor of the Berlin journal *Musikblätter*, thus: "Beside him [i.e., Josef Greindl as King Philip], young Fischer-Dieskau's Posa made its mark because of his incredibly secure, inner intuition."[25]

But there was something else: the young man's fierce desire to shape a role, and his determination to do it better than his predecessors. This can be seen most clearly in his Lieder recital programs; there were no more of those varied programs, so popular in pre-war days, and even as late as the 1950s. Poem and music, music and poem, should be an entity. Thus, the programs presented the works of one poet or one composer. Even a musician like Wilhelm Furtwängler doubted whether the public would accept a Beethoven program on its own, but was that really such a novelty?

The Beethoven program, something almost unique in the repertoire of a Lieder recitalist, was described by Fischer-Dieskau himself: "It is true that the expressiveness and character of these confessional miniatures, so personal to Beethoven, fragmented, stormy, even untamed, are never met with anywhere else in the history of music." It continually reappeared in Fischer-Dieskau's repertoire, however, precisely for the above reasons, and it also appeared as a recording (with Jörg Demus) in April 1966. (There had been an earlier issue of two LPs of Beethoven's Lieder with Hertha Klust as accompanist, as early as 1954. *Trans.*) The order of the Lieder in this program confirms the thematic range of the compositions:

"In questa tomba oscura" (In This Dark Tomb), Giuseppe Carpani
"An die Hoffnung" (To Hope), Christoph August Tiedge
Sechs Lieder (Six Songs), after Christoph Fürchtegott Gellert
"Der Wachtelschlag" (The Song of the Quail), Samuel Friedrich Sauter
Song cycle: *An die ferne Geliebte* (To the Distant Beloved), Alois Isidor
    Jeitteles
"Adelaide," Friedrich von Matthisson
"Wonne der Wehmut" (Joy of Sadness), Goethe
"Mailied" (May Song), Goethe
"Sehnsucht" (Longing), Goethe
"Neue Liebe, neues Leben" (New Love, New Life), Goethe
"Mephistos Flohlied" (from *Faust*) (Mephisto's Song of the Flea),
    Goethe.

And the question once again: Was that really such a novelty?

Fischer-Dieskau felt himself to be truly part of a great tradition when he gave a recital:

> I had the good fortune to have been overwhelmed by my impressions of a Lieder recital when I was quite young (I was nine), and I have never forgotten them. Among those memories were the recitals given by Emmi Leisner (1885–1958), the great Lieder singer of the 1920s and 1930s, who, probably because she had a firmly based intellectual public in Berlin, could afford to hold a subscription cycle every year in the Beethoven Hall. These were all "closed" programs, that is, song cycles, or programs on the works of one composer (Max Reger or Hans Pfitzner). This contralto, who had a vocal timbre never heard nowadays, was, however, by no means the

first to make up a program like that. Brahms's friend, Julius Stockhausen (1826–1906) really started it off, and he was emulated by Raimund von zur Mühlen (1854–1931) [who died in Sussex] and Johannes Messchaert (1857–1922). So, you see, there were precursors.[26]

Yet it does seem that we have to go a long way back to find such precursors, and Fischer-Dieskau has now clearly become a trailblazer with his Lieder programs. Few keep to their precepts as strictly as he does; he much dislikes merely trying to please an audience. Amazingly, audiences were so willing to be led and to accept—clearly and gladly—the singer's ambitious demands.

Or did they actually misunderstand him? These were not, of course, new audiences, at least, not the majority that filled the concert-halls from the 1950s on, but rather the same music-lovers who had enjoyed those former, sometimes ill-prepared recitals of Lieder mixed with operatic arias. Nor could one assert that recital audiences after 1945 were exactly looking for a "new style of singing," or even for "something new." No, they all wanted to hear the same old, beloved Lieder—but then along came a singer who clearly demonstrated that it was Heinrich Heine's "alten bösen Lieder" (the old, evil, songs) [from his poem in the cycle *Dichterliebe* (Poet's Love) set by Schumann] and, above all, the sad songs, that reminded those audiences of what could be neither forgotten nor explained away.

The misunderstanding, if there was one, was not limited to the 1950s, however. What is it, one could ask, that attracts a public of thousands to an art form in which people sing so often about suffering and death as they do in the Lieder of German Romanticism? Why is the saddest work of all, Schubert's *Winterreise* (written, furthermore, in the last years of his life in 1827–1828), such a magnet for modern audiences? What is it that they hear in it? The attraction of a voice? Or more perhaps—an intellectual and musical statement created by virtuosity? Fischer-Dieskau has always felt himself fortunate to have been able to employ his voice both emotionally and intellectually. He has never lightened the sadness, the dark melancholy that broods over German Lieder, never let it descend to a pretty, soothing vocalizing, but rather he let it be heard to the full, as perhaps no other singer before him. He showed the memento mori of this art form, warts and all, so to speak—and his audiences lapped it up. One cannot deny either that during his interpretations, moments of hope and of (swiftly fleeting) happiness can be savored more deliciously than with anyone else's. Yet not only were these great moments of joy and sadness, however important a part of the literature of the German Lied they may be, so immediately convincing, but Fischer-Dieskau also appreciated the humor of many Lieder and brought it out: for example, in the song "Zur Warnung" (A Warning) from Hugo Wolf's Mörike Lieder, which was sung in a wonderful, "hung-over" voice to represent the man who had had "one too many"; or in Wolf's "Abschied" (Farewell), in which a none-too-welcome critic is booted downstairs and the piano postlude turns out to be a riotous Viennese waltz; or in Schumann's "Sitz' ich allein" (When I Sit Alone) from Goethe's *West-östlicher Divan* (The West-East Divan), a collection of poems with oriental themes:

> *Sitz' ich allein*
> *Wo kann ich besser sein?*
> *Meinen Wein*
> *Trink ich allein*
> *Niemand setzt mir Schranken*
> *Ich hab' so meine eignen Gedanken.*

> When I sit alone
> Where can I be better off?
> When I drink on my own
> Nobody can set me limits;
> So, I have my own thoughts.

Did audiences notice the "new credibility" that Ivan Nagel spoke about (see above)? From what culture of listening does or did it come? At any rate, it does seem that from these very first Lieder recitals in Berlin, a bond was established between Dietrich Fischer-Dieskau and his audiences that remained firm for the whole of his career and was validated by audiences all over the world; a phenomenon that has to do with his voice, his talent, his craftsmanship, and his art, with listening and understanding, with the aura of his personality, and probably also partly because this singer, through his musicality, his integrity—in short, his whole attitude—incorporated the durability of values. He seemed to validate—or perhaps actually did validate —values that were collapsing or seemed to be collapsing all around.

Of course, the unity of a Lieder recital that Fischer-Dieskau was striving to achieve had already been established by the song cycles of Schubert, Schumann, Brahms, et al. Yet single songs from Schubert's *Winterreise*, or more often from his *Die schöne Müllerin*, would be regularly included in a program by, say, the German baritone Gerhard Hüsch (1901–1984), who, of course, also sang the complete cycles. In contrast, *Winterreise* and *Die schöne Müllerin*, Schumann's *Liederkreis* cycles (Opp. 24 and 39), and Brahms's *Die schöne Magelone* (Op. 33) became the cornerstones of Fischer-Dieskau's repertoire. Many other cycles were added: apart from Mahler's orchestral cycles, the *Lieder eines fahrenden Gesellen* (1883) (not too well translated as Songs of a Wayfarer; the young man is really an "apprentice" journeying from job to job, *Trans.*) and his *Kindertotenlieder* (Songs on the Death of Children) (1902). There were also the more modern cycles, written sometimes especially for Fischer-Dieskau by contemporary composers such as Hans Werner Henze (b. 1926), Siegfried Matthus (b. 1934), or Benjamin Britten (1913–1976). When he sang a cycle such as *Lebendig begraben* (Buried Alive) (Op. 40, 1927) by the Swiss composer Othmar Schoeck (1886–1957) to poems by his countryman Gottfried Keller (1819–1890), a work that lasts almost an hour without an intermission, it too sounded as though it had been written just for him. The recordings of these works give the same impression, even if Lieder recitals and recordings in a studio obey their own laws. To receive the original impression, concert excerpts are more helpful, such as the CDs made by the Orfeo firm from recitals between 1957–1965 at the Salzburg Festival, but these, too, remain a far cry from the immediate experience in the concert hall, simply because they lack the singer's attitudes and gestures. In many cases, the record will give us a compilation, rather like a collection of materials; one has to know what to do with it.

A Fischer-Dieskau Lieder recital follows dramaturgical precepts, not thematic principles; these are quite separate from the chronological order. The order of keys is as important as the change from soft to loud, from slow to fast. One adagio song after the other will lull an audience to sleep. Fischer-Dieskau's precept is: What is the effect of the song? The beginning is as important as the conclusion. Fischer-Dieskau prefers to jump in with the first song, without any preamble, and he always looks for an impressive conclusion to the final song—which one hardly ever finds in Brahms's Lieder, for example!

The following Schubert program, regularly given over many years, will give some idea of Fischer-Dieskau's method. The keys listed are the ones that the singer actually sang; therefore, the songs quite often had to be transposed down from the composer's original key. The very first Schubert song was in B-flat major; Fischer-Dieskau transposed it to A major. Schubert, who himself sang tenor, wrote for tenors, so in many cases the transposition for the baritone voice follows as a matter of course. Fischer-Dieskau took great care with transpositions but did not avoid them, always having the piano part in mind, for, as he stated, the piano must not be allowed "just to growl":

1. "Des Sängers Habe" (The Bard's Possessions), Schlechta, D832. This is in A major and begins *forte*, "Schlagt mein ganzes Glück in Splitter" (Break my happiness to smithereens!), and it ends quietly with the image of death's slumber.
2. "Der Wanderer" (The Wanderer), Schlegel, D649, in D major, begins in a slow walking tempo, "Wie deutlich des Mondes Licht /

zu mir spricht" (How plainly the light of the moon / speaks to me), and it ends just as quietly. The "steige mutig, singe heiter" (Climb bravely, sing joyfully) sounds thoughtful, almost with a suspicion of doubt, in the recording with Gerald Moore made between 1966 and 1969.

3. "Der Strom" (The River) (probably by Stadler, D565), is in D minor and begins *presto*, in agitated tone-painting: "Mein Leben wälzt sich murrend fort" (My life struggles on, grumbling the while).

4. "Das Zügenglöcklein" (The Death Knell), Seidl, D871, is in F major and is a Ländler-like melody in 4/4 tempo in which the funeral bell rings almost joyfully. (Fischer-Dieskau reports that this song was rescued for posterity by the tenor Karl Erb. *Trans.*)

5. "Freiwilliges Versinken" (Death by Choice), Mayrhofer, D700, is in F major / D major. It begins majestically with strong accents and ends with an elegiac scanning of the distant heavens.

6. "Der Tod und das Mädchen" (Death and the Maiden), Claudius, D531, is in D minor and has a slow rhythmic beginning; the vocal part is very emotional. The alternating dialogue determines the song's character. (As is well known, Schubert used the theme in the second movement of his *Death and the Maiden* quartet, No. 14 in D Minor, D810 (1824). *Trans.*)

7. "Gruppe aus dem Tartarus" (Scene from Hades), Schiller, D583, is in D minor and C major. It begins *presto agitato* but ends slowly.

8. Nachtstück (Nocturne), Mayrhofer, D672, is in A minor and begins slowly, strongly accented, until the harp accompaniment mirrored in the piano part unleashes an emotion which then becomes lyrical.

9. Before the intermission: "Totengräbers Heimweh" (The Grave-digger's Longing for Home), Craigher de Jachelutta, D842, in E-flat minor, begins *lento*, gains speed, then slackens before speeding up again and finishing *piano*.

10. The first song after the intermission is "Der Wanderer an den Mond" (The Wanderer Speaks to the Moon), Seidl, D870. It begins in a walking rhythm, then gradually quickens: "Ich auf der Erde, am Himmel du" (I on earth and you in heaven).

11. "Abendstern" (Evening Star), Mayrhofer, D806, is in G major. It begins slowly but movingly: "Was weilst du einsam an dem Himmel" (Why do you linger so lonely in the sky).

12. "Selige Welt" (Blessed World), Senn, D743, is in A-flat major, begins *presto*, accented, and becomes lyrical in the second verse: "Eine selige Insel sucht der Wahn" (Folly will seek a blesséd isle).

13. "Auf der Donau" (On the Danube), Mayrhofer, D553, begins *lento* in E-flat major and flows on in a broad rhythm: "Auf der Wellen Spiegel schwimmt der Kahn" (The barque flows on, on the mirrored waves).

14. "Über Wildemann" (Above Wildemann; Wildemann is a town), Schulze, D884, in B minor, is stylistically in the region of *Winterreise*; it begins *presto*, emotionally: "Die Winde sausen am Tannenhang" (The winds rage round the fir tree's slopes).

15. "Der Kreuzzug" (The Crusade), Leitner, D932, is in D major and is a slow narrative song right up to the uplifting conclusion: "Es ist ja auch ein Kreuzeszug / In das gelobte Land (For this is also a crusade / towards the Promised Land).

16. "Des Fischers Liebesglück" (The Fisherman Lucky in Love), Leitner, D973, is in F minor and begins slowly, quite emotionally, and stays so to the end.

17. "An die Laute" (To the Lute), Rochlitz, D905, in C major, begins in a dancing, gradually quickening rhythm: "Leiser, leiser, kleine Laute" (Ever more softly, little lute). It sounds cheerful, just what the key signature promised.

18. The last song, "Aus Heliopolis II" (From Heliopolis II), Mayrhofer, D754, begins in C minor and accelerates quickly to the stormy conclusion: "Wenn die starken Stürme brausen / Findest du das rechte Wort" (When the mighty storms rage / You will find the right word).

There is no pedantic schematic pattern here, but rather a variable one, given here in the keys actually sung: A major, strong tone, measured; D major, slow, walking rhythm; D minor, *presto agitato*; F major, gentle tempo, Ländler-like; F major / D major, strongly accentuated; D minor, slow, very emotional; D minor, accentuated; A minor, slowly, strongly accentuated, becoming lyrical; E flat minor, quickly accelerating tempo, then subsiding; F minor, gently accelerating; G major, slow, emotional; A-flat major, accentuated, quick, emotional; E-flat major, flowing broadly; B minor, quick, emotional; D major, narration up to the uplifting conclusion; E minor, slow, gently emotional; C major, a dancing measure, slowly quickening; C minor, accentuated, fast; and then, following all that, usually seven encores in the major: F, D, G, F, A-flat, G, and A.

Fischer-Dieskau's Lieder repertoire also included programs based on single composers: Beethoven, Schubert (four distinct programs during a concert tour and many variations in the course of time), Schumann, Liszt, Brahms, Wolf, Pfitzner, Mahler, Schoeck, Hanns Eisler, Hermann Reutter, Arnold Schoenberg, Alban Berg, and programs of contemporary composers such as Boris Blacher, Wolfgang Fortner, and Aribert Reimann, to name only the most significant. Programs on the poems of one poet were in the minority; after the Goethe Lieder were settings of Eichendorff, Hölderlin, Heine, and Eduard Mörike (although, in the latter case, Fischer-Dieskau almost always sang the settings by Hugo Wolf). A Lieder recital dedicated to the poems of Richard Dehmel (1863–1920), a poet of German Realism, was really on the periphery of a repertoire that grew with the years yet remained faithful to the basic patterns established at its beginning; it was later extended to at least twenty-two different tour programs. The singer emphasized once in conversation that he had never chosen programs with the time and place of the recital in mind, nor with nations or nationalities. Art must be valid, wherever it was presented. Promoters who expressed doubts about any particular choice of Lieder found little sympathy, and the international conference of professors and lecturers in German Studies who had chosen "The Controversial View of Goethe" as their theme had to accept the (musically justified) rationale of a program of Goethe Lieder. Dutch organizers could not be convinced that a song cycle without an intermission (and without a cup of coffee) was tenable.

The order of songs in a Goethe program was not always the same, quite apart from the fact that Fischer-Dieskau never missed the opportunity of giving a Schubert program devoted solely to settings of Goethe. There were always the basic pieces, and variations. The two Goethe programs below might illustrate the point:

Franz Schubert	"Am Flusse" (By the River)
Carl Friedrich Zelter	"Gleich und gleich" (Like to Like)
	"Um Mitternacht" (At Midnight)
Johann Friedrich Reichardt	"Tiefer liegt die Nacht um mich her" (The Night Lies Deeper All Around)
Ludwig von Beethoven	"Mailied" (May Song)
	"Wonne der Wehmut" (Joy of Sadness)
	"Sehnsucht" (Longing)
Franz Schubert	"An die Entfernte" (To the Distant One)
	"Auf dem See" (On the Lake)
	"Erlkönig" (Erl King)
Robert Schumann	"Sitz' ich allein" (When I Sit Alone)
	"Setze mir nicht, du Grobian" (Don't Smack the Jug Down, You Oaf)
Johannes Brahms	Serenade
	"Unüberwindlich" (Unconquerable)
Ferruccio Busoni	"Schlechter Trost" (Poor Consolation)
	"Zigeunerlied" (Gypsy Song)

Othmar Schoeck	"Nachklang" (Echo)
	"Höre den Rat" (Hear the Advice)
	"Dämmrung senkte sich von oben"
	(Twilight Sank from on High)
Hugo Wolf	"Frühling übers Jahr" (Forever Spring)
	"Anakreons Grab" (Anacreon's Grave)
	"Der Rattenfänger" (The Ratcatcher).

The second program of Goethe Lieder emphasizes the chronological order more but retains the powerful effect of the concluding Wolf songs:

Duchess Anna Amalia	"Auf dem Lande und in der Stadt"
(of Weimar)	(In the Country and in the Town)
Carl Friedrich Zelter	"Gleich und gleich" (Like to Like)
Ludwig van Beethoven	"Mailied" (May Song)
	"Neue Liebe, neues Leben"
	(New Love, New Life)
Franz Schubert	"An den Mond" (To the Moon)
	"An Schwager Kronos" (To the
	Coachman Chronos, i.e. Father Time)
	"Meeres Stille" (The Silence of the Sea)
	"Erlkönig" (Erl King)
Robert Schumann	"Freisinn" (Free-minded)
	"Sitz' ich allein" (When I Sit Alone)
	"Setze mir nicht, du Grobian"
	(Don't Smack the Jug Down, You Oaf)
Johannes Brahms	Serenade
	"Unüberwindlich" (Unconquerable)
Richard Strauss	"Gefunden" (Found)
Othmar Schoeck	"Dämmrung senkte sich von oben"
	(Twilight Sank from on High)
Max Reger	"Einsamkeit" (Loneliness)
Ferruccio Busoni	"Zigeunerlied" (Gypsy Song)
Hugo Wolf	"Wanderers Nachtlied"
	(Night Song of the Wanderer)
	"Frühling übers Jahr" (Forever Spring)
	"Anakreons Grab" (Anacreon's Grave)
	"Kophtisches Lied" (Coptic Song)
	"Der Rattenfänger" (The Ratcatcher).

The comparison might give some idea of how deep and lasting the influence of Goethe's poems was on composers of German Lieder—and how much, unfortunately, it belongs to the past. Dietrich Fischer-Dieskau wrote

once that one could see that Goethe's poems (which Goethe himself preferred to call "Lieder" and "cheerful") as the alpha and omega of the art of
the Lied, for Goethe's poems were the first that could be turned into Lieder:

> The musical fallout is so great that the program-maker has the great
> problem of choice—if you except the two most important setters of
> Goethe's poems, Schubert and Wolf. I was attracted by the enormous
> range of possibilities offered by Goethe's lyrical language—right
> into our own century.[27]

Such considerations (although the above are from recitals in the 1960s)
preceded the choice of Lieder for a recital on a tour; however, the prepara-
tions of a Lieder program went far beyond the scores and the poems set.
Fischer-Dieskau was not satisfied with the old idea (still prevalent in literary
scholarship in the 1950s) of studying only the poetic text of the work to be
performed. It seemed quite natural to him to study also the historical,
literary, musical, and socioeconomic background as well. To know about the
poets as well as about the composers seemed important to him, to know from
what circumstances they had come to their poem or their setting, to understand their place in society and the world of their times.

His own position in society and the world also had to be determined, for,
thanks to his musical and interpretative genius, he had risen quickly into the
ranks of elite singers. This meant a societal status, too. A certain liking for
middle-class customs was not lacking either. Memories of a childhood in a
headmaster's house with its cultural figurehead in the shape of a father
prominent in the life of the school and the town, played their part as the
young Fischer-Dieskau began to set up home. House concerts, given regularly over the years, began in the flat in Charlottenburg with the harpsichord
virtuoso Edith Picht-Axenfeld. Yet Fischer-Dieskau continued to give his
gramophone record evenings with his own commentaries, a contemporary
form of "house concert." The later introduction of television helped to
perfect the mix of pictures, music, and commentary.

To one of these record evenings came a music-loving young man who
wanted nothing more than to work near the singer: Diether Warneck soon
became Fischer-Dieskau's secretary and remained with him for the next
thirty years. Fischer-Dieskau, the host, related once:

> In 1952, I began to hold musical evenings in my house, for no
> particular reason. The research needed to find out the background
> to the various vocal works I had to sing brought so much incidental
> work that it just needed a little touch of communicativeness
> (ineradicable in every artist!) to prompt me to organize a meeting
> of friends. The preparation was very easy: texts from various books I

had come across were spoken on tape. I dug out suitable records to illustrate them, and, finally, I selected whatever relevant pictures and slides I had in my enormous collection and showed them on a screen—and the lecture was ready. I didn't have time to do any more but, all the same, in the course of eleven years, it mounted up to about a hundred such evenings . . . .

We were able to listen to, and compare the careers, the personal remarks, and analyses of the works of composers from [Heinrich] Isaac [c. 1450–1517] to [Paul] Hindemith, and I think everyone got something from them.[28]

But such solemnity was not always the rule at these most thoroughly prepared musical evenings. The theme "English Music after Purcell, to Edward Elgar" was presented by Fischer-Dieskau on a 78 rpm record from which one could hear only a loud hiss!

His passion for collecting was always related to his artistic interests: records, books, old photographs, all document his craving for knowledge, and this is also shown in a more playful way in the crossword puzzles that he used to make up in the 1950s for his own amusement and to test other people's knowledge.

The life of the young Fischer-Dieskaus only later began to be different from that of other postwar couples because of his ever-increasing number of engagements. A letter of Irmgard's to her parents in Freiburg at the end of 1950 describes the situation fairly drastically:

I'm sending you the sugar, quite a packet, in time, I hope, for Sunday. We no longer get as much as we want here either, but enough all the same. I'm also sending you some new material—we bought it as a mat for our books on the wall-shelves and had to take a full roll, which is why there is so much left over. Can you do any-thing with it? . . . Please send me the recipe for the potato soufflé and the order of the ingredients. I'm such a fool, I've forgotten most of it already. My new treasure really is a treasure. She does everything on her own whereas you have to tell others a thousand times. She is a very good and thrifty cook and shopper, cleans remarkably carefully—and she's nice and quiet. I've got enough to do, running here and there, and I often have a long nap after lunch—and I'm beginning to practice regularly again. Everything is fine with the heating—it came on 1 October. On Monday, we preserved thirteen bottles of tomatoes, tomorrow the same again, exactly to my (or rather Mom's) instructions.

The Fischer-Dieskaus were settling in. Six months later they became a real family, when, on 10 February 1951, the first of the three Fischer-Dieskau sons, Mathias, was born.

The new father's firm-standing engagement with the Städtische Oper was only one of his many professional activities; nevertheless, he remained on the opera house's books for six months of every one of those early years, which meant, of course, that he was in Berlin, and at home, during this time—and he wanted these six months to be properly utilized. He wrote in 1951, and repeated it almost word for word in the following year: "It was my most fervent wish to take part in two premieres during this time," and that could only have pleased Heinz Tietjen, the theater director. Did he foresee that his new baritone would very soon be satisfied with only one premiere, since other opera houses—Munich and Vienna in the vanguard—also wanted him, and Fischer-Dieskau obviously also wanted time for Lieder recitals as well? The intendant must have been thinking particularly of the revivals. In the 1951–1952 season, these included the singer's unloved Troilus in Zillig's *Troilus und Cressida*, Don Giovanni, the King's Minister in *Fidelio*, Ottokar in Weber's *Der Freischütz* (much praised by the critics, though in Fischer-Dieskau's opinion there was not really much to praise, since not much vocal skill was required), Valentin in Gounod's *Faust* (called *Margarethe* in German), and then Marcello in *La Bohème* beside Helge Roswaenge (1897–1972), the celebrated Danish tenor. It did sound rather patronizing when, after a *Don Giovanni* in 1953, Tietjen announced to Fischer-Dieskau that he

> had proved once again the great talents which lie within you and which with systematic direction [referring to himself] could lead you to an international career.

Although Fischer-Dieskau had quickly outgrown such "direction," his letter to Tietjen in 1954 when the latter left the Städtische Oper (and Berlin) did have the ring of truth about it:

> and so let me thank you for taking the lanky lad up into the "company of the Saints" at that time, despite his fear of "childish illnesses," for the considerate, sparing treatment of his sensitive voice, and the truly fatherly generosity with which you watched over him when it was a case of building up the material existence of his little family.[29]

Anyone who had lost his father as early in his life as had Fischer-Dieskau would be grateful for such paternal help. Rarely did he need it, in all honesty, for the loss of his father, the war, and the POW camps had freed him from any need for security or dependence on others. His rapid rise to fame, and his exclusion from a normal lifestyle, had only strengthened the feeling of loneliness that he had had from his early youth. It was wonderful, however, to be standing on the stage or on the platform and receiving so much acclaim, although from those early days on, physical and emotional problems began to show themselves. He wrote to a school-friend in December of that year:

> In the meantime, the pressure of engagements began to become so great that I had to cancel an important premiere (Verdi's *La forza del destino*) (The Force of Destiny, 1862), since I would have been "rejected and outsung."

It is interesting that the twenty-four-year-old already knew his Wagner by heart: "Versungen und vertan" ("rejected and outsung" are the last words of Wagner's *Die Meistersinger* at the end of Act I). In fact, the part of Don Carlos avenging his father's murder in *La forza del destino* went well beyond his vocal capabilities at that time, as he himself was well aware.

Similar precautionary cancellations were quite common in his early days in opera. An irritation or an inflammation of the mucous membranes was very common. Suppurations of the maxillary sinuses were treated with punctures until an operation corrected the trouble. The young singer's constitution could hardly be called robust, and perhaps that, along with the lack of food and the deprivations of those early postwar years that had left every second German weakened, was part of his particular endowment. Does what Goethe said to his secretary Johann Peter Eckermann, toward the end of his own long life, about the connection between "talent" and "constitution," not seem to refer directly to Fischer-Dieskau?

> The extraordinary achievements of such people presuppose very delicate constitutions, which make them capable of rare emotions and enable them to hear the voices of angels.[30]

Intelligent circumspection and a certain shyness prevented the singer from confronting the really great challenges of his art too early. On the other hand, he did sing difficult roles such as Doctor Faust (Busoni), Wozzeck (Alban Berg), and Mathis der Maler (Hindemith)—these all displayed the range of his abilities. Looking back on Fischer-Dieskau's enormous repertoire does refute the charge that he had always wanted an even larger share of roles. Ambition—never lacking—and caution were held in balance. Even Furtwängler experienced this when he invited his young protégé to sing the role of Count Almaviva in *The Marriage of Figaro* at the Salzburg Festival at the beginning of the 1950s. He was informed that the singer's health had necessitated a change in his schedule; trouble with his thyroid glands had needed treatment. Perhaps, so Furtwängler was told, Fischer-Dieskau would be able to sing the part later "in a manner suitable for the Festival" after he had prepared it more thoroughly by singing it elsewhere, at other venues.

His first appearance at the Salzburg Festival in 1951 was, in fact, at Furtwängler's invitation. Fischer-Dieskau's interpretation of Mahler's *Lieder eines fahrenden Gesellen* (Songs of a Wayfarer) had brought Furtwängler a little closer to a composer of whom he had never thought much. (And Fischer-Dieskau himself is very doubtful about the quality of many— though, of course, not all—of the Austrian composer's works.)

Not everything was always so earnest and so respectful in that narrow circle of great artists, among whom, despite that inborn and acquired shyness, the newcomer was not at all unhappy. One day, he was standing with Furtwängler and the bass Josef Greindl at a window of the old Salzburg Festspielhaus, looking out onto the street. A young girl went past beneath them. "She's pretty," said Furtwängler, and he turned to Greindl: "Whoever gets down first—gets her!" The young man, blushing and embarrassed, watched his heroes dashing down the stairs!

That was never his way, however, even when he had to step over a female admirer who had lain on the steps of his apartment during a later Salzburg Festival. The next day, a bathtub full of lilies barred the way!

Salzburg 1951 was the pre-Karajan era, although Herbert von Karajan (1908–1989) had already conducted Gluck's opera *Orpheus and Eurydice* (1762) in the Felsenreitschule and Mozart's *Marriage of Figaro* in this, his hometown, in the summer of 1948, as well as concerts that included Beethoven's Fifth Symphony and Brahms's *German Requiem*. Fischer-Dieskau later sang the latter work twice under Karajan's baton, and persuaded him to dispense with the applause and leave the platform after the last note.

In 1949 Karajan gave only two concerts, having rejected Salzburg in favor (temporarily) of Bayreuth. As a result, Furtwängler's influence increased again in Salzburg, but it was always much less absolute than Karajan's. One anecdote throws a little light on the limits of Furtwängler's assertiveness. When Karl Böhm suggested putting on Alban Berg's opera *Wozzeck* for the 1951 Festival, Furtwängler demurred: "You cannot present a work at the Festival that shows a wife's death on the open stage!" Whereupon Böhm, quick as a flash, said: "And you, Herr Doktor, you want to conduct *Otello?*" *Wozzeck* was produced in Salzburg![31]

In those first postwar years, several generations of great conductors, apart from Furtwängler and Böhm, conducted the Vienna Philharmonic Orchestra: Bruno Walter (1876–1962) had returned to Austria; Otto

Klemperer (1885–1973) and Hans Knappertsbusch (1888–1965) were there; Artur Rodzinski (1892–1958) and Leopold Stokowski (1882–1977) had come from America; Eugen Jochum (1902–1987), Georg Szell (1897–1970), Ferenc Fricsay (1914–1963) (Fischer-Dieskau's first influence), Josef Krips (1902–1974), Sir Georg Solti (b. 1912), still going strong; and Rafael Kubelik (b. 1914)—all were in Salzburg. What an array of talent!

In 1951, Friedrich Gulda's debut as a pianist was greeted with amazement, and Furtwängler's "suspect" *Otello* was acclaimed. Karl Böhm, Oscar Fritz Schuh, and Caspar Neher created a spectacular *Wozzeck*, with Josef Herrmann in the title role and Christel Goltz as the downtrodden Marie, and Gustav Gründgens, one of the postwar stars of the theater, directed the German version of Shakespeare's *As You Like It*. It was, in all senses, a year of great theatrical events. In all this gorgeous feast of music, one single voice was noticed. In one of the many concerts offered, Furtwängler conducted one of Mendelssohn, Bruckner, and Mahler. On the platform stood the twenty-six-year-old Dietrich Fischer-Dieskau—and he was "discovered" anew:

> The sensation of this concert was the interpretation of Mahler's *Lieder eines fahrenden Gesellen* by the twenty-four-[sic]-year old baritone Dietrich Fischer-Dieskau. This singer, discovered last year in Vienna [a great honor for Vienna, where, in fact, he had only given one, albeit remarkable, recital of Beethoven's Lieder!] stood now on the world's stage in Salzburg and conquered an international audience. Not by his bravura, not by a great volume of tone, but, above all, by a *pianissimo* that was completely transparent, spiritualized, and so had an almost ethereal effect. This singer, still quite young, has already immersed himself completely in the literary and musical meaning of these four very beautiful songs (which are to be found again in part in Mahler's First Symphony), yet he scarcely allowed the *fortissimo* that lies hidden in his voice to be heard, but sang quietly in his own way, and so attained an effect that was truly unique. Here is a great and gifted artist . . . . Let us note his name. In the last few decades, it is probable that Central Europe has never produced such a talent.[32]

The Joy, and the Price, of Success

That same year, 1951, brought the first invitation to the Edinburgh Festival.[1] This invitation opened up the world to the young singer. He had sung in London on 7 June 1951 in a performance of Frederick Delius's *A Mass of Life*, a 1905 setting of Friedrich Nietzsche's *Thus Spake Zarathustra* (1883–1891). [Delius (1862–1934), born in Bradford, Yorkshire, of German parents and a friend of Grieg's, had been particularly championed by one of Britain's leading conductors, Sir Thomas Beecham (1879–1961), and it was Sir Thomas who conducted his own Philharmonic Orchestra at the London performance. *Trans.*] *The Times* wrote on 8 June:

> Herr Fischer-Dieskau has a high baritone of ringing nobility and a remarkable range of colors through all its registers; he sings, as the best Germans do, on his consonants, but more than that, he threw immense conviction into his enunciation of the German text, so as to touch poetry in Zarathustra's soliloquy at midnight.[2]

(It is true that the voiced consonants have to be sung like that; Fischer-Dieskau has done this from the very beginning.)

Here then, for the first time, a writer who was not a native German speaker had noticed the singer's clarity of diction, and how important it was. It was a point on which opinions were later to differ.

From that year on, Salzburg and Edinburgh had a special place in Fischer-Dieskau's engagement diary. It was different with Richard Wagner's Bayreuth. In contradistinction to Salzburg, which had been able to carry on its traditions without a break (apart from the fact that Arturo Toscanini did not return), Bayreuth had been the center of controversy for years. Wagner's own anti-Semitism, the reverence shown to Bayreuth by the Nazi regime, Hitler's friendship with Winifred Wagner, all threw deep shadows over Wagner's operas and the all-too-visible place where they were venerated. In 1947, indeed, the prospect of performing Wagner in Munich had horrified so sensitive an author as Alfred Andersch. "*Richard Wagner redivivus*" was the title of his article in the journal *Der Ruf* (The Call, the journal of Alfred Andersch and Hans Werner Richter, the forthcoming leader of the

Gruppe 47, mentioned above). In the article, Hitler's and Wagner's respec-
tive triumphal progresses were compared and condemned.[3]

The controversy about Wagner and what came after him has never been
silenced. At the first postwar Bayreuth Festival in 1951, Wagner's grandchildren tried to block any further political discussion; the reason that came
down from the *Grünen Hügel* (the Green Hill, on which the theater stands)
sounded rather quaint: "Only Art matters here!" Wieland Wagner's so-called
"clearing out of all the junk" (Entrümpelung) really did seem to be directed
toward the obliteration of all traces of the past. Any critical discussion of
the philosophical currents in Wagner's operas had to wait for later interpretations of the works.

Decades later, when such dictatorial attempts at explanation and clarifi-
cation had long been forgotten—including Patrice Chéreau's at first
violently opposed and then later much celebrated strokes of directorial
genius—Fischer-Dieskau was asked the question about "Wagner and what
came after." He answered his interlocutor in his own, very typical way. He
described himself first of all as one of those anti-Wagnerians who succumb,
again and again, to the magic that Wagner's music evokes, his genius for
catching us unawares. Then, the seemingly familiar cliché: "Only, I also see
what came after Wagner." (Pause.) "Came after?" Could he mean then
something radically different from the much-bruited handing-on of an
ideology through his operas? But Fischer-Dieskau was on a quite different
track. He was thinking about *music*: "For that's what concerns me. A plant
was cut down too quickly. Had it appeared just a little later, it would have
been able to blossom more freely."

The question that historians dare not ask: "What would happen if . . . ?"
can be asked by a musician. If Schubert had only had more time (says
Fischer-Dieskau), his music would have had a much greater influence on
the nineteenth century. Yet this retrospection about "Wagner and what came
after" does contain within it an unambiguous vote for the performance of his
music, if, that is, one listens carefully not only to the music and libretti, but
to what lies between the notes and the words. So, even this very personal
connection with Wagner's works concerns "only Art," too, and this is not a
defense but simply an understanding.

Thirty years before that comment, when Fischer-Dieskau stepped onto
the Bayreuth stage for the first time, he must have approached his role,
Wolfram von Eschenbach in *Tannhäuser*, much more innocently. His attention was focused on the image of the role that he had fashioned for himself—
a good example of how he saw himself expressly as a singer-actor and of how
he put into practice what he later so often told his students: "Become the
character who is singing."

As Wolfram von Eschenbach in Wagner's opera *Tannhäuser* in his debut in the role at the Städtische Oper in Berlin in 1949.

Friedrich Herzfeld, a contemporary eyewitness of Fischer-Dieskau's early years on the operatic stage, wrote about his Wolfram:

> Dietrich Fischer-Dieskau as Wolfram was an ideal casting. The inner tensions of this lyrical character corresponded so completely to his natural personality that we all believed that he had found his true *métier*. After this Wolfram, no one would have believed that Fischer-Dieskau could also have been able to play completely different roles with any success.[4]

But all were to be surprised, and soon. There was general astonishment when audiences heard him sing the part of Count Almaviva in Mozart's *Marriage of Figaro*, first of all in German in Berlin, and then in Italian in Salzburg—truly a very different character from Wagner's Wolfram.

As a sort of counterpoint to Herzfeld, this is what the music critic Karl Schumann wrote about his Salzburg Almaviva in the *Süddeutsche Zeitung* for 23 September 1965:

> All eyes and ears waited expectantly for Dietrich Fischer-Dieskau's Count. The over-sensitive Lieder singer, the other-worldly Wolfram in *opera buffa*? An almost youthful-looking feudal lord appeared, built like a mediaeval warrior, right hand resting imperiously on

his hip, his soft, broad features set in folds of discontent, able to command every humorous nuance of the *parlando* as well as the full power of the *cantilenas*. Fischer-Dieskau, the actor, is about to catch up with the singer of the same name. Salzburg has found one more attraction.

The actor and the singer "of the same name" had also shaped the character of Wolfram to his own design, or should we say, rather, had brought it to light? Just as with his interpretations of Lieder, his portrayal was drawn from his knowledge of the background, the context of the music, the text, and the intentions of the creator, but also from the circumstances of Wagner's own life. Friedrich Herzfeld's description supports this view:

> In *Tannhäuser*, Wagner describes the struggle between sacred and profane love. He was able to portray profane love from his own experience of it, and so found powerful, illuminating colors. Sacred love, on the other hand, he could only feel as a longed-for possibility. This led then to Tannhäuser's becoming an active, dramatically exciting role, Wolfram's a lyrical, suffering one. Most traditional interpretations have simply underlined this fact, so that the "Song to the Evening Star" in Act III sounded all too often like a song inserted in the style of a sentimental romance.

It was different, of course, with Fischer-Dieskau.

Another eyewitness, already quoted, was Ivan Nagel (Ch. 4, *n*. 23), who saw the singer as Wolfram several years later in Munich. He asked himself whether Fischer-Dieskau's charisma did not come from a personal magnetism, so that one could never ignore a single note or want to miss a tenth of a second of that voice. He wrote about that Wolfram:

> When at the beginning of the second act, he had brought the hero and the heroine together, he went straight to the rear of the stage and stayed there, his back to the audience. The "old hands," the Elisabeth and the Tannhäuser at the front of the stage, could duet away to their heart's content, you could not take your eyes off that motionless, averted third character.

That is what Fischer-Dieskau achieves in his characterizations: he does not re-invent the character, he brings to life what the creator has put into the character. In Ivan Nagel's words:

> It was not Fischer-Dieskau, but Wagner who worked out, and wrote, Wolfram's long silences. But who else could have understood, or portrayed, so well what it means to *be* that third character?

And Friedrich Herzfeld again:

> In Wieland Wagner's rather abstract production where everything
> was constructed on spirituality, Fischer-Dieskau's Wolfram domi-
> nated the whole action even more, if that were possible.

1954, then, was Fischer-Dieskau's Bayreuth debut. Apart from Wolfram,
he also sang the role of the King's Herald in *Lohengrin*, a role which thus
gained an unexpected prominence and became—through word, presentation, and music—the dominating character of the scene and, as the
Rhein-Ruhr Zeitung's review put it, "the key to an understanding of the
opera." In his memoirs, Fischer-Dieskau has related the background to the
circumstances surrounding his time in Bayreuth; despite all the success, all
the acclamation with which the Festival audiences greeted him, he never felt
as welcome there as he did elsewhere. Indeed, one day, he was to see himself
unceremoniously shown the door.

Yet he was Bayreuth's Wolfram in 1954, 1955, 1961, and 1962, Amfortas
in *Parsifal* in 1955 and 1956, and, in the latter year, also Kothner in *Die
Meistersinger*. As has already been hinted, some time would elapse before his
Hans Sachs. In a letter of 10 March 1960, he wrote to Wieland Wagner: "I
shall be forty in 1965. From that date (no matter when) you can reckon with
my Hans Sachs at Bayreuth, that is, if I remain 'in your dreams' till then."

Wieland Wagner had already written to him (on 20 February 1960) of
"your Bayreuth Sachs in my dreams," had even thought of bringing Wagner's
early (1842) opera *Rienzi* into the Bayreuth canon, and had asked Fischer-
Dieskau whether he would be "happy at the thought" of singing the part of
Adriano. Neither suggestion bore fruit. As early as 1958, indeed, Wieland
Wagner had been complaining about having wooed Fischer-Dieskau so often
in vain. He said that he had offered the singer everything that his grandfather
had written "for a voice like yours—and you wanted to sing Mathis . . .
lucky Hindemith!!! Poor Richard, still poorer Wieland Wagner." Then, on
26 December 1958:

> Dear Herr Fischer-Dieskau,
> Will you not sing the Dutchman? Courage! The Dutchman =
> Mandryka divided by two, expressed mathematically.

According to Fischer-Dieskau's singer's mathematics, however, the formula
was still the same: "The Dutchman = Mandryka times two." It lay too low for
him, he wrote, and would be so for most baritone voices, and so he has never
sung the part on the stage.[5]

After the third Wolfram of 1961, there was no further room for Bayreuth
in the singer's calendar. Was that because he had not answered Wieland

Facial transformations:

Gianni Schicchi   Wozzeck

Wagner's siren calls often enough—or was it his refusal to wear a costume that cut out the acoustics, which really upset the Festival director? It was sad, both for Bayreuth and for Fischer-Dieskau, that they never got together again. Fischer-Dieskau has never really fully exhausted the possibilities that lay open for him in Wagner's operas. (We shall have a word to say later about his Wotan in *Das Rheingold* and, above all, his Hans Sachs.)

In this first decade of his work in opera, Fischer-Dieskau managed to work on a major share of his standard roles from Posa in Verdi's *Don Carlos*, via Jochanaan (John the Baptist) in Richard Strauss's *Salome*, Wolfram von Eschenbach in *Tannhäuser*, Amfortas in *Parsifal*, the eponymous hero in Mozart's *Don Giovanni*, Count Almaviva in *The Marriage of Figaro*, the Minister in Beethoven's *Fidelio*, Renato in Verdi's *The Masked Ball*, Mathis in Hindemith's *Mathis der Maler* (Mathis the Painter), and, finally, Verdi's *Falstaff* and Ferruccio Busoni's *Doktor Faust*. Wolf Völker and Richard Kraus, the director and the conductor of the production of Busoni's opera, had to urge the singer, literally for hours, to get him to sing a role really meant for a *Heldenbariton*, for, to begin with, he found neither the role nor the opera very convincing. Yet it proved to be a very useful experience for him (after he had agreed to sing it and to collect the music, letters, and other documents pertaining to Busoni). Although it was by no means the first score of the "New Music" that he had encountered (works by Winfried Zillig,

Don Giovanni   Cardillac

Boris Blacher, and Wolfgang Fortner he knew already), he felt that this work was an important bridge to an understanding of modern music. Busoni himself had thought of his *magnum opus* as having that very function, both in its details and in the whole concept; this is why he built into it some of his earlier compositions to express the continuity in the change of the music. But these connections lead much further back in the case of Busoni, who, both as pianist and as conductor, took Bach as his own point of departure:

> I've been playing Bach since my earliest days, and practiced counterpoint. At that time, it became a mania for me, and it is certainly true that in all the works of my young days there is at least one *fugato*. The continual, hidden work of Mother Nature had had an unconscious effect on me, and I became aware of unexpected qualities that had matured within me. Of all of these, one of the most valuable was the *newly emerging harmony created by the unconditional polyphony.*[6]

This also characterized the score of the *Faust* opera. Heinrich Kosnick's phrase "the link of continuity" is the key one in the metaphorical sense as well. It was a familiar-sounding concept for Dietrich Fischer-Dieskau.

There was a concert performance of *Doktor Faust* in Munich in 1969 under Ferdinand Leitner and the Bavarian Radio Symphony Orchestra, and there is a 1969 recording, too, with Fischer-Dieskau's imprint on it. After that production, Igor Stravinsky said, somewhat surprised: "I didn't think Busoni was such a good composer!"

Fischer-Dieskau feels that he always has to penetrate as completely as possible the music, the libretto, and the character—once again, to "become the character who is singing." This commitment went so far that Walter Franck, the actor and, later, a friend of the singer, said in a public meeting: "The most gifted young actor of recent years isn't an actor, but a singer." Yet once Fischer-Dieskau had fashioned the character to his liking, one found only slight changes in nuances in future productions. Audiences in Berlin, Munich, and Vienna (he had signed guest contracts in the latter two cities) had become used to this, as had the critics; indeed, they expected that Fischer-Dieskau would give them his very own interpretation of the role and would justify it at a very high level. But . . . Falstaff?

H. H. Stuckenschmidt wrote after the Berlin premiere:

> I admit that I had my doubts when I heard of the project; how could the Romantic dreamer, the singer of Schumann's and Wolf's lyrical Lieder, of Busoni's Faust, of Wolfram von Eschenbach, of Posa in *Don Carlos*—the very essence of moral aristocracy—how could he become the comic money-grubber and ladies' man, the despiser of honor, the wine-bibber and capon-guzzler?

Nor was the idea all that acceptable to the singer. When Carl Ebert, Heinz Tietjen's successor in Berlin, announced it to him, only much later, during the recording of Francis Poulenc's *Le bal masqué* (The Masked Ball) (1932) in 1975, with its punning phrases and its hilarious bravado, did he recall his first Falstaff. His view was that he had had difficulty with the comedy insofar as the vocal part needed a very particular slant to fit the comic intention:

> It's a question of what is possible in practice. And there was no one who could have taught me how to do it—before Carl Ebert. I was accustomed to singing *Winterreise* and very serious Lieder programs. But someone had to teach me to unwind and how to point lines with assurance. I just didn't have that in my nature. I'm a North German, after all—and a Prussian to boot.

It is true, of course, that humor is not the first thing one thinks of when the name of Dietrich Fischer-Dieskau is mentioned, because of the nature of German lyrical poetry and of German Lieder and, in particular, the Lieder of Schubert, Schumann, Brahms, and Hugo Wolf with whom his name is always associated. Yet he had already given his Count Almaviva characteristics that could be laughed at, although this was far removed from

making him a "comic" character. His Almaviva held all the terrors of a
lecherous tyrant—a domineering man who reveals his weaknesses unwillingly and who is eternally duped. This is why he is secretly laughed at. The
singer would have liked to have played him as the old slavering lecher
of Beaumarchais's play of 1784, but operatic—and Mozartian—tradition
forbade that.

As far as opera goes, there is not really much humor to be found in the
genre. People who know the more mature Fischer-Dieskau discover a very
humorous man who can parody and imitate and is a gripping story-teller.
Listen to him reciting the correspondence between the composer Richard
Strauss and the poet and librettist Hugo von Hofmannsthal (taking turns
with the actor Gert Westphal), full of high spirits and, literally, eloquent
humor. For the young Fischer-Dieskau, however, humor was more of a
challenge. He conquered it as early as 1957:

> There he sits in Caspar Neher's medieval English pub stage-set:
> depraved and lovable, curls round his bald head (and one in the
> middle on top!)—amused, roguish eyes peeping over his turned-up
> nose, with dimples and a mouth that can change in a flash, from
> joyful smiles to an old campaigner's temper. His body is enormous,
> "this superb specimen" with a colossal belly on huge, thin legs: He
> stands there like a Jupiter and begins to sing. Notes flow from an
> inexhaustible cornucopia of registers, of parodying and *bel canto*
> colorations, from the depths of the bass up to an extraordinary
> falsetto—that female voice: "I am Sir John Falstaff's!" Then the
> rhetorical questions to poor Pistol are growled out: "Can honor set a
> broken shin? No. Or mend a foot? No. Or a finger? No. Or a hair?
> No!" Then there is the transfigured *pianissimo* after the enjoyment
> of the sardine, and the nimble A major *parlando* of "Quand' ero pag-
> gio" (When I was a page). It is all there, absolutely right, emerging
> from a perfected vocal art, moved by an inner emotion, a masterly
> performance *sui generis*. But what would it be without the addition-
> al mimicry and gesticulation! Fischer-Dieskau's hands, when he dis-
> misses the word "honor" into the air as an empty sound, when he
> touches Alice lecherously, yet also chivalrously, on her décolleté,
> when he peers out of the half-open basket-top into the lovely wood-
> en wainscot of Mistress Ford's house. Every moment is just right, has
> been studied, becomes artistically controlled life. This Falstaff is one
> of the most joyous Shakespearean characters seen on a Berlin stage
> since 1945.

This hymn of praise on the successful attempt of the thirty-two-year-old
Fischer-Dieskau to make a character from world literature his own through

music and poetry, comes again from the pen of H. H. Stuckenschmidt—but Fischer-Dieskau heard similar critiques from all quarters.[7]

Yet in many of his letters from those years, one can nevertheless read of those "crazy demands." His success begins to militate against his own private laws. How does a singer's yearly engagement diary look—a singer who so often said "No" so as not to burn himself out, a singer whose constitution was not all that robust? As an example, we might take the year 1960 and the engagements noted in his *Hauptbuch* (engagement diary), which records, without omissions, all his performances since 1948. This is also fairly typical for the second half of the 1950s:

January

5, 17   Berlin, Städtische Oper, *Falstaff*

February

2, 9   Berlin, Städtische Oper, *Wozzeck* (première)

5   Zurich, Frank Martin: *Sechs Jedermann-Monologe* (Six Monologues from *Everyman*)

7   Basel, Lieder recital, Schubert, Schumann

15–19   Berlin, recordings, Richard Wagner: *Der fliegende Holländer* (The Flying Dutchman) (title role)

23   Berlin, evening of cantatas, Handel

26–28   Berlin, recordings, Handel/Bach cantatas

March

13, 16, 19, 22, 25   Berlin, *Falstaff*

27   Berlin, *Wozzeck*

29   Recording, Rezniček: *Vier ernste Gesänge* (Four Serious Songs)

April

1, 4   Berlin, Recording, Dvořák: *Biblische Lieder* (Biblical Songs)

5, 6   Berlin, recording, Schumann Lieder

11   Berlin, recording, Handel: *Giulio Cesare* (Julius Caesar) (scenes), conductor Karl Böhm

14, 16, 19, 20   Berlin, recording, Hugo Wolf Lieder

23   Berlin, Lieder recital, Hugo Wolf, with Gerald Moore

26–30   Munich-Freiburg-Karlsruhe, Lieder with orchestra, Beethoven, Mahler, Wolf, Vienna Symphony Orchestra

May

2   Stuttgart, orchestral concert, Beethoven, Mahler, with the Vienna Symphony Orchestra

4–31   Lieder tour—Munich, Heidelberg, Frankfurt am Main, Bonn, Düsseldorf, Cologne, Essen, Münster, Kassel, Hamburg, Bremen, Hugo Wolf: Lieder of Eduard Mörike and Goethe, with Günther Weissenborn

June

3   London, Tribute to Kodály with the London Symphony Orchestra, conductor Zoltan Kodály

8   Vienna, Lieder recital, "For Robert Schumann's 150th birthday," with Jörg Demus

10   Vienna, Lieder recital, Wolf: Mörike Lieder, with Jörg Demus

12   Graz, Lieder recital, Wolf: *Spanisches Liederbuch* (Spanish Song Book), with Irmgard Seefried, Erik Werba, and Günther Weissenborn

15–17   Vienna, Richard Strauss: *Arabella* (as Mandryka) at the Vienna State Opera

20   Vienna, Mahler: *Lieder eines fahrenden Gesellen* (Songs of a Wayfarer)

July

28   Salzburg, Lieder recital, Wolf: Goethe Lieder, with Gerald Moore

31   Salzburg, Lieder recital, Wolf: *Spanish Song Book*, with Irmgard Seefried, Erik Werba, and Gerald Moore

August

8, 16,   Salzburg, Mozart: *Marriage of Figaro* (as Almaviva),
26   conductor Karl Böhm

As Mandryka in Richard Strauss's opera *Arabella* with Lisa della Casa in 1958 in the Salzburg production by Rudolf Hartmann.

11, 23, 31	Munich, Richard Strauss: *Arabella* (as Mandryka), conductor Joseph Keilberth
14	Munich, Chamber concert, Handel

18, 28   Munich, Verdi: *Falstaff* (as Sir John), conductor
Ferdinand Leitner

21   Munich, Lieder recital, Wolf: Goethe Lieder, with
Gerald Moore

September

2, 4   Berne, Lucerne, Lieder recital, Wolf: Mörike Lieder,
with Karl Engel

7   Lucerne, Orchestral concert, Mahler: *Kindertotenlieder*
(Songs on the Death of Children), conductor George Szell

9   Montreux, Orchestral concert, Frank Martin: *Sechs
Jedermann-Monologe*, conductor Joseph Keilberth

14   Hanover, Lieder recital, Wolf: Goethe Lieder, with
Günther Weissenborn

13–23   Berlin, recording, *The Marriage of Figaro*, conductor
Ferenc Fricsay

25   Berlin, Lieder recital, Wolf: *Spanish Song Book*, with
Irmgard Seefried, Erik Werba, and Gerald Moore

29   Berlin, Alban Berg: *Wozzeck* (as Wozzeck), conductor
Richard Kraus

October

2   Berlin, Gustav Mahler Celebration with Karl Engel
(*Five Early Songs*, Three Lieder of Friedrich Rückert)

4   Berlin, Berg: *Wozzeck* (as Wozzeck)

8, 9   Berlin, recording, Bach: *Bauernkantate* (Peasant Cantata) and
Kaffee-Kantate (Coffee Cantata), conductor Karl Forster

12, 13   Dresden, recording, Richard Strauss: *Elektra* (as Orestes),
conductor Karl Böhm

17–21   Berlin, recording, Wagner: *Tannhäuser* (as Wolfram),
conductor Franz Konwitschny

24   Paris, orchestral concert, Wolf, Mahler, conductor
Paul Kletzki

As Count Almaviva in Mozart's *The Marriage of Figaro* in 1974, in a performance with Erika Köth in Japan.

26 London, orchestral concert, Mahler: Rückert Lieder, conductor Jascha Horenstein

28 London, Lieder recital, Wolf: Goethe Lieder, with Gerald Moore

30 London, orchestral concert, Mahler: *Kindertotenlieder*, conductor Jascha Horenstein

November

2   Paris, Lieder recital, Schubert: *Winterreise*, with
Günther Weissenborn

6–20   Montreal, Pennsylvania, New York, Los Angeles, Claremont,
San Francisco, Lieder recitals, Wolf: Mörike Lieder, with
Paul Ulanowsky

23   Chicago, orchestral concert, Mahler: *Songs of a Wayfarer*,
conductor Walter Hendl

24, 25   Chicago, orchestral concert, Hans Werner Henze: *Fünf
neapolitanische Gesänge* (Five Neapolitan Songs),
conductor Walter Hendl

December

1–3   Berlin, recording, duets with Victoria de los Angeles

These were just the dates of performances. The preparation (every role, every Lied had to be learned or relearned in Fischer-Dieskau's own particular way, that is, by studying the whole background to the works), rehearsals, and travel still have to be added. How much time can be snatched from these engagements? Can we trace a clearly felt loss here—even though so much "vocation" went along with the "profession"? Almost forty years later, the singer delineated that problematic situation in which he found himself as a young singer:

> If anyone—like me at that time—only wants to work with, and know about, music, he can easily become misanthropic and soul-starved. An exaggerated concept of "Art," the egocentricity of those who put sounds together, can seriously damage everything that is alive in one's own life. The job, the resulting *tour de force*, prescribed the rules and our daily life. So there was a hidden danger of avoiding reality, of losing one's identity, of living in constant contradiction with one's self, unaware of life's banalities, ignoring the cares of one's young family, and rejecting day-to-day affairs as a waste of time.[8]

In his memoirs there is a remarkable sentence: "I worshipped my profession and my career," followed by: "I was under the spell of opera and my recitals." This confession has to be read in connection with his visits to a music-loving London psychotherapist called Walter Schindler. They were private visits, yet it was obvious that the singer, already world-famous at the end of the 1950s, was hoping to find help. They talked about having "more time amid all the hard work" (that must have been a tried and tested theme in the Fischer-Dieskau household) not to spare himself but to be able "to undertake more profound studies to widen his horizon—but at *leisure*." "I still live mainly by Schindler's precepts," Fischer-Dieskau wrote in *Nachklang*.[9]

It was welcome advice from Schindler, a student of Sigmund Freud—almost a confirmation of the lifestyle that he was practicing. But what had given life to those musical evenings in the house in Charlottenburg? How had he managed to make those works his own, if not through his efforts to deepen the "psychology" of the particular musical interpretations? Yet the one thing that is peripheral to the singer's daily activities is leisure. On the other hand, receiving such high praise from all sides laid a weight on the other side of the scales. Schindler wrote to him:

> Your voice production doesn't dwell, as is usual, outside the listener, but goes unbelievably deep, right into my inner emotions, so that it makes me feel at one with the spirit of the music. What joy for you, too, to be a medium of such experiences![10]

In the review of a Lieder recital during the 1958 Salzburg Festival, a critic wrote: "During the whole evening of Brahms Lieder he gave the impression that there was nothing more important to him than this music." Therein lies, to be sure, part of the appeal of his singing; what was written about a single Brahms evening holds for all his work as an artist, maybe even for his whole life. Was there nothing more important than music, or, more bluntly, nothing more important than his profession, his career? What, then, is the meaning of the word "worshipped" above? A comet-like rise to fame, such as was achieved by, granted to, or imposed on Dietrich Fischer-Dieskau, hardly permits a quiet consideration of what life has to offer. If you have discovered that you can make the world happy, truly happy, then you must be prepared to give up your leisure time—and will you then not almost inevitably expect that the world will trim itself to *your* needs and conform to *your* wishes?

Once again, we have this idea of an "artistic egotism," an egotism that rises far above many of one's own interests. Stated another way: the price that an exceptional talent has to pay for its continuing "top form," its fame, and its career, can be very high indeed, and the artist has to pay for it with some of those possibilities which life otherwise has to offer. The gift of a great talent proves to be a continual challenge that can sweep a human being off his feet.

Without wishing to diminish or extenuate Fischer-Dieskau's own testimony, it should be added that he attached himself too much to the bourgeois

As Don Giovanni. Rehearsal with Lisa Otto in 1961 at the opening of the Deutsche Oper Berlin.

tradition of self-education, which is, of course, connected with character training and a conscious pedagogic sense of responsibility toward himself and others, to ignore the danger that always lies in a rise to fame and the consequent continual highwire act that great art then demands. Nothing could be less typical for him than to use his exceptional talents as an alibi for a selfish life. "I want to merge completely with her," he said, thinking of his wife, Irmel. He wanted to be a father to his family and a friend to his friends, and he was concerned when he could not entirely, or even only partly, fulfill what corresponded to his marked feeling for harmony in the world.

His dissatisfaction with what he felt to be the incompleteness of his life has never left him, and the shadow that it cast over him influenced only too clearly what he sang. At its highest stage of perfection, art speaks of what is unfinished, of vain hopes and shattered happinesses, and only by speaking about them can it bring comfort.

Letters, reviews, and essays in their hundreds grant Fischer-Dieskau's art a human dimension that can be added to the artistic ones he himself posits. One of his confidantes wrote to the nineteen-year-old once: "Your perception of things cannot be changed—all beauty goes on hurting," and the stormy course of his life has never let him forget that he spotted the imperfections in others' lives as he did in his own, and his "very delicate constitution," which made him "capable of rare emotions," also made him feel failure much more acutely than most people. If the price was high, however, what he received was likewise incalculable—love and admiration a thousandfold. A word from one expert witness must stand here for many others. The great soprano, Lotte Lehmann, who certainly knew what she was talking about, began her letter with the word "perfection" and finished with the word "fulfillment":

> Dear Dietrich Fischer-Dieskau,
> They say that perfection is an ideal that can never be attained. This is not true; that *was* perfection in the subtlest and the most movingly true sense. I can only say: thank you for the experience of this Lieder recital. . . . What you gave there can never really be understood by "the masses." Only a singer, only a poet, can appreciate it *fully.*
>
> I recall a conversation in Santa Barbara when you said that only the voice (and therefore the soul) and one's facial expression should speak in a Lied. But oh, you spoke *from head to foot*, which delighted me more than I can say. You were so wonderfully free, freed from all reservations. *You just sang*—and, for me, that was the final fulfillment, the absolute apogee of Lieder singing. . . .
>
> God bless you—I hope I can see and hear you often. My love to you and your charming wife.
> Your Lotte Lehmann.[11]

Fischer-Dieskau's outward appearance had changed considerably in the course of the first twelve to fifteen years of his career. How could it not have? The tall, rather thin, rather clumsy youth had become a powerfully built man, who was now accustomed to dealing with the world, and not just with his art, even if he did not particularly like what is usually called "the world." His extreme politeness, never false, served among other things as a shield against hypocritical familiarity. If asked, he would say gladly: "I'm a happy man!" He was—and he knew it. His life was filled with work, work that he loved, and the catalog of fresh high points in his career seemed to be endless.

His fame grew, too, honors and awards rained down upon him—from the Art Prize of Berlin in 1950, the Golden Orpheus of the town of Mantua in Italy in 1955, election to the Academy of Fine Arts in Berlin in 1956, the Federal German Cross of Merit, First Class in 1958 (which was followed by the awards of the other classes), to his designation as a Bavarian *Kammersänger* (an honorary title awarded to singers by the state of Bavaria) in 1959 and the inaugural Edison Prize of 1960. Then came three honorary doctorates of music (from Oxford, Yale, and the Sorbonne in Paris), the Order of Merit for Science and the Arts, and, finally, the order of a Chevalier of the French *Légion d'honneur*, to name, as they say, but a few.

Dietrich Fischer-Dieskau accepted all of them calmly and with great pleasure, without any false modesty or refusing any with displeasure, nor was there any reason for so doing. He took particular pleasure in the award of the Hans von Bülow Medal from the Berlin Philharmonic Orchestra (named after their former conductor and the rejected husband of Wagner's future wife, Cosima) and the honorary membership to the Deutsche Oper Berlin.

Apart from all this public approval and fame, money also came his way, although in his particular circumstances, it went quickly too, since it contributed to the securing and the extension of the civilized comforts of living. The house in Charlottenburg had now been bought, and soon it became their own. One day, they divided it—the basement for the parents and the upper floor for the children (after Mathias had come Martin, on 17 June 1954)—but if readers think that *division* meant *separation*, they are wrong. The children soon came to enjoy the freedom that was now theirs, including the huge roof-terrace that henceforth belonged to them and on which they were able to cycle around. As in other families, the mother now became the central person for the children, although she would often accompany her husband on his concert tours. The absences of their parents did not seem to have harmed the happy years of early childhood of the two children. Only later did these absences become a source of conflict.

The celebration of art and success can sometimes contain an element of the grotesque. In 1956, Bonn's officialdom, led by Chancellor Konrad Adenauer and Federal President Theodor Heuss, celebrated at the Hotel Exzelsior in Cologne the 200th anniversary of Mozart's birth. Fischer-Dieskau described his contribution, later curtailed, between the main course and the dessert, with great good humor. It is worth reading.[12] But there is another memory, an infuriated Irmgard Fischer-Dieskau's memory of the continual and continuing farce of the relationships between the high and mighty and art:

> Dear Dr. Berg,
> I was very pleased and, at the same time, very comforted to meet you on 27 January at that remarkable "Mozart celebration." Had that not happened, I do not know what would have been the consequences

for my husband. . . . I never guessed that the artist, after his contribution, would be left on his own in the servants' quarters. That was
a real *coup d'état*, I must say. . . . But could my husband have
guessed that his singing on the day of Mozart's 200th anniversary,
in front of the German government, would become an item of
amusement between the roast venison and the pineapple?

Then, in her justified anger, she perhaps rather overestimated a little the
musical knowledge of Germany's first federal chancellor, for she continues:

Dr. Adenauer presumably never thought it possible that they would
ask such an artist to sing during a meal. Nevertheless, would it not
have been possible, that, after the Mozart arias (which were better
sung than ever before), he would have been interested enough to
ask who the singer was . . . , namely, a German singer through
whose efforts—which could be placed alongside our diplomacy—
Germany was restored to a position among other countries after the
War; who was the first German to perform in Norway after 1945, the
first spontaneously to break the ice there, and who reawoke in most
countries a true understanding of Germany's major contribution to
music—the Lied.[13]

As in most things, Irmgard was right here, too. The singer's foreign tours,
with programs that seemed to represent everything that was German, were
not immediately accepted by everyone, even if skepticism soon melted at his
voice, his art, his credibility. This letter was quoted also to characterize
Irmgard Fischer-Dieskau, her naturalness, her passionate *engagement*, and
her temperament, which could be aggressive. Her inborn happiness, which
she retained with such conviction and which is seen in the early letters to her
parents, never corrupted her critical intelligence. Thus, probably no one else
at that time could have seen, could have named, the strengths and weaknesses of her beloved husband. She had been there at the awakening of his
genius and, something not quite so obvious, had never been small-minded.
She had accepted his artistic superiority and placed herself behind him. So
it remained, with arguments colored by her temperament, accepted as
unavoidable, but a matter of give and take for both partners. "Enjoy this very
rare destiny," Gerda Riebensahm wrote to them. She, a pianist herself, belonged, with her husband Hans Erich Riebensahm, a pianist and university
teacher in Berlin, to the group of really close friends of the Fischer-Dieskaus.
Riebensahm had decisively influenced the musical intellect of the young
singer and had opened up for him the world of piano music, as his own
teacher, Artur Schnabel, had done for him. He was also a confidant in
private matters, which his wife Gerda has remained to this day. How well she

With his sons Mathias and Martin.

understood the other side of the destiny of someone who has conquered the world, and that of his wife, is proved by the wording of that whole sentence:

> Enjoy this rare destiny—I shall enjoy it with you in my thoughts—and love each other over all the abysses; then none of them will be too deep, and I will be very happy.[14]

Was there a shadow over Irmel's life that she had given up her profession as a cellist after they had given concerts together in the first years of their married life? There were, of course, still concerts together, with the superb oboe soloist of the Berlin Philharmonic, Lothar Koch, and with Karl Engel, Aurèle Nicolet, and Edith Picht-Axenfeld. In each of the years 1959, 1961, and 1962, they made records together: songs by Debussy and Ravel with Karl

Engel (piano) and Aurèle Nicolet (flute) in 1959, then a recording of Scottish folksongs with the same accompanists in 1961, and Telemann Lieder with Edith Picht-Axenfeld (harpsichord) in 1962.

What was certain, and Irmel's realistic cast of mind most certainly told her so, too, was that she would never reach the same heights with her instrument as he would with his. So, she gave him strength, acted now and then as a corrective, and was undoubtedly always a safe refuge. That role betokens a close understanding, which lay at the heart of their life together. Alas, it did not last long enough.

Many years later, the eighty-year-old Italian author Zenta Maurina wrote to Dietrich Fischer-Dieskau that it was on the day after recovering from a serious illness that she had understood the secret of his art. It was his interpretation of Mahler's *Lied von der Erde* (The Song of the Earth) that had brought this realization:

> You sing not only the music and the words, you sing about the tragic love for our infinitely beautiful, infinitely cruel, mysterious earth. The gentleness of your *piano-pianissimo* can bring about one's recovery.

Then, quoting the text, she went on:

> "He dismounted and handed him the parting-cup"—in that line your singing tells us that our life is only another word for an uninterrupted leave-taking.[15]

The leave-taking that struck Fischer-Dieskau on 13 December 1963 was the death of his wife. She died of eclampsia upon giving birth to their third son, Manuel.

Grete Busch, the widow of the conductor Fritz Busch (1880–1951), wrote to the singer in the spring of 1964: "I find it difficult to imagine how you have been able to get through this black winter," and she spoke about her husband and of the fulfillment that Fischer-Dieskau's art had given him. Then she wrote about the deep impression that his interpretation of a particular piece of music had made on her, a piece

> that was my favorite, but that, sung by you, became a revelation, and, in a moment, I felt a pain that Fritz Busch had never heard that, had never been able to make music with you! . . . You show us in friendship the way out of the vale of tears.[16]

"The Way Out of the Vale of Tears"[1]

Most of the people close to Dietrich Fischer-Dieskau at the time of his wife's death in 1963 were not thinking of Wolfram von Eschenbach's "presentiment of death" and his hopes. Another image presented itself to them: that of Orpheus. It was very apt, yet the stricken singer was not thinking of beautiful images:

> In any case, I find it more presumptuous than ever to think of me as an Orpheus, for in the face of death, I have become terribly aware how ill-prepared I was, how much my whole being was, and is, rooted in living.

Yet in no way did this belief in "living" mean that he wanted to, or could, return to his normal ways. In that letter of January 1964 he went on:

> Now I must try to trace long-lost, forgotten threads back into the past. They weave a picture, however incomplete, of two lives threaded into one. I want to know how that really was so that I can carry on with my life.[2]

Instead of yielding to the pain, he wanted to have clear vision. Nor was there any lack of self-reproach, as always happens when one loses one's nearest and dearest.

Yet, somehow, all those who wanted to comfort him, managed to do so: "Your singing, your art, will lead you out of this vale of tears," and the singer himself put it quite bluntly, if you like, quite existentially: "I'm forcibly drawn again to air, light, and food," and, for him, that meant back to his work as a musician, although that was more easily said than done. Normal people can go on with their work with clenched teeth, even though sadness clutches at the throat, but a singer, for whom it is all important to be able to open up and not to shut oneself off—must there not have been a moment when he felt that he would never be able to sing again?

The pianist Jörg Demus, who had been one of Fischer-Dieskau's regular accompanists since the beginning of the 1950s, came to Berlin and settled in Fischer-Dieskau's house. Lieder recordings had been planned for January 1964, and these had to be canceled, of course, or at least postponed. But the accompanist—and here the word takes on a pleasant double meaning that often is reflected in their correspondence over many years—came and stayed and began to play. Music regained its natural place in the scheme of things: "He used to make thematic comparisons on the piano, say, between sonatas and certain passages in songs, and, without thinking, I hummed along with him."[3]

The correspondence between Demus and Fischer-Dieskau was usually limited to an exchange of technical information about the particular work in progress, but it also shows the difficulties in arranging and agreeing on schedules between singer and pianist, which could often lead to unpleasant disagreements. It was also concerned with the program arrangements and sometimes with requests for transpositions, but it always contains a certain glow nevertheless, which also was visible in their collaboration on the platform.

Jörg Demus described what working with Fischer-Dieskau meant, in connection with Schubert's *Erlkönig*, a piece of music whose piano part "is one of those rare exceptions where playing it leads one to one's own physical limits." The professional accompanist, wrote Demus, has long ago discovered the passages where he can spare himself a little, but

> nothing of the sort could help me when, years ago in Vienna, I had to begin a Lieder recital with *Erlkönig* for the first time. Even at the final rehearsal, I couldn't keep up with the tempo Fischer-Dieskau wanted. I got tired and tensed up half-way through. I clearly remember how I went onto the platform that night, terrified, and how, still terrified, I launched into the introduction without any prior warm-up. But, from the minute he began to sing, I cannot remember anything about my own playing! I only had ears for, only thought of, Fischer-Dieskau's wonderful declamation–recitation–singing of the ballad. I followed all the twists and turns, all the colorations, all the nuances, and became just the mediating servant of that single-minded performance, while my wrists pounded out those hundreds of racing triplets without a single pause—and without feeling in the least tired.[4]

All the artists who have worked with Fischer-Dieskau have experienced the same phenomenon: his demands went unquestioned, and his dominant role, almost never challenged and often gratefully accepted, was credible, not only because of his incomparable musicality but also because of his conceptual thinking. His most recent accompanist, Hartmut Höll, in conversation after a decade of working with Fischer-Dieskau said: "I've never felt myself dominated." During their preparation and rehearsals, Fischer-Dieskau had always listened carefully to his partner's comments and had tried to put them into practice. During the recital, however, on the platform, there came that interplay of forces which puts soul into the work being performed. Höll remembered with pleasure how Fischer-Dieskau had accustomed himself to wishing the younger man "gute Reise" (*"Have a good journey"*) just before they went on to the platform—and those recitals were a journey, but a journey on which there was so much to experience. What differentiated Fischer-Dieskau from other singers, he added, was his knack of always looking forward, always driving on. He had hardly ever experienced him breaking off in a song because, as can happen to any singer, he had forgotten a line of the poem. No, on he went "either with his own text or perhaps even on one word." Höll recollects that, once, several lines of Heine's poem "Schöne Wiege meiner Leiden" (Lovely Cradle of My Sorrows), set by Robert Schumann, were sung on the one word, "Lebewohl" (Farewell)!

Such "driving on" by the singer made the pianist's errors shrink into insignificance. All the hard preparatory work was subsumed in the mutual experience of making music, which is then carried over to the listener, for the good relationship between the performers encourages the listener to allow himself to be actively involved in the music. Looking forward creates what was once called "the joy of art," a joy that does not reduce the

With the accompanist Jörg Demus in the recording studio in Berlin in 1958.

seriousness of the performance but increases it: "Whoever looks forward, looks cheerful," is one of Fischer-Dieskau's favorite quotations from Busoni's opera *Doktor Faustus*.

Yet, at the beginning of 1964, after the death of his wife, that maxim was difficult to follow: "Yes," he wrote to Gustav-Adolf Trumpff in Darmstadt, "I've begun again, even if the feeling of being left on one's own is therefore all the more acute."[5]

He began with the "outsider" opera, Verdi's *Macbeth*, in a production in the Deutsche Oper Berlin, on 20 February 1964: it was actually Gustav Rudolf Sellner's 1963 production. For the music critic Werner Oehlmann, however, it was not until Oscar Fritz Schuh's Salzburg production (also in 1964) that he saw what Fischer-Dieskau was capable of in this role. To this critic, it seemed to be yet another breakthrough:

> Only a larger-than-life Macbeth could hold his own on this enormous stage—the magnificent ambience of the Felsenreitschule. Dietrich Fischer-Dieskau was a blonde giant, grave, gloomy, aware of the witches' dark magic, yet capable of a powerful majesty, eaten up by the demons of ambition as well as by those of contrition. When he stumbles after the apparition of the dagger that his own murderous lust has conjured up, he reveals in the recitative the stormy, conflicting emotions within him, until the silent night and the mute earth lull his conscience to sleep, and, in a mighty outburst, his decision is made *fortissimo*.

After he had described how this Macbeth acted some of the most important episodes of the part, Oehlmann went on:

> That was the achievement of an actor whose powers of expression have grown beyond belief, of a singer who has transcended national stylistic boundaries: Italianate in the breathing in the *cantilenas*, in the dramatic pregnancy of the recitatives, German in the almost frightening spiritualization, in the heavy weighting of those dark, murderous emotions. This is a figure of world stature in opera.[6]

The opera stage in another sense, the whole world of music itself, had quickly repossessed the Lieder singer and the singer-actor. He belonged once again to the music industry, which he then each time just as quickly left behind him.

The critic Hildegard Weber wrote:

> He dedicates himself to music; he will not let himself be diverted from getting to the fundamentals of a work of art. His success has not

been an easy road, he has paid dearly for it by setting himself such high standards.

That statement sounds just like the echo of a phrase often attributed to him: "I live for my work."

So life went on again, from February 1964 on: Fischer-Dieskau made a recording of Richard Strauss Lieder with Jörg Demus on 29 February, and at the beginning of March, he had decided to record the same composer's *Krämerspiegel* (The Shop-keeper's Mirror), Op. 66, and a few well-known Lieder, but also to dig out from a trunk the seemingly dusty melodrama *Enoch Arden* (the poem by Alfred Lord Tennyson is spoken to a background of Richard Strauss's piano music). He wrote in his letter to Gustav-Adolf Trumpff: "So I'm moving once again in the actor's pastures. It is fun to do this, and I hope that the result will be a little bit more than a mere museum-piece." Once again, he was looking for something new in what seemed to be a very out-of-the-way work, even when he had to restore it himself to do justice to the original: "I almost had to recast completely Tennyson's original poem, to scratch off the paint from the century-old translation."[7] (In 1994, he retranslated the text, and he performs it occasionally now as an actor since he has given up singing. *Trans.*)

1964 was no different from all the other years as far as the number of performances and productions was concerned. In April, he gave performances of Mahler's *Das Lied von der Erde* (The Song of the Earth) with Fritz Wunderlich and the Bamberg Symphony Orchestra under Joseph Keilberth, and Lieder recitals, mainly of Brahms's cycle *Die schöne Magelone*, in six and eight German towns, respectively. In May, he sang in Paris and Basel; in June in Zurich, Stockholm, Vienna, and Amsterdam; in July and August in Amsterdam, Milan, and Salzburg; in September in Edinburgh, Ottobeuren, and Göttingen; and then during the Berlin Festival weeks. In October, only two performances were scheduled, of Benjamin Britten's *War Requiem*, but then in November it all started up again: Cologne, Frankfurt, Vienna, New York, Washington, and New York again. In December, he gave performances at the Deutsche Oper Berlin, and at last he was back home in the house in Charlottenburg, where, it must not be forgotten, he was often to be found for weeks (albeit sporadically) during the rest of the year. He had not heaped this massive program upon himself in order to "forget"—he would be the last person to want to forget. No, it was just the normal year's itinerary—and did it not mirror the fulfilled life of a musician to whom life meant work? The need for a partner did not vanish with Irmel's death, and he was always plagued with worries about his three young children, one of whom was still a baby. He wrote to friends in Sweden who had written wondering whether his concert with Mahler's *Das Lied von der Erde* would now be canceled:

Of course I'm coming to Stockholm. Irmel would not have wanted me to lie down, brooding and grieving, but sometimes, being alone becomes almost unbearable for me—I was so accustomed to the harmony of our life together. And I don't really know what the future holds for me, for, however lovingly and selflessly my relations look after the children and the house, I see very clearly how little of a spiritual home I can make for them on my own.[8]

"Excruciating, but a success" was his verdict on the first *Macbeth* performances, written in that same letter to Stockholm. "Recordings with Jörg Demus and Gerald Moore still to come," he added.

The partnership with the British pianist Gerald Moore was similar to, yet different from that with Jörg Demus, whose career as a pianist ran parallel to Fischer-Dieskau's as a singer. Moore (1899–1987) was already a very experienced, internationally famous accompanist when he first heard of the young German baritone. That was in March 1951:

No more than six months later, this young giant walked into the recording studio in London with his beautiful wife. He had only to sing one phrase before I knew I was in the presence of a master.[9]

At that time Gerald Moore was fifty-two and Fischer-Dieskau twenty-six —half the accompanist's age. Both have written in their memoirs about each other, and these include personal anecdotes from their long years of cooperation:

It is not enough to say that his voice is wonderful, that he has an incredible technique which enables him to do what he will; it is not enough that his enunciation is flawless, with perfect marriage of word and tone. If I had to put my finger on the key to Fischer-Dieskau's supremacy, setting him apart from every other singer, I would say, in one word, rhythm. That is the life-blood of music, and he is the master of it.[10]

And what did the singer write?

It was rhythm, just what he emphasized about me, that was one of his cardinal virtues, unity with the partner, which means that the fundamentals of tempo and breathing would not be sacrificed or lost in details but would faithfully follow the composer's grand design right to the end.[11]

Without this mutual confidence in their musical integrity, the enormous task of recording 466 Schubert Lieder could never have been undertaken. Following their first performance in 1964 after Irmel's death, Gerald Moore wrote a caring letter to the singer that stands out significantly in their huge

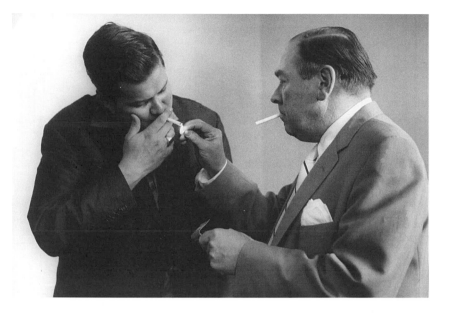

Pause for a smoke with Gerald Moore during a rehearsal in Salzburg in 1960.

correspondence, which is full of technical expertise and questionings on matters musical, but also of a quiet friendship. Moore wrote on Easter Sunday 1964:

My dear Dieter,
I feel I must write to you, to put in a letter what would have been too embarrassing to say face to face. It was wonderful, not only to work with you again, but to witness the heroic way you are applying yourself again to your art. This is what Irmel, your darling, would wish.

One can also read in Moore's book of how Fischer-Dieskau, who seemed to care only about classical music, once took quick leave from him after a Lieder recital in Washington with the excuse that he had to catch a plane rather quickly to New York to attend a concert that night featuring Ella Fitzgerald and Duke Ellington: "Who knows whether I'll ever get to see them again?"

How much Fischer-Dieskau thought of the cooperation with this "true gentleman" and born musician Gerald Moore, how much he valued his confidence and trust, can be seen from his attempts to encourage his friend to undertake new enterprises, even after Moore had retired in 1967. Gerald Moore's answer reveals him again as someone rather special: "Dieter, it is better to get out knowing one is still wanted than to stay upon the order of one's going." (The near-quotation from *Macbeth* was rather apt, and Fischer-Dieskau himself realized the sense behind it one day, after almost fifty years of public performances. *Trans.*)

There had been twenty years of music-making with Gerald Moore, including recitals, mostly in English-speaking countries (and one celebrated recital in Iceland) and many, many recordings; Schubert's songs comprised the lion's share, of course. It all began with *Die schöne Müllerin* in October 1951 (the famous ALP 1913 from the 78 rpm DB 21388-95)—they recorded that work alone four times: 1951, 1955, 1961, and 1971.

The success of such an exceptional enterprise—the recording of almost all of Schubert's Lieder for the male voice—depended on many coincidental factors. The first had to be a proven artistic cooperation between singer and pianist, which hardly needs any further comment in this case. The pair understood each other, without words, without signs, thus permitting the minimum of recording time. Gerald Moore had accompanied many great singers during his long and distinguished career, and he was amazed at how few repeat-takes Fischer-Dieskau needed. If one were needed, Fischer-Dieskau preferred to re-record the whole song; with the longer songs, he might re-record particular passages, but very rarely single phrases. All of this certainly contributed to the unity of a particular recording.

The quality of a Lieder recording does not depend on the singer and pianist alone. Fischer-Dieskau had only praise in the case of the Schubert recordings for the technicians in the studio, or more accurately, in the studios, since the recordings were made in two places, in Lankwitz and in Tempelhof in Berlin. He was particularly impressed by the natural balance between singer and piano that was achieved in both studios. Hans Schweigmann, the director of recording, had found an ideal position for the microphone, which remained unchanged during all the many recordings. It was a disc microphone, which, as Fischer-Dieskau recalled, was placed some five meters above his head. Rainer Brock was responsible for the musical quality of three-quarters of the recordings, and he had, as Fischer-Dieskau put it, "unbelievably good ears" and could judge what seemed good and what was poor. The other quarter was Cord Garben's province, and, by and by, this developed into a growing musical partnership.

How many accompanists did Fischer-Dieskau have during his long career? He guesses between 120 and 130, but he points out that that figure includes all the pianists who accompanied him, even if only once. Yet change was part of his philosophy:

> Each new partner means a new world with whose tricky problems one has to come to terms. Of course, in many cases, musicians soon agree on most points, but, in each case, each partner must make his

views clear, so that the other can make adjustments accordingly, and that includes giving a new shape to the work to be performed. That dare not contradict the text, of course, however spontaneous the new version may sound. The pleasure of such changes in musical partnerships lies in the extension of one's vision, keeping an open mind vis-à-vis the temptations of what one is used to.[12]

Did he ever know these, the "temptations of what one is used to"? It probably is one of his great life achievements that he used the spur of his strong willpower to combat the inertia that had characterized his ancestry and the philosophical views of the society in which he lived.

Yet this enormous number of accompanists is really reduced to a handful of recurring names when one examines the list more closely. Change remains the principle, but concentration on a few partners came naturally, if only on the grounds of practicality. When we look at the recordings of the 1950s and 1960s, after Hertha Klust, with whom so many of those early recordings were made, the main partners were Jörg Demus, Gerald Moore, Karl Engel, Günther Weissenborn, and Hermann Reutter (the composer). Later came Daniel Barenboim, Christoph Eschenbach, Wolfgang Sawallisch, Aribert Reimann, and finally Hartmut Höll. Among the less frequent names, perhaps those of Alfred Brendel and especially Sviatoslav Richter stand as synonyms for the really great hours of music-making.

Fischer-Dieskau could be certain during the whole of his career that each accompanist was only too glad to cooperate with him in his work. The only real problem came when he had to choose between partners, although it was not only by chance that the main reason for choice of partner was the composer to be recorded.

Before Aribert Reimann (b. 1936) influenced Fischer-Dieskau's involvement with modern music in a major way, Hermann Reutter (1900–1985), himself a significant composer, as was Reimann later, represented modern music for the singer. It was a temperate sort of modern music, as befitted Reutter's age and style of composing. Paul Hindemith, Wolfgang Fortner, Darius Milhaud, Othmar Schoeck, and a few of Reutter's own works were to be found in their recital programs, with recourse now and then to Mahler and Pfitzner.

Fischer-Dieskau considered Hermann Reutter a creative musician, with a particular sensitivity to poetry. He has always rated the composer's settings of poetry very highly, and appreciated in them the ability of the composer to "illuminate with his music the words and their poetry from behind, as it were." The literary pantheon of Reutter's settings also attracted him: Matthias Claudius (1740–1815), Friedrich Hölderlin (1770–1843), Theodor Storm (1817–1888), Thornton Wilder (1897–1975) and James Joyce (1882–1941) were among the poets set, to the joy of an avid reader like Fischer-Dieskau, who expressly admitted that he had gained "a great deal from Reutter's close acquaintanceship with the human voice." If the direct cooperation between singer and accompanist was not so extensive as with others, and the number of recitals together relatively few, Fischer-Dieskau probably found the right reason when he wrote in a letter in July 1954: "I think that in your heart of hearts, you can do without the extroverted platform manner that makes mock of any sign of shyness," and the singer knew full well what he was talking about, for every performance had meant his conquering that very shyness—although he did conquer it in the end, and his performances made him, and others, forget out of how hermetic a world of creative rediscovery he was communicating.

The connection to and friendship with Reutter continued up to the latter's death in 1985. Recordings from 1970 and 1971, and a correspondence from the 1980s centering on works and performances together, are proof of this.

The accompanists, as well as some of those who were near Fischer-Dieskau as his career progressed and some of those pianists who accompanied him only rarely, became very good friends over and above the professional cooperation. They became closer friends than, say, singers and their conductors, probably because of the intensity of the cooperation. Such a friend, from the beginning of the 1960s, was Günther Weissenborn, a pianist and university teacher in Detmold in the state of North Rhine-Westphalia. The whole Weissenborn family became part of this friendship, and it is the glow that the music-making casts on the mutual participation in the more normal areas of life that is so attractive. From the Weissenborns, the Engels, the Demuses, and the Moores, *et al.* comes a warmth into the human relationship brought about by this very particular set of circumstances, which is usually far removed from the "delights of ordinary things." There is a very refreshing technical language at work here, too, as shown in this letter from Günther Weissenborn, for example:

> Dear Dieter,
> I think that there are still some errors of transposition in "Wanderers Gemütsruhe" (The Wanderer's Peace of Mind):
>
> | | |
> |---|---|
> | 3rd measure, last note: | right hand E-flat, G |
> | 4th measure, 2nd chord: | left hand B-D-F |
> | 5th measure, 1st chord: | left hand, A-flat–D-flat–F-sharp |
> | 6th measure, 2nd chord: | right hand, F-sharp |
> | 17th measure, third last note: | right hand, D(?) |
> | 19th measure, third beat: | left hand, E-sharp–E-sharp(!) |
>
> If I don't hear from you, I'll assume that my guesses are correct and I'll go on quietly practicing just as I wrote. Easter greetings from all of us,
> Your Günther.

The friendship with Karl Engel prospered in the same way, although this correspondence is enlivened by the cheery temperament of the Swiss pianist from Basel, who loved to sign himself "Carolus Angelus Basiliensis." He used to write music to verses about the singer, and as early as 1957 wrote generously: "Everything that I experience with you and in your surroundings is the real joy of living for me." Fischer-Dieskau worked out a huge repertoire with Engel, which included the Lieder of Beethoven and Brahms, and Schubert too of course, and eventually Ravel, Mahler, Darius Milhaud, Hermann Reutter, Othmar Schoeck, and the Austrian Gottfried von Einem. If there was a single emphasis in the repertoire worked with Jörg Demus, which encompassed almost the whole field of Lieder, it was on the Brahms Lieder; and that was then taken over by Daniel Barenboim. Christoph Eschenbach was the pianist for the complete set of Schumann recordings made between 1975 and 1977. Schubert's Lieder became the focal point of his work with Gerald Moore because of the three boxes of twenty-nine LPs of recordings of Lieder for the male voice made between 1969 and 1972, but they had already been central (in 1958–1959 and again in the 1960s) to his work with Demus. (*Die schöne Müllerin* with Demus is regarded by Fischer-Dieskau as one of the best recordings of the cycle, although it was never published.) Schubert's Lieder in general are central to Fischer-Dieskau's career, and

With the pianist Alfred Brendel at the end of a Lieder recital at the Schubertiade in Feldkirch, Austria, in the summer of 1989.

many happy hours were spent later with Barenboim, Brendel, Richter, and not least though in point of time actually last, with Hartmut Höll and András Schiff.

We rely on these old recordings nowadays to experience Fischer-Dieskau's art. They are numerous indeed, and their number enables us—as far as recordings can, of course—to gain a powerful impression of his voice, the fullness of expression, and the poetry that he transmitted from the platform or stage. He himself puts the immediate experience of platform and stage performance above all the fidelity of record players, with their stereophonic wonders and their "divided effect," about which he is only moderately enthusiastic—and we must agree. On that first series of mono recordings made live in Salzburg in 1957 (and now available on CD), he found the voice "and sometimes even the interpretation" clearer and more faithfully reproduced than the newer stereo recording techniques have managed to do. As far back as 1955, he wrote to a musical friend in Switzerland:

> People attach far too much importance to the technical super-quality of the latest recordings. All reproduced art, even when it is technically at its most refined, should give way modestly to a performance *in natura* and, of course, accept willingly a subordinate place, as it were.[13]

This serious point of view was not entirely contradicted by the fact that Fischer-Dieskau was then in the process of becoming the most recorded singer in the world.

"Fame mushroomed, the honors accumulated"—this is what we read in the German magazine *Der Spiegel*, which devoted its lead story to Dietrich Fischer-Dieskau on 12 August 1964. There he is, looking out of the front page, friendly, intelligent, but a little skeptical too. Even if the Hamburg journal does not claim to be particularly competent in matters musical or artistic, it certainly knew how to publicize a man and his career. Fischer-Dieskau had not only become a musical authority, but his phenomenal success had made him a "superstar"—a description, incidentally, that he would never use of himself.

Der Spiegel during this period was not only a media product dedicated to revelatory political journalism, it could also be useful as a barometer of careers. The first mention of Fischer-Dieskau (on 27 July 1950) reviewed his appearance at the Bach Festival in Göttingen, the second, on 22 September 1954, reviewed a Schubert recital with his friend Hans Erich Riebensahm, sponsored (even in those far-off days) by the cigarette firm Muratti.

The number of reviews grew steadily, and Fischer-Dieskau had a certain status, a particular significance, as a counterbalance to the protagonists of the ordinary musical roundabout. In 1963, Herbert von Karajan's so-called

The German magazine *Der Spiegel* titles its cover "Mastersinger Fischer-Dieskau," 12 August 1964.

"star-promotion circus" was attacked in *Der Spiegel*. This was because of the cult status of the Austrian conductor (before one of whose Beethoven concerts a concert-goer is reputed to have been looking forward to enjoying "Karajan's Ninth," *Trans.*), and also because none of the great stars could reputedly escape from it. *Der Spiegel* printed the friendly comment: "Exceptions to this rule are normally only valid for those who are exceptions themselves. Thus, Dietrich Fischer-Dieskau, for example, sings operatic roles almost exclusively in Berlin" (not quite accurate either, of course, for apart from the various music festivals, the Vienna State Opera was at least one of his regular venues). The 1963 *Der Spiegel* article continued:

> Apart from the fact that Fischer-Dieskau can defend this personal decision also on artistic grounds, it is particularly easy for him to afford himself the luxury of turning down engagements. In the opinion of the majority of critics, he has been the best Lieder singer in the world for years. . . . Dietrich Fischer-Dieskau is of the opinion, absolutely justifiably, that limiting his operatic appearances benefits everyone.

While the tried and tested practice of limiting the number of performances is indeed given praise here, voices were also raised asking: "What else can he possibly sing? Operatic roles, Lieder, sacred music—can one person really sing all these different types of music?" Fischer-Dieskau's high level of achievement in all of these would be answer enough, but the insistent references, despite all these proofs to the contrary, to the monotonously repeated "cobbler-and-his-last" (i.e., stick to what you know best) attack, goaded the singer—quite early on—to answer them: *"Pro diversitate"* was the title of his article, which the *Österreichische Musikzeitschrift* (The Austrian Music Journal) published in its January 1965 number:

> Mozart's Count Almaviva, Schubert's Lieder, Brahms's *German Requiem*, that is, opera, Lieder recitals, and oratorio, were listed for me on last year's program of the Salzburg Festival. Everyone was amazed, and they all asked: "How can you move from one so very different type of music to another? And is it really even possible to use your voice, technically speaking, equally efficiently when one type follows another so quickly?" People looked at me as if I were a chameleon or a ne'er-do-well who dragged up secret and dubious magic potions to use in his performances. Since such things do not exist, I can only assure you of my enormous pleasure in the great variety of music and poetry, ignoring those technical boundaries which, out of a traditional love of order, people have always wanted to erect.

Any attempt to answer this question has to be tackled from quite different points of view. This ability to be versatile, so admired by so many, loses its point when one considers the common denominators: Can the human voice not perform in all of these types of music? The ability to do that is, of course, also a question of technical know-how, indeed, of a short-term ability to change one's character, but, more than that, it is a question of an intellectual adjustment.

That was in 1958. How far the singer's fame had traveled was shown by a scene from Bernhard Wicki's 1961 film *Das Wunder des Malachias* (The Miracle of Malachi). During the cold buffet lunch of the *nouveaux-riches*, we hear a scrap of conversation: "Fischer-Dieskau was in superb form again, we only listen to Fischer-Dieskau these days."[14] In Max Frisch's 1960 novel, *Mein Name sei Gantenbein* (translated as A Wilderness of Mirrors), the eponymous hero puts on a record: "*Don Giovanni*. All listen. Lili beams, blissfully happy, not just at Fischer-Dieskau, although he is wonderful."[15] [Patricia Highsmith pays him a tribute, too: her character, Mr. Tom Ripley, is known to be a Fischer-Dieskau fan in her 1980 novel, *The Boy Who Followed Mr. Ripley*. A more modern German author, Ingrid Noll, in her 1993 novel *Der Hahn ist tot* (The Cock Is Dead) has a boss christen a member of his staff's dog "Dieskau," because it has a fine baritone howl![16] *Trans.*]

The story in *Der Spiegel* was long overdue, and when it appeared in 1964, its readers were somewhat surprised that in a magazine in which mockery was the order of the day, the great singer was hardly attacked at all. The tempo indication printed on the page of music on which the singer's face was superimposed did indeed read "Sehr mässig" (molto moderato), which sounded malicious and was probably meant to, but it also corresponded to Hugo Wolf's original marking for his song "Der Musikant" (The Musician) (although Eichendorff's poem does describe an itinerant, rather lazy one). This was certainly the score of the music in the illustration. Inside, the author of the article discussed the material that he had gathered, though without abandoning the well-known *Spiegel* journalistic jargon—how could he? It quoted *Time*: "the greatest living Liedersänger (sic)"; the London *Sunday Times*: "A genius"; the *New York Times*: "a very rare mastery"; and the *Süddeutsche Zeitung*: "the greatest talent that has appeared on Europe's concert platforms since the Second World War"; and also faithfully reported the record applause at Fischer-Dieskau's first Lieder recital in the Royal Festival Hall in London on 12 October 1951. There, "the 3200 listeners kept applauding with unrestricted enthusiasm half an hour after the final song," and *The Times* of London wrote: "When voice, poetic and musical imagination are matched as they are in Mr. Dieskau's singing, the effect comes near to stunning the emotional centers."

That happened not only in London. But something the readers probably heard about for the first time was a private partiality of the singer's. The report in the German paper quoted above continued:

> Only when the hall staff had put out the lights did the audience depart and the much applauded singer get back to his hotel and, as he always did after a successful concert, treat himself to his favorite semolina pudding with raspberry syrup—

which, of course, is also not quite accurate!

The main story in *Der Spiegel* gave a sketch of the singer's life and career, followed by a catalog of his musical favorites and praise for his pioneering deeds:

> Heedless of the limitations of the public's interest and much against the wishes of concert promoters, Fischer-Dieskau, unlike almost any other modern singer, includes the Lieder of modern, of the most modern, composers in his programs: Othmar Schoeck, Alban Berg, Wolfgang Fortner, Frank Martin, and Aribert Reimann.

Then, but almost by the way, a few criticisms clouded the portraiture, an inevitable concomitant of the continual paeans of praise for his triumphs on concert platform and stage and the admiring echo from fans all over the world.

So there were also criticisms of *Time's* "greatest living Liedersänger," but had such flattering descriptions as those and the following not called forth criticism before? The British music critic John Amis, writing after one of Fischer-Dieskau's Lieder recitals during the Edinburgh Festival, finished his review in *The Scotsman* with these words:

> Providence gives to some singers a beautiful voice, to some, musical artistry, to some (let's face it) neither, but, to Fischer-Dieskau, Providence has given both. The result is a miracle, and that is just about all there is to be said about it. It is difficult therefore to write a long notice about Fischer-Dieskau. Having used a few superlatives and described the program, there is nothing else to do but write "finis," go home, and thank one's stars for having had the luck to have been present.[17]

Such a modest view is not typical of how all critics regarded Dietrich Fischer-Dieskau, yet not all skeptical or negative criticism can be explained away by a sort of general sense of justice—in the avoidance of "fine words," for example—or even to envy of a successful artist, although such obvious motives can be noted here and there. It is not usually the worst critics who get annoyed with a singer's manner of artistic presentation, when they avoid the temptation to be preceptors. Almost every critic wants to say something to the artist himself—beyond his readership or his listeners, really beyond his own public. The success rate is notoriously small. One need not go as far as Martin Walser, the contemporary German author, who had to put up with a good deal of criticism in the 1960s and 1970s, and who wrote once: "I have had reviews that I could call attempts at assassination."[18] Dietrich Fischer-Dieskau has also experienced this. What was the burden of the criticism of those who disliked Fischer-Dieskau's singing of Lieder? He himself was quite surprised at it (and that, too, was often criticized) not in the sense of being "wakened up out of a beautiful dream," but rather because of the overwhelming approval that otherwise reached him from the press, the public, and, unanimously, from his colleagues.

Here, to prove the point and as an example among hundreds, is Edith Picht-Axenfeld's impressions of a Hugo Wolf recital:

> It was a wonderful concert, wonderful poetry, wonderful music, wonderful presentation. I was also delighted with the order of the songs you sang; the placing of *Grenzen der Menschheit* (The Limits of Man) with *Prometheus* is only one example. Highest level of reflection, yet singing of complete and relaxed simplicity. The words were incorporated in the music, in the color and the line, and yet, at the same time, porous enough for that unutterable quality they produce to be experienced.[19]

Here was the nub of the matter—words incorporated into the music—in the arguments for and against Dietrich Fischer-Dieskau's interpretations of Lieder. *Der Spiegel* wrote about the music critic who, during a broadcast, compared the French baritone Gérard Souzay's recording of Schubert's *Der Atlas* (Atlas) with Fischer-Dieskau's. The main criticism: "an almost violent form of expression"—but surely, that is what is in the score?[20]

Without wishing to refute this criticism, which was indeed often repeated elsewhere and is only mentioned here as a sort of prototype of a serious discussion (yet one that should be made relative, to put it in correct perspective), we should add here the point of view of the singer who was compared with his German colleague—Gérard Souzay. He wrote (in French):

> Cher Fischer-Dieskau,
> What you bring to music is unique, and I have such a feeling of respect and sympathy for your art, that, without knowing you, I dare to consider myself one of your friends.[21]

Though certainly not an answer to the criticism of "an almost violent form of expression" in interpretation, or to other, different formulations by other critics, the Frenchman's words do illuminate the discussion.

The criticisms, which had been heard even before the *Spiegel* story and continued after it, became for a time something of a fashion, concentrating on two points: on the one hand, they said that Fischer-Dieskau, like hardly any other singer, studied every song that he had to sing, every operatic role that he had to play, with the whole background—as indeed every instrumentalist really has to do—and "mit Leib und Seele" ("with body and soul"). That formulation "with body and soul" is important here, for the doubts that some critics expressed concerned the *head*, which had to do all this preparatory work. The tag *cantor doctus*, "the singer as professor," coined first of all by Max Kaindl-Hönig in the *Salzburger Nachrichten*, was a gift for the critics, but the rather crude conclusion that followed was: Does he not know too much and so can no longer feel emotion?[22] The imputed antinomy between intellect and emotion led to a prejudice that eventually narrowed down to a charge, difficult to categorize, of "unnaturalness" or "affectation." Fischer-Dieskau once wondered whether there were a norm by means of which the accuracy of the written word or of an interpretation could be measured. As for the "form of expression" or "naturalness" or "artificiality," well, even Schubert had difficulty with contemporary critics on that score. One critic felt of his Lieder that

> this sort of Lied is too artificial to be a true German Lied. In consequence, one could justifiably allege that this popular composer had actually *mis*-composed in this case. True, Herr Schubert's melodies are not trite or artificial, but his harmonies are; and, in particular, he modifies so disturbingly and often so suddenly into the most distant keys like no other composer, at least of Lieder and other short vocal pieces.

So, "disturbingly" and so "suddenly"? Was this then also an "almost violent form of expression"?[23]

Fischer-Dieskau answers these questions of what he thinks about the criticisms of his overemphases, of his going beyond the limits of expression in a Lied, usually rather stoically: "I just sing what is in the notes," he always says. But this rather curt formulation is an understatement. He also sang what lay between the notes, and he himself has defined "interpretation" as "the search for a true expression." Yet, as early as the article in the *Österreichische Musikzeitschrift* of 1955 (above), the comparison made there between a stage-part and the Lied gave him a welcome opportunity to write:

> I hate it when a singer of Schubert's *Der Doppelgänger* (The Double) is accused of treating it like an aria, just because he obeys Schubert's demands for an *fff* at the climaxes. That Lied—or, more

correctly, that monologue—is almost a *scena*, and is a perfect example of what I am trying to say.

Stranger still, many critics also took umbrage at one of the singer's attributes, which would seem to be a virtue for the average listener, what Gerald Moore called his "flawless diction." Even texts in foreign languages are comprehensible when Fischer-Dieskau sings them. The suspicion that he might prefer the words to the music and the reproach that he actually did so, must have hurt a musician as sensitive as Fischer-Dieskau, for he knew that that had never been his intention, and that good articulation had been a cardinal virtue of singers since time immemorial.

Thus, this view about interpretation of the text became confused in critically biased reviews with the impression of his preference for "the words." He tried every so often to correct this impression:

> The "pedantic interpretation of the text" arises, as far as I am concerned, solely from the demands of the music, and if you think that you can detect the stressing of a word, then, in truth, it is at most an expressivo, which is always made in line with the composer's wishes.[4]

A cliché that has become fixed in many a critical head over the years—that Fischer-Dieskau lives for the principle that his task is to serve up an exegesis of the poet's words by singing them, pursued to the extent of the music being a commentary on the text—is one diametrically opposed to the singer's point of view. He wrote on the point to a friendly critic, starting by quoting King Mark in Act II of Wagner's *Tristan und Isolde*:

> Mir dies? Dies mir? (for me, this, this for me?) On the concert platform, you don't bother about a commentary, only about the song. That must come alive at the moment of the performance and must be, above all, what the composer wanted . . . . True, I don't blush when I don't ignore the poem . . . , but, with the best will in the world, I cannot remember ever having subjected the poem to a philological examination, ages before singing the song.
>
> Long live the music, heavens above, with all the emotions that the composer has put into it. "Philologists" are really those people who, although they may hear something, do not really understand it—or am I wrong?

He then dropped into south German dialect: "Nemmans bitte nix für unguat, Herr Doktor (Don't take offense, Doctor) begs your Dietrich Fischer-Dieskau."[25]

Professor Joachim Kaiser managed to collect all the criticisms of the singer's interpretion of art in an article entitled "The Genius of Fischer-Dieskau," and, without denying any of them, took them *ad absurdum*. Part of this critic's stylistic method was to allow the reader to participate in a monologue, as it were, allowing himself in the process to question his own judgments, or at least to put them to the test. Such a technique, a "dialectic" if one wishes, makes the presentation something of an enigma, which, at the same time, raises its credibility in the eyes of the reader: "People are always striving to find out what is so fascinating about the most famous Lieder singer of our times," begins a review of a Schumann Lieder recital. "Is it the effortlessly produced voice, the ease with which Fischer-Dieskau changes or unites registers, letting a *fortissimo* follow a *pianissimo*?" But then it occurs to the reviewer that the singer is often not at all concerned with a "beautiful sound," and that other singers sing with "a more bewitching melodiousness." Kaiser mentions the "intelligence at the singer's command," but he cannot claim that as the definitive factor of his effect on his audiences. Then, right in the middle of his article, comes a provisional answer to the question about the singer's appeal, and this answer also encompasses all the criticisms mentioned above. While Kaiser allows the reader to share his thoughts about where "the extreme limits" have been passed, "to the point where he [Fischer-Dieskau] can go too far," he goes on to query (in brackets, as it were): "Who has the right anyway, to permit or to forbid anything?"—and that is the point.

After this interjection, the critic, in a conciliatory manner, writes more ingratiatingly, and while he is thinking about it, states:

> Fischer-Dieskau resurrects Lieder whose texts are difficult, whose solitary dry-as-dust contents have left them buried in the two rarely used volumes of the [Max] Friedlaender edition. He finds (and invents) ways of interpreting these songs, which possess the purest, most admirable magic.

With two key-words, "genius" and "danger," Kaiser filtered out the difficulties troubling a few of Fischer-Dieskau's critics.[26]

In connection with Schubert interpretations in general—and not with Fischer-Dieskau in mind, since it was actually Alfred Brendel who was mentioned—there appeared a later (1993) article on "Musico-sociological Corrections to the Schubert Image":

> Schubert's Biedermeier image has long since vanished under the attacks of musico-sociological criticism. It gave way to the view that his music was a protest of despairing inner emotion against the

political and social conditions of the age of Metternich [Prince Metternich (1773–1859), Austrian Foreign Minister 1809–1848, much opposed to liberal forces]. One consequence of this change of perspective is a new interpretation of Schubert that offers not only more realistic readings of the music, but, as Alfred Brendel does, presents a less idyllic image of Schubert.[27]

More realistic (actually, more accurate) readings of the music could be heard already in Fischer-Dieskau's interpretations—and that was something new, if not "outrageous," in the 1960s.

The whole argument about the overaccentuation and the primacy of the word over the music, proceeded (when one views it rationally) from a very conventional view of Lieder singing, namely, that a "correct" interpretation would be given if one were guided by what had been heard before, and this meant, of course, an orientation on great singers of the past. But a historico-musical dimension was relevant here as well—the very development of Lieder composition. There was not a single book on Schubert, Schumann, Brahms, Wolf, or Hans Pfitzner that did not mention the fusion of words and music, the equality of status of the piano and the vocal line. [Gerald Moore's admirable book *Am I Too Loud?* (1962), which traces the rise to equal status of the accompanist, might serve as a monument to the principle. *Trans.*] The justification for the whole questionable argument seems to start from this point. Yet it might just be worthwhile to bear in mind here Fischer-Dieskau's first recital and the audience's amazement at the newcomer's unexpected approach to the largely familiar repertoire. At last, here was a singer who did what audiences had originally wanted. Of course, it was the voice, the singer's instrument, that, above all, gained the young singer the unqualified admiration of the audience—but was there not also this new, credible comprehension of the Lied, touched on already? And what they heard, psychologically dramatized—did it not always concern the music as well as the words? Had one or other of these critics perhaps only listened to the words, and not to the music? If we consider the matter more closely, we can see that Fischer-Dieskau is not, in fact, concerned with the dualism of "word and music," but about the work as a whole. This fresh view taken by the interpreter needed to be accompanied by a new way of *listening*.

Not only in the field of Lieder has there been a great change in ideas of interpretation in this century. The phenomenon of a Fischer-Dieskau would probably be easier to appreciate if one were to compare him, not with the singers who went before him, who all grew up in a different, relatively hermetic tradition, but rather with those great instrumentalists of our own days, pianists such as Alfred Brendel (b. 1931) or Sviatoslav Richter (b. 1914), who, like the singer, represent a new understanding of interpretation. It is the *musician* and not just the singer Dietrich Fischer-Dieskau whose variations of interpretation are explained when we have him before us on the platform. Perhaps a quote of what the music critic of the French paper *Paris-Presse* had to say about Richter and Fischer-Dieskau is relevant here:

> To say of Richter that he is the greatest living pianist seems insufficient—without a doubt. Richter is (with Fischer-Dieskau) the greatest living *artist*.[28]

Unmoved by praise or criticism, these "miracles" progressed through the 1960s. Those who did praise the singer had difficulties in finding new formulae. After the performance of Mahler's *Songs on the Death of Children* at the Lucerne Festival of 1960 with the conductor George Szell, H. H. Stuckenschmidt wrote:

> Dietrich Fischer-Dieskau has a rapport with these Lieder that allows for many variants. He sings them nowadays with a suppressed passion that is forced out of the intellectual center of his being. There is a wealth of *pianos* and *pianissimos*, an economy of colorations, a security of attack and of phrasing that puts all previous interpretations to shame.[29]

The "variants" mentioned by the critic form an essential element of Fischer-Dieskau's life as a musician. He never loses his sense of curiosity; he is always looking for something new and fresh. Just as Fischer-Dieskau once asked Paul Hindemith for some new music, the young composer Hans Werner Henze (b. 1926) received an urgent call at the end of the 1950s from the singer, hungry for new music. The date was 9 January 1959:

> Dear, naturally also much-respected, Henze,
> Your friendly New Year greetings and my recent listening to the amazing music from your pen, make me write to you. Please excuse me!
>   Since Hindemith's *Marienleben* (The Life of Mary) for women's voices only, there has been no piece for the human voice that could fill an evening and still a hunger!

Fischer-Dieskau wrote that he "wanted this secret wish to become unsecret," and he went on to speak of the practicality of its becoming reality:

> Ingeborg Bachmann's poems [the Austrian poet born in 1926 who died tragically in 1973] would be an ideal place to start, as has already been proved. There should be between ten and twenty . . . . There should also be only one accompanying instrument, so that a

With the pianist Sviatoslav Richter during a rehearsal for a Lieder recital in Salzburg in 1965.

singer can travel around with the work without any hang-ups and without the promoters causing trouble (the piano would still be the most colorful one). Free the young recitalist from the damning burden of the past; surely, we want to be able to speak at last in the language of our own times.[30]

This letter began a cooperation that was of great significance, not only for the singer and the composer, but also for contemporary music.

Nevertheless, a month later, when he had a selection of Ingeborg Bachmann's poems in front of him, Fischer-Dieskau had grave doubts. Henze, who was living in Naples at the time, had written to him, omitting the usual capitals on German nouns: "Read Bachmann's *der grosse baer* (The Great Bear) and *die lieder auf der flucht* (Songs of Emigration)." Fischer-Dieskau replied to his "dear Neapolitan":

Of course the poems are wonderful, and I was very moved by them, but only at the very end did I realize that it was a woman who was talking, and I couldn't forget that all evening. Old-fashioned it may be, but I don't think that a woman should sing *Dichterliebe* [Schumann's 1840 song cycle of very "politically incorrect" poems by Adalbert von Chamisso].

In the same letter, there are suggestions and words of encouragement, and, once again, practical comments on the venue for the premiere and the number of possible recitals.

It would not have been their first cooperative venture. In 1956, Fischer-Dieskau had recorded Henze's *Fünf Neapolitanische Gesänge* (Five Neapolitan Songs) with the Berlin Philharmonic under Richard Kraus — indeed, only at Fischer-Dieskau's urgent request; this was the first recording of a Henze work. Henze had written these *Gesänge* spontaneously under the influence of an orchestral concert in Naples where Fischer-Dieskau had been the soloist. What now emerged at the beginning of the 1960s, however, instead of the much desired solo Lieder, was a stage role, that of the poet Gregor Mittenhofer in Henze's *Elegie für junge Liebende* (Elegy for Young Lovers) to a libretto by W. H. Auden and Chester S. Kallman (from whose libretto Stravinsky's *The Rake's Progress* had been composed ten years earlier). Dietrich Fischer-Dieskau thanked "dear, admired Hans . . . for the solid food that you have given me with this part." As in the premiere in Schwetzingen near Heidelberg in 1961, Fischer-Dieskau sang the part of the egocentric poet Mittenhofer at the Berlin premiere in 1962 (and then recorded it in 1963 with Thomas Hemsley, Liane Dubbin, and Martha Mödl with the orchestra of the Deutsche Oper Berlin, conducted by Henze himself, *Trans*.).

From Gregor Mittenhofer
to Hans Sachs and Lear:
His Major Operatic Roles

The Mittenhofer role belonged to a group of thematically related parts, which then became the major operatic roles of Fischer-Dieskau's career. When he was asked in an interview with Karla Höcker about the various strands that connected these parts—Mozart's Don Giovanni, Busoni's Doktor Faust, Verdi's Falstaff, and Henze's Mittenhofer—Fischer-Dieskau touched on the similarities and dissimilarities in the characters:

> One can indeed make a connection between Mozart's and Busoni's works, insofar as the theme of both is the daemonic in man, and, in each case, in such a way that the listener's sympathy is evoked. That is the case also with Mittenhofer. All three characters have their revolting aspect: Don Giovanni's is his unscrupulousness and his lasciviousness; Faust's is his search for life's pleasures, which makes him trample over corpses; while Mittenhofer seems to be a creative character who is trapped between his life and his work, a man who renounces human integrity in an almost tragic fashion, even resorting to crime, to create the perfect work of art.

The musical aspect of such connections he finds also naturally and readily:

> You can find strands of connection to Mozart's music in all of these works, for Busoni's as well as Verdi's were in debt to Mozart's music—and you can say that of Henze too. This is shown by the character of the *Elegie [für junge Liebende]*; it is a "number-opera" [i.e. an opera with arias and duets] and employs a sort of super secco-recitative; in addition, there is a limited but lucid accompaniment for a small orchestra.

Yet Fischer-Dieskau knows the dangers of seeking such links:

> But if you try to make these links too generously, you run the risk of over-simplification—that hybrid creation, opera, often creates

As Gregor Mittenhofer in Hans Werner Henze's opera *Elegie für junge Liebende* (Elegy for Young Lovers), here with the composer in 1962.

extraordinary things that defy classification. And that's the only way it can progress.

Defying classification, always ready to progress, could well be Fischer-Dieskau's own motto. The 1960s became, in fact, an almost perfect example of his deep-seated desire to go on, to progress, not to stand still. That was the only way to get over Irmel's death, the only way, so it seemed to him, to re-establish his family life on which he hung his hopes.

In artistic fields, there was much to harvest — and much to sow. Another contemporary composer seeking to develop something new out of old traditions became, just at this time, both a companion and a stimulus. In February 1961 Fischer-Dieskau had received a letter from "The Red House" in Aldeburgh in Suffolk, on the east coast of England. In it, the British composer Benjamin Britten (later Lord Britten, 1913–1977), described his *War Requiem*, Op. 66, to poems by Wilfred Owen (1893–1918), the British poet killed just before the Armistice in 1918. The poems had been set for tenor and baritone. Britten wrote: "They will need singing with the utmost beauty, intensity, and sincerity." The score was a setting of words from the *Missa pro Defunctis* and the poems of Wilfred Owen, and the character of the work was epitomized by the extract from a poem by Owen that prefaced the published score: "My subject is War, and the pity of War. The Poetry is in the pity . . . . All a poet can do today is warn."[1]

Peter Pears, Britten's close companion, would sing the tenor part, and now Britten ("with great temerity") asked whether Fischer-Dieskau would take the baritone role, which represented the German enemy. Fischer-Dieskau agreed with enormous pleasure and sang in the premiere on 30 May 1962 in Coventry Cathedral, a significant venue that had been bombed (or "coventriert," "coventrized," as Goering put it) by the Luftwaffe in 1940 and had been lovingly restored, partly by financial, and partly by practical aid from the Federal Republic. Irmgard Fischer-Dieskau was present on that occasion, and Britten, who had always been enthusiastic about her cello playing, hinted that he might write some music for the cello for her—but, alas, time ran out. Fischer-Dieskau sang Britten's *Requiem* frequently, in Berlin under Karajan, for example; but Fischer-Dieskau told Britten after that performance:[2]

> In spite of all excellent facets of his interpretation, I only must repeat that I missed you at the rostrum. The hall was packed and a spell-bound silence at the end. [Fischer-Dieskau's own English. *Trans.*]

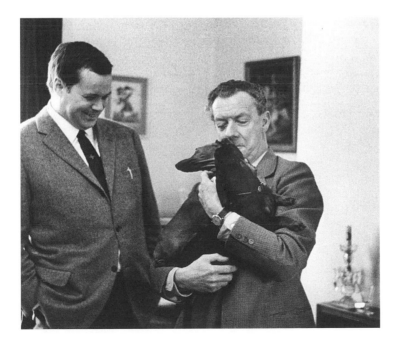

With Benjamin Britten (later Lord Britten) in Britten's London flat, 1963.

As one might have expected, Fischer-Dieskau, so passionately keen to "speak in the language of our times," soon began to speak to Britten about new songs—but not only about songs. Alas, only the *Cantata misericordium*, Op. 69, performed by Pears and Fischer-Dieskau on the centenary of the Red Cross in Geneva at 11 A.M. on 1 September 1963, came to be written. Next came a reworking of a Purcell cantata with an accompanying piano quintet ("When Night Her Purple Veil") and, finally, *The Songs and Proverbs of William Blake*, which the two also recorded in 1965. Yet Fischer-Dieskau began to discuss his favorite project with Britten as early as the beginning of the 1960s: an opera on Shakespeare's *King Lear*, an idea that Verdi had considered for so long but then lost his nerve and abandoned. Again, as with the songs, nothing came of that project either. *The Songs and Proverbs of William Blake* were written for Fischer-Dieskau after his wife's death, and Britten's dedication: "To Dieter, the past and the future," was meant to point beyond her death. The friendship that Lord Britten felt for Fischer-Dieskau was expressed, not only in a letter of 15 February 1964 in which he and Peter Pears admitted that "you and she became so quickly part of our lives," but also when he spontaneously offered practical help by inviting Fischer-Dieskau's two boys, Mathias and Martin, over to Aldeburgh to enjoy sailing and tennis while their father was touring.

The pleasure in their work together, in the creative process that they shared, had also made Hans Werner Henze a good friend. The composer's enthusiasm, shown in his letters, was equaled by the singer's quiet authority and his 100% *engagement*, for example, in the arranging of recordings and performances. There was no doubt that Henze's remarks about Fischer-Dieskau's interpretation of Bach's *Kreuzstab* cantata pleased the singer enormously, for he was well aware that this was from an experienced musician who knew what he was talking about: "Waves of thankfulness, reasons for going on living, swept over me," wrote Henze.

When Fischer-Dieskau agreed to sing in Venice and Rome in the premieres of Henze's oratorio, the cantata *Novae de infinito laudes* (1962; to a text by Giordano Bruno, 1548–1600), the composer answered enthusiastically:

> Many thanks for making yourself available. When I received your telegram, I immediately put a terrific baritone cantilena into the oratorio and hope to think up more in the near future.

How close a friend the composer had become can be seen from the fact that Henze was one of the very few to whom Fischer-Dieskau explained why his second marriage with the German actress Ruth Leuwerik had broken up.

The relationship between the couple had started with a very wary friendship, since both had had to suffer the heady air of fame. Frau Leuwerik, a German actress of the stature of a Myrna Loy or Anna Neagle, had a long series of famous and popular films behind her: *Die ideale Frau* (The Ideal Wife), *Die Trapp-Familie* (the original family of *The Sound of Music*), and *Taiga*, and also TV films such as *Der einsame Weg* (The Lonely Way), an adaptation of the play by Arthur Schnitzler (1862–1931), and, even at the end of 1965, *Ninotschka*, in which Leuwerik, a modern woman, challenged her famous predecessor, Greta Garbo, in her own, if slightly parodistic manner. With these films, she had gained her own particular niche in German film history and lived as far away from society, publicity—and gossip—as Fischer-Dieskau himself. Fita Benkhoff, a close friend of Ruth Leuwerik's, watched the growth of the friendship and was a witness at their private wedding in Zollikon near Zurich in Switzerland on 4 September 1965. Jörg Demus was Fischer-Dieskau's best man.

There seemed to be every chance of a real give-and-take relationship between the couple. Literature (so said the singer) had played an important role in it. His great interest in books coincided with the actress's own deep knowledge, and she, in turn, let herself be inducted (with great enthusiasm)

Wedding with the actress Ruth Leuwerik in Switzerland in September 1965.

into the deeper secrets of music. Both were thinking of a quiet private life centered on the three sons, but this could only have been possible if both had been able to agree to cooperate on the demands of the singer's extraordinary and never-decreasing professional commitments.

Fischer-Dieskau, however, was determined that this would happen, but his determination made him underestimate what could only have been an illusion. Did it have to stay an illusion? He was well aware of the difficulties and was determined to combat them. He wrote to Hilde Poppen, the mother of his first wife:

> For the three boys, Ruth, and myself, the attempt to live together entails a whole host of problems; to solve them, means everyone putting everything they can into it. After long and painful consideration, it is clear to me that that will only be possible in the enclosed circle of our new family of five.

That letter, in which he passionately pleaded for the independence of this narrowest of family circles, obviously caused the writer great difficulties. He knew, of course, that his thanks for the Poppen family's time spent looking after his three children during that terrible period of his "descent into the abyss" would be devalued by a request not to be further helped. Everyone must feel that the creation of this new family group was more than a fervent wish—it was a truly vital decision.

What the children recalled about this period, whether from their own memories or from the stories and surmises of older people (these are very difficult to separate when one is looking back at one's own childhood) was their father's long absences. He, on the other hand, remembers quite clearly what happened when he was at home; the puppet-theater he built—a reminiscence of his own artistic beginnings—the first music lessons, and the first practicing on the piano together. There is no doubt at all about the extent of the father's influence on, or example to, the sons. The youngest boy, Manuel, once spoke very openly about his complete identification with his father's art, particularly when the children saw him on the stage or platform, as they often did. At these times he, who was so often far away, was very close to them.

The break-up of the marriage with Ruth Leuwerik was painful for both parties. In his letter to Hans Werner Henze, Fischer-Dieskau even used the word "tragic," a word that he otherwise rarely used. He wrote to Henze on 31 March 1967:

> First of all, I have to tell you the latest tragic event of the past six months. Ruth and I were divorced a few days ago. We have both tried to create something like a lasting partnership, but you probably

cannot confuse marriage with love, particularly when it is with a person who is so independent and freedom-loving as Ruth.

At the end of this very private and confidential letter was the hope "to be able to keep Ruth's friendship and our close relationship."

For a woman who relatively recently had lived for her profession as a film star, at the height of her fame and popularity, and in a state of carefree independence, it was certainly no small matter to find herself the mother of three sons, the youngest really a baby still, and the companionship of a man whose career had reached its apogee.

The secret world that Fischer-Dieskau had created for himself as a child had never really merged with the "normal world," if one may call it that. That had been, on the one hand, the premise for his artistic career, but, on the other, whoever entered this private world had to obey its laws and be prepared to become a part of it. This, however, does not mean that such complete cooperation could be attained only by a less independent partner —as his later successful partnership with Julia Varady has proved. How difficult it was to find an agreement in this microcosm, despite a mutual understanding, good will, and all the pains taken, is shown by the breaking up of this union of two human beings who seemed to be so like one another in so many of their predilections and emotions. So, two years after the very private marriage, came the equally private separation. For the public—not well-informed of news of the private life of a couple who lived, professionally, always in the glare of publicity—life could go on as usual.

Seemingly unaffected by these happy and not-so-happy events, Fischer-Dieskau's artistic work went on as before. The strict discipline that he showed at this time could, of course, be regarded as partly due to his typical Prussian inheritance, but one cannot rely on that forever—it has to be constantly renewed—and that is just what Fischer-Dieskau did.

1965–1967 saw a series of great artistic successes. During the Munich Opera Festival of 1965, he sang *Cardillac* (Hindemith's 1926 opera), the story of the goldsmith Cardillac, who murders for the sake of his art. With Joseph Keilberth conducting, Fischer-Dieskau revived a modern classic. They produced the original 1926 version without the modifications of Hindemith's extended 1952 version. The recorded opera, made in 1968, again with Joseph Keilberth, also followed the score much influenced by the Expressionist libretto of Ferdinand Lion. Karl Schumann wrote in his review of the recording:

> For Dietrich Fischer-Dieskau, Cardillac is a role after his own heart;
> an interesting character, possessed, pathetic and pathological at one
> and the same time, the most extreme example of the fanatical artist.

Fischer-Dieskau offers what the ideal actor for the part should offer—intelligence, the power of a *Heldenbariton*, musicality, the mastery of nuances, and the fascination of the exceptional case. You won't find a better.[3]

The next high-point was *Falstaff* in the Vienna production of Luchino Visconti and Leonard Bernstein. Visconti stared rather horrified at the huge German when he first met him, and his young assistants did the same. "*That's* our Falstaff?" But he, too, observed—and relished—the amazing transformation from the tall, rather reserved Lieder singer to the energetic, fat-bellied Falstaff with his all-conquering sense of humor: "Tutto nel mondo è burla" (Jesting is man's vocation)—it had never sounded so convincing.

Then came the second tour of Japan with the Deutsche Oper Berlin: Fischer-Dieskau sang Germont in Verdi's *La traviata* in the new production of Gustav Rudolf Sellner and the conductor Lorin Maazel. His famous interpretation of the Speaker in Mozart's *Magic Flute* made surprisingly clear what a central figure this character is, because Sarastro's whole world appears for the first time here. There is no break at this point. A new sound creates a new reality. On he went then with the part of Gregor Mittenhofer in Henze's *Elegie für junge Liebende,* Mahler's *Lieder eines fahrenden Gesellen* (conducted by Eugen Jochum), and *Winterreise* in Tokyo and Osaka. In London, in 1967, he sang Mandryka in Richard Strauss's *Arabella* under Georg Solti, and then that much-discussed *Falstaff* at Covent Garden. From the middle of March to the beginning of April, he was in New York and Washington for four recitals, all with Gerald Moore, and four orchestral concerts.[4]

Paris, Basel, Geneva, and Zurich were still to come; and that was only one year taken at random, which proved the almost unbelievable scope of the performances, as well as the strength and the physical, psychic, and artistic condition of the singer.

Along with Berlin, Munich had become the major venue of his stage performances. 1967 closed with two Lieder tours in the second half of October and the first half of November, followed by his Iago in Verdi's *Otello* on 7, 10, 17, 20, and 25 December in Berlin.

Beside the one major question of where he found the strength and the breath to carry out such a program, there is a second, which with hindsight is connected with future happenings, not all that far off. That question was: Did this world voyager notice that the world of music had begun to change? His professional career had begun in the immediate postwar era and had been not a little influenced by the events of the time: by the Berlin crisis, the hopes of a defeated nation for something to hang onto, something that perhaps art could give, and that his art promised to give—and gave.

As Falstaff in Luchino Visconti's Vienna production of Verdi's opera in 1966.

Between these years 1965 and 1967 much had happened that had an indirect, perhaps even a direct, influence on life in Germany and, if not on Fischer-Dieskau's own art form, on artistic life in general. The war in Vietnam escalated in 1965. In the same year, diplomatic relations between the Federal Republic and Israel were established. In 1966, the radical right-wing party, the NPD (National-Democratic Party of Germany) gained seats in the Länder (States) elections, while in Bonn, the Federal capital, the

Grand Coalition was founded by the right-wing CDU, the Christian Democrats under Kurt-Georg Kiesinger, joining with the left-wing SPD, the Socialist party under Willi Brandt. In 1967, we had the Entlaubung (the "defoliation") of the demilitarized zone between north and south Vietnam; Israel's Six-Day War affected the whole world; in Berlin, during the visit of the Shah of Persia, the German student Benno Ohnesorg was shot; and Ché Guevara, then a guerilla leader, died in Bolivia.

The questions of the connections between art and politics, between art and society, between elite culture and mass culture became even more urgent, and later fueled the now-historical revolt of the students in Berlin, Berkeley in the USA, Nanterre in France, and other universities throughout Europe and the West. This revolt was clearly not just a German phenomenon, but was an expression of the mood of young, thinking people throughout the western world; and it was also aimed at "art" and this so-called "élite culture." It was a time for young Germans to ask whether Schubert, Schumann, and Brahms, the Romantic poets such as Mörike and Eichendorff, and the older "classical" writers Schiller, and even Goethe had any relevance still for this new generation. They really did seem to be calling for the nineteenth-century philosopher Nietzsche's Umwertung aller Werte (reevaluation of all values).

Fischer-Dieskau lived through all of this with a certain feeling of shock, for he was experiencing the language and actions of these rebellious young people not at second hand, but at home, from two intelligent young sons, one fourteen, one seventeen, who brought the Zeitgeist (the spirit of the times) unfiltered, as it were, from school back into the family home. Neither as a normal citizen and father nor as a professional musician could he ignore all the discussions. Thus, 1968 became for him the exemplar of that old argument: Should art mingle with politics?

He found the argument on his own doorstep as a consequence of the interrupted premiere of Hans Werner Henze's oratorio *Das Floss der Medusa* (The Raft of the Frigate *Méduse*), written to a libretto of Ernst Schnabel and scheduled for the Planten-un-Blomen hall in Hamburg on 9 December 1968. Théodore Géricault's famous painting from the Louvre in Paris (*Le radeau de la Méduse*) (1819) was meant to arouse the sympathy and excite the emotions of all mankind. The intellectual impulse — both for Géricault's painting and Henze's oratorio — was the cruel consequences of the sinking of the frigate *Méduse* for those sailors cast into the sea on their hastily constructed raft. Most died, left in the lurch by those who commanded the ship and who had saved themselves. Schnabel's text, a literary collage, given some intellectual body by its quotations from Dante, ends with the description of the few survivors: "They came back into the world: enlightened by reality, they were feverishly determined to overthrow that world."

Klaus Geitel, writing in the *Neue Zeitschrift für Musik*, said: "The final line of the libretto is really the only one which calls for direct action to change society."

Our interest here is not so much in the contents of the picture, nor in Schnabel's symbolical treatment of the theme—which Fischer-Dieskau later described as "wolkenreich" (very cloudy) in a letter to Ingeborg Bachmann —but in the circumstances that lay behind the interruption of a premiere that really never began. Not only had the RIAS chamber choir and Fischer-Dieskau himself flown from Berlin, but also a group of students, who delayed the start of the concert with their chanting and the throwing of certain objects that they brought with them. Wolf-Eberhard von Lewinski, writing in the *Süddeutsche Zeitung* of 11 December 1968, described how they had decorated the platform

> with a picture of Ché Guevara, to whom the composition is dedicated, with a rather tawdry banner with the one word, "Revolutionary," and a red and black flag. A large section of the audience, then the choirs, above all the guest choir from Berlin, left the platform, because they did not want to sing in front of the red flag. Henze shouted that they should allow the concert to begin and prepared to start to conduct, but all the choirs were determined to leave—and did so.

As did Fischer-Dieskau also. He has described the spectacle in his memoirs—and he did not forget to mention the "operetta-like arrival of the police, who planted themselves in front of the platform, in battle-order, with loud shouts and cries."[5]

Although the premiere itself fell apart in this way, the dress rehearsal had in fact taken place. It was broadcast by North German radio and recorded by Deutsche Grammophon in the same month (but only released in 1970). Not for nothing did Klaus Geitel (who attended the dress rehearsal) comment on the "stereophonic effects" that were employed so dramatically for the recording, so that the choir of the survivors could be heard gradually moving to the other side, where the dead lay, during the recording. Geitel continued his review:

> The superbly rehearsed performance under Henze's own direction had, as soloists, Dietrich Fischer-Dieskau (who sang the part of Jean-Charles, who takes over command of the raft) and Edda Moser (Madame La Mort) and also on stage, the Speaker, Charles Regnier. . . .
>
> Fischer-Dieskau sang his part with the greatest urgency and with beautiful tone: an immaculate interpretation. Edda Moser mastered the enormous interval leaps and the artistically fashioned

musical phrases of her part with a melodious intensity. The choirs and the orchestra showed their independence, even if their reasons for striking at the premiere were not really justified, but they have certainly convincingly demonstrated them now—on extra-musical grounds as well.

Those who lived through these times knew that such events were commonplace. They have gone, and are now a piece of history, but the discussion about Fischer-Dieskau's behavior at that time has never ceased. First of all, however, came the explanations between the two friends, for must Fischer-Dieskau not have felt himself rather betrayed, by being, all unsuspectingly, placed in front of a red flag? Henze was able to make him believe that it had not been his, the composer's, intention to involve him and the colleagues who had agreed to sing with him in a possibly scandalous situation. Yet he had been unable to bring himself to remove the red flag, as can be seen from Fischer-Dieskau's answer to a letter about "that ghastly evening." Fischer-Dieskau wrote:

> The same feeling of shame that would not allow you to conduct without the red flag would have forbidden me to support a political attitude that is not mine.[6]

Once again, Fischer-Dieskau found himself placed between two stools: "Not to have a political opinion" meant for him, above all (and this is how he put it once) to allow other people to have their own opinions—which is why he had agreed to sing in that premiere in the first place.

The basic question about the attitude of the artist came in Henze's answer, referring to Fischer-Dieskau's own point of view, dated 16 March 1969:

> I read your last letter with gratitude. I don't have it with me at the moment, but I'm thinking of your sentence: The artist's attitude must be to concentrate on his work. A nice sentence, but it can also be challenged. For example, we could say: The mistake made by many artists is that they only concentrate on their work and that they therefore forget what is going on around them. When they do look up, they despair—and find themselves alone. Life is passing them by.
>
> Then again, I really have to ask you: If you concentrated less on your work, would you be as great an artist? So you see, I'm not absolutely certain.

Fischer-Dieskau has rarely argued so much about his attitude to the arts and their influence with anyone else than with Henze, from whom he still expected so much, musically speaking. Nor did he ever believe that the composer would exchange the concert platform for the political pulpit—and certainly not for the barricades. But he is just as little a friend of the esthetic attitude to the arts: "Everything I sing is full of earthly squabbles," he wrote once to a musical friend.

Just about this time, too, Fischer-Dieskau's mother had died, at the age of eighty-two in 1966. She had watched over his meteoric rise to fame as a world-renowned musician almost from his first contact with the professional world of music, when she took the sixteen-year-old into the artists' room after a concert by the celebrated Lieder singer, Emmi Leisner, whose interpretations of Brahms's *Four Serious Songs* and Schubert's *Winterreise* he had never forgotten. His mother was close to him, and yet had remained far away, as mothers almost always do—how much more so with a son who had reached such unimaginable heights of his art. Nonetheless, she had always been there, a living connection with the world of his childhood—and she had always listened. Whether one is a singer or not, it is always essential that someone is listening. She had done this in two ways: Her love of music had enabled her to listen to him as a singer before all the others discovered him. It is worth noting that a musician of the caliber of Wilhelm Kempff wrote of her death: "As far as I am concerned, I shall miss this ideal listener terribly," while a British friend, John Russell, the art critic of *The Sunday Times*, described her as

> the representative of the old upright Germany where people instinc-
> tively knew what was decent and would never dream of doing
> anything else. Wherever she was, there was a little piece of the old
> Europe[7]

—a nice epitaph for a woman who had seen "the upright Germany" literally fall about her ears when her house was bombed in 1943 and she had to aug-ment her small pension by giving English and French lessons, thus handing on something of "the old European" tradition. Twenty years later, when Daniel Barenboim's mother died, Fischer-Dieskau wrote to him: "I lost my beloved mother once, too, and it was a real setback to my life."[8]

In the autumn of 1966 came that second visit to Japan. Fischer-Dieskau experienced once again the extraordinary reaction of Japanese audiences to music. During his whole career, that country remained his favorite concert venue. He always recommends to his musician colleagues that they try to enjoy such an experience, although he found that Japan, and especially the huge city Tokyo, did not improve between visits. He wrote (albeit not until

1970) to his stepbrother Achim in Berlin: "In the meantime, Tokyo is moving from the beauty of Asiatic filth to the ugliness of uniform glass boxes—everything is becoming uniform." Yet Japan remains his Promised Land. America, which feted him as only Americans know how, has left him with mixed impressions—even though *Newsweek* once listed him among the ten greatest men in the world! Of course, there is the incomparable New York, where the huge number of listeners of Jewish origin makes its mark, but there is also something specifically American. He wrote once after an American tour:

> I love being in America—as always. The myth of vanishing concert activity has not reached America yet. On the contrary, one has the feeling of never having encountered such awakened, fresh, and inquiring audiences. How dreary and unspontaneous old Europe seems beside them![9]

Spontaneous impressions do often hit the mark—and yet:

> In accordance with my habit of regularly inspecting my feelings about America after my tours, it was the showy character of peoples' relationships to one another that scared me, the constant overemphasis on "business," but above all a sort of impersonal over-friendliness, behind which is usually—nothing. New York makes you sick in the long run. It is radical, hard, and always violent under the surface.[10]

Both pictures are in fact accurate.

There is a line from Queen Elisabeth of Spain in Friedrich Schiller's play *Don Carlos*: "In meinem Frankreich war's doch anders" (In my France, it was quite different). Here is Dietrich Fischer-Dieskau in a letter to the conductor Wolfgang Sawallisch:

> Facing a French audience made me realize once again what it means to be carried to greater heights of performance by one's listeners. That true union of heart, mind, and spirit that is manifested there (by the audience as a whole, of course), does not need to be expressed by rapturous applause. You feel it above all before the concert.[11]

To be fair, it should be added that Fischer-Dieskau found audiences in Britain, Scandinavia, and Holland, and also in Germany, that could listen—or be made to listen. Usually the singer knew from the moment he came onto the platform whether he would be able to establish a rapport with his audience. He could also say this about American audiences:

If an audience could be taken as a yardstick for the country, then it would confirm my old impression that, in this country, candor, assent, and vitality are united in the happiest mixture of all possibilities in the world. You feel reborn.[12, 13]

Perhaps this little mosaic of his impressions of his audiences and their countries is the best way to make clear how every singer is dependent on the mood of his audience, always bearing in mind the promise of "the highest standards" that Fischer-Dieskau demands from himself. Of course, it makes a great difference when most of the audience has studied the program before the recital (a necessity in Japan), whether by reading the scores or by listening to the various songs, or at least some of them, beforehand on records.

Audiences, however attentive or dull they might have been here and there, could be relied upon for one thing all over the world: They packed the halls to the doors whenever Dietrich Fischer-Dieskau performed. To experience his Almaviva, his Don Giovanni, or his Falstaff, they would travel for miles.

Audiences might have had to lose the actor Fischer-Dieskau much sooner than they actually did—even then much too early, or at least the singer felt that it was, and was very pessimistic about what actually happened. He had just taken the next step into the world of Wagner's operas by singing the part of Wotan in Herbert von Karajan's production of *Das Rheingold* (The Rhine Gold) at the Salzburg Easter festival in 1968 when an accident occurred on the way back from Salzburg. At 11:15 A.M. on Tuesday, 16 April, his car ran into a car in front near Holzkirchen on the Salzburg-Munich autobahn. His secretary, Diether Warneck, who was driving, escaped with shock, but Fischer-Dieskau suffered a complicated fracture of his upper arm ("probably the only person who was seriously injured") and feared the end of his stage career. The doctors' diagnoses did not help much either. On 4 June 1968, he wrote to Karajan:

Dear revered Maestro,
The avalanche caused by my accident is looking more unpleasant than originally anticipated. According to what the doctors have so far diagnosed, I shall only be able to move the broken arm in a very limited way—which has made me come to the decision to give up all my operatic work for the time being, since half-mobility is useless.

He was communicating his decision very early, he continued, so that the conductor could recast the roles and arrange the rehearsals in plenty of time:

Please imagine the enormous sorrow that these cancellations give me. To have to give up the stage will, in the long run, cause me more pain than my arm does at the moment.

As Danton in *Danton's Tod*   As Don Alfonso in Mozart's *Così*
(The Death of Danton) by   *fan tutte* in Günther Rennert's
Gottfried von Einem, Berlin, 1963.   Salzburg production in 1972.

Fischer-Dieskau had got to know Karajan as a friendly man who regarded an interest in, and an understanding for, the careers of the singers who worked with him as a matter of course: "He was calmness and kindness personified." He had been highly enthusiastic about Fischer-Dieskau's Wotan for, as was usual with Karajan, the recording had been made before the stage production. On 20 February 1968, he wrote:

Dear Herr Fischer-Dieskau,
Five days ago, I heard the first pressing of the *Rheingold* recording. There are times when one says to oneself that all difficulties and obstacles have been swept away and all that remains is what one believed in most sincerely. What you achieved at the first attempt is so colossal that people will need some time to appreciate it fully. You have realized to perfection the style that I had in mind. *Symbol* was the key word above all; and in this symbol of deep humanity, (and that is why it is so convincing), there is a model terseness and

As Giorgio Germont in Verdi's opera *La traviata*.

As Iago in Verdi's opera *Otello* in the Berlin production by Gustav Rudolf Sellner in 1969.

a bel canto at the same time. And something else—the character has taken on the fascination of a late Renaissance prince.

Fischer-Dieskau was ideally cast as Wotan—"a lyrical fairytale, a restrained transition from prehistoric harmony to the coming universal catastrophe" was *Die Zeit's* reviewer's comment—and the recording of December 1967 to January 1968 can bear this out still.[14] In the *Mannheimer Morgen*, Kurt Heinz, after hearing Fischer-Dieskau's very human god, asked:

> Is it just that we have got used to it that we cannot forget that wonderful lyrical baritone, the Wolfram von Eschenbach? Will he—should he—go on, Valkyrie-Wotan, Siegfried-Wanderer?[15]

But no, he did not follow that path, thus avoiding almost too circumspectly a beginning of something that could not really be achieved to his own exacting demands, even when, as in this case, someone like Karajan would have gladly gone along this path with him. One step along this road—that is, for those who would like to see a singer continue along the trodden path, or who had a picture of the artist as they would like to see him—was his Dr. Schön in Alban Berg's *Lulu*, sung a few weeks before his Wotan.

Yet only *Der Spiegel* (which did not review the performance in the Deutsche Oper Berlin) felt that his Dr. Schön was not erotomaniac enough; the journal only reviewed the recording of March 1968 under Karl Böhm. Otherwise, there was unanimous praise for the perfect fulfillment of the production's and the music's concept by the director Gustav Rudolf Sellner and Karl Böhm, which

> presented the maximum of dramatic drive and orchestral color, tonally beautiful, richly differentiated, and significantly well-ordered, presented by the cast with a burning intensity—above all, by Fischer-Dieskau, who, as Dr. Schön, sings and plays out with unbelievable urgency his tragic fate behind the mask of the serious elderly gentleman.

That was in *Die Welt* of 19 February 1968. The opera's libretto is not the most distinguished, but Fischer-Dieskau's recorded performance does seem to raise its standard. Thus, it was not just the "morally pure" characters such as Posa or Wolfram that Fischer-Dieskau loved to play—the Posa or the Wolfram with whom his worshipping public identified him, that public which nevertheless had gladly become accustomed to his very personal version of Mozart's Almaviva or Don Giovanni. The tortured souls of a Macbeth, a Dr. Schön, and also of an Iago, also fascinated Fischer-Dieskau, as they do all good actors.

The recording of Verdi's 1887 opera *Otello* conducted by Sir John Barbirolli, with James McCracken as Otello and Gwyneth Jones as Desdemona and Fischer-Dieskau as Iago, was made in August 1968. It held fond memories for the seventy-year-old Sir John, who recalled the beauty of Fischer-Dieskau's singing of Iago's Dream, while a German critic wrote: "Here we sense the breath of Hell."[16] Fischer-Dieskau wanted to present the whole cosmos of characters that opera could offer. His curiosity for "something new" in music was closely related to the ever-changing presentation of the human personality. Was this now all to finish, at least as far ahead as he could see, because of a broken arm?

Rolf Liebermann, then intendant of the Hamburg State Opera, who had been looking forward to a production of Richard Strauss's opera *Salome* with Fischer-Dieskau as Jochanaan (John the Baptist), refused to accept this pessimistic conclusion. How often, he wrote, had he seen such obstacles disappear; anyway, Jochanaan was a completely static role: "You don't need your arms for this part. You just stand at the edge of the fountain and sing the music as beautifully as you always do!" The singer could only laugh at the suggestion—and perhaps that was Liebermann's idea.

Teresa Berganza, the Spanish mezzo-soprano, wrote cheerily, "to the best singer in our field today":

> I am happy to hear that it is only a broken bone . . . and nothing more serious. . . . Broken bones heal. Did you have an accident, or did some beautiful girl twist your arm?

As Jochanaan (John the Baptist) in Richard Strauss's opera *Salome,* with Leonie Rysanek in the 1971 Munich production by Günther Rennert.

It had nothing to do with the accident, but there was a "beautiful girl," and one of the caring young ladies who wanted to look after the unattached singer read in a letter from him "that I intend to marry again shortly, so that my 'walks' are fully booked up, as you can imagine."

Kristina (Pugell), the lovely young American who had met Fischer-Dieskau during one of his American tours, was the daughter of a singing teacher, among whose pupils had been Tito Gobbi and Jan Peerce, the American cantor and operatic tenor. Kristina seemed made for such a union; she had grown up, not just with music, but with Fischer-Dieskau's recordings, which she had greatly admired long before she met him for the first time face to face. The whole affair really looked like an American version of the old story of the poor girl and the fairytale prince, but it was Fischer-Dieskau who was entranced in this case. Was this not the woman who would be everything for him, and he not the man who would solve all her problems?

For the next few months, it did seem that both their dreams would come true, and reports from others confirmed this. An old friend, who had stayed with them, wrote in a letter: "Kristina was a great success, not only with the men—that goes without saying"—but the women, too, had enthused over her charm and intelligence. In the very first year of their marriage, Fischer-Dieskau told his closest friends: "Kristina has been an angel this last year; the children are in seventh heaven,"[17] but in truth, Kristina never felt at home in the singer's world.

Fischer-Dieskau sent cheerful letters home from the US tour at the beginning of 1971. Here, in a letter from New York dated 29 January 1971:

> I almost didn't have enough time before leaving Minneapolis to thank you for your welcome letters. We're off again in a mad rush, but I cannot leave you without a sign of life from me. . . . Mathias's report on the cozy (gemütlich) (oh, how suspect I've always found that word!) hours with Achim [Fischer-Dieskau's step-brother] made me very jealous.

Then follows a slightly ironical description of the three concerts in Carnegie Hall, which "were a sensation," and about which "even the critics" had nothing to complain. The letter went on good-humoredly:

> In the audience were such stars as R. [Rudolf] Serkin (who went on once again about our music-making together), Isaac Stern (now the co-director of Carnegie Hall), Alexander Schneider (who has been promoting the Casals Festival in Puerto Rico for twenty years), Alfred Brendel (very enthusiastic, particularly about the Schumann duets), Jackie [Jacqueline DuPré], of course (who always sheds a

Wedding with Kristina Pugell
in October 1968.

few tears), [and so on]. . . . Daniel [Barenboim] played and
conducted superbly as always. . . . This orchestra [the Philadelphia]
is just heavenly.

He goes on to describe the program of the gala evening of 23 January 1971
in Philadelphia. Before that, there was a Wolf-Mörike recital with Daniel
Barenboim and a recital of duets with the British contralto Janet Baker.

The gala evening had begun with the slow movement from Beethoven's
seventh symphony:

> Then came the overture to [Weber's] *Euryanthe*, my Mozart arias,
> Anneliese's [Rothenberger] Strauss Lieder, our *Arabella*-scene, the
> Saint-Saëns cello concerto, and Liszt's *Les Préludes*. So, a real
> hotchpotch of a menu for a gala! But then, unfortunately, so was the
> audience. Never again concerts for a pension fund! Meanwhile, I
> went round the villages (New Brunswick—a Schubert recital in an
> enormous gymnasium), and today, Minneapolis, where [Antal]
> Dorati was in charge for so long. Still to come, a recording with
> [Jean-Pierre] Rampal and three with the Cleveland Orchestra.
> Then a baroque music concert, a Lieder recital in Boston and the
> Juilliard Quartet . . . but we are more than halfway through. And
> Kristina is feeling wonderful. (Of course, it's the home air!)[18]

Later, a shadow falls over the reports. The end result was that "a part of life full of love, consideration, and suffering" ended with a separation, followed by a divorce. Fischer-Dieskau wrote at the time:

> It was not to be—and, as I see it, you're putting your life to rights. It's probably easier for you than everything that has gone before, for, at heart, you want to learn what it is like to have, and to keep, your independence.

The collapse of a second marriage bore more heavily on Fischer-Dieskau than would appear from the extract above, which was written long after the separation; he could easily have made excuses about the behavior or the character of his young wife, particularly since he was exposed at the time to the violent protests of his two older sons (now teenagers). A second failure—that is how the heavy shadow thrown over him appeared. Perhaps the psychological advice that he tried to seek at the time might have told him whether the gulf caused by the death of his first wife Irmgard in 1963, with whom his adult life had really begun, was not yet ready to be closed by a new union. For a man whose whole life was based on the two premises of "conservation" and "faithfulness"—which his own art form continually proved—such a result of his attempts to form a union could only entail grief.

We shall see that he allowed himself to be rescued from this abyss; that Edith Schmidt, the cousinly confidante of his youth, was proved right when she claimed that despite everything, he was a Sunday's child and had been born under a lucky star.

There was one unquestionable mountain-top experience in his professional life during these troubled years—in 1971, the first concert tour of Israel to be made by a German musician after World War II:

> Just think, it's only a year since we performed the final movement of Beethoven's Choral Symphony in the original language, German! It was normally sung, either in Irwit [New Hebrew] or English, and now this: a whole evening of German Lieder, in German!

Wolfgang Lewy, a horn player with the Israel Philharmonic Orchestra and the spokesman for the Israeli musicians, himself born in Berlin, said this to Klaus Geitel, music critic of *Die Welt*. Geitel's report began:

> A whispering in the tumultuous applause. The audience was astounded, moved, relieved. "That is a—how do you say it in German—a standing ovation!" The artist receiving the applause is Dietrich Fischer-Dieskau. Nothing unusual in that—least of all for this singer. But this is Tel Aviv, and we are in the huge Frederic R. Mann auditorium with its 2700 seats (and the steps, like the

platform in the hall, are packed full), and here, many are holding their breath.

(It must not be forgotten, however, that the music of Wagner and Richard Strauss was still banned in Israel for a long time after this event. *Trans.*)

It was different, too, for the singer from the thousands of other recitals that he had given. He said to Geitel:

> I came onto the platform and saw as usual the vague crowds in the background, but also the faces in the front six rows—all turned toward me, expectantly, but perhaps also anxiously; although they were silent, those faces spoke to me. And I understood their language straightaway. These were the faces that I always miss among my audiences in Germany—and, of course, I know, and my whole generation knows, the reason why, and will never forget it. Although belonging to strangers, these were familiar faces, easy to pin down: Frankfurt, Berlin, Baden-Baden. But other names pushed these place-names to one side. Terrible names. And even without knowing them, it is still not very easy to sing Schubert. But, in this case. . . .[19]

He sang Schubert in Tel Aviv and in Jerusalem, accompanied by Daniel Barenboim; on another evening, Beethoven Lieder, and, finally, Mahler's *Lieder eines fahrenden Gesellen* (Songs of a Wayfarer) with the Israel Philharmonic.

During the rehearsal for these Lieder with the orchestra, Klaus Geitel made an illuminating comment on Fischer-Dieskau the musician:

> The rehearsal begins. Fischer-Dieskau has discovered that the orchestra has not played Mahler for fifteen years. He also knows that Barenboim was not a particular admirer of Mahler. Fischer-Dieskau turns to the orchestra, and helps it, and Barenboim, to appreciate the work. He sings it to the musicians, corrects tempi and entries. Barenboim, eager to learn like every young genius . . . willingly repeats every phrase that doesn't sit as it should, a conductor of subtle energy, and a first-rate accompanist, with the orchestra too.

Not long afterwards, Fischer-Dieskau wrote to Barenboim, in English, the language they always used with one another: "It has to come out of me. Working with you is always the most fulfilling experience of music-making that I have experienced in many years."

A young man, Barenboim (born in 1942) received a great deal of encouragement at that time from Fischer-Dieskau, who sensed in the younger man a passion for music the same as his own. He loved to listen to Barenboim and his young wife Jacqueline du Pré playing together. ("Jackie"

DuPré, born in 1945, died tragically early in 1987.) Fischer-Dieskau has never forgotten the picture of the two of them as they made music together:

> When I saw Daniel and Jackie Barenboim in Rome—they had just been married during the Six-Day War [5–10 June 1967]—a fire, a drive, came from these two brilliant musicians. It wasn't difficult to see in Jackie a superlative interpreter of music . . . . I knew that there were no artistic limitations for this woman on the platform in front of me who played, now dreamily, now tempestuously.[20]

The meetings with Sviatoslav Richter (b. 1914) were also "all music." One sees how little the difference in age matters when it is a question of art and artistic collaboration—neither with Barenboim, seventeen years younger, nor Richter, ten years older.

After the recital with Brahms's cycle *Die schöne Magelone* in Salzburg in 1970, Ivan Nagel described the "inexplicable tension" of Richter's pianism and how it can blend so perfectly with these songs:

> There was never the hint of a need for the one to accommodate the other. There was a fusion—so difficult to imagine for anyone who has not heard it—a dual unfolding of the richest, most complete independences. Probably no one else today but Fischer-Dieskau can afford to let Richter play so independently, as if he were playing solo a Brahms Intermezzo. The advantage that this adds to a penetrative illumination of a Lied was shown before the end of the first song.
>
> Before the words "so bleibt das Alter selbst noch jung" (thus does Age itself stay young), Richter allowed his instrument to play the theme with a constrained, undemonstrative naturalness, which Fischer-Dieskau then had to repeat. This introduction of the beautifully sensuous row of notes, later repeated, which then fill the last fifty measures, does not need to presage too obviously the singer's reply. Fischer-Dieskau then eased himself in quite simply, as if hovering above the music, wrapt in himself, unaffected, it seemed, by the earlier piano entry, thus giving the listener the surprise of the inevitable. The words sung by the baritone voice followed the wordless song of the piano with that illuminatingly beautiful inevitability with which an uttered word follows an unuttered thought, or realization follows an idea.

People will never be able to understand the life of an artist like Dietrich Fischer-Dieskau without taking account of moments like these of supreme musical artistry. Fischer-Dieskau wrote in later years to his son Martin, who had become a conductor:

Take every struggle as part of your profession and of learning. Your reward will then be the few very special moments of happiness, which most of the others will never know.[21]

The gods ensured a good many misgivings before such "moments of happiness"—even if they were only the perpetual arguments about the acoustic problems of a concert hall or recording studio, or the very variable qualities of a recording. The following list of a few "requests for improvements" after the recording of some Schubert Lieder in 1970 gives some idea of the labor required to perfect a recording.

> *Leichenphantasie* (Funeral Fantasy): Can the reprise at the end not be exchanged line for line for the mistakes at the beginning? As far as I can see, the music is the same for long stretches, and you could correct . . . ?
>
> *Der Jüngling am Bache* (The Youth at the Stream): "Der Knabe" (the boy) in the first line is terribly imprecise. Can we alter it?
>
> Page 1, *Der Taucher* (The Diver): "Er mag ihn behalten, er ist sein *eigen*" (He can keep it; it is his *own*): The sound is quite inaccurate. Have I ever done it better?
>
> Page 1, *Die Laube* (The Arbor): The whole piece has gone wrong, but we probably cannot take it out, because the book with the texts is already printed. Perhaps we could at least save the "Abschied" (Farewell) in the last line?

And so on—little details that nobody notices later. The pitfalls to be avoided with the acoustics of halls and studios are seen in concrete examples from the following two excerpts from his letters. On 9 April 1987:

> There were quite different problems here in the concert hall, the Rosbaud studio of SWF (Südwestfunk) [South West German Radio]. The acoustics of the rather small room conjured up for me the idea of a "Herr FD" somewhere out there in the audience, but from my place in front of the piano, I could hardly hear a thing. I have never experienced "die Tücke des Objekts" [i.e., that things have a will of their own] so strongly before. So they pushed me around on the platform, hoping that the sound would improve—forward, backward, forward again. The trouble was (in my opinion) that we were really too near the middle of an almost square room—and behold! . . . when we made that alteration, everything seemed different.[22]

Yet where, in concert halls built in the new and the latest architectural styles (for example, where nothing can be moved "forward or backward"), the singer almost always comes off the worst! On 8 June 1986, Fischer-Dieskau wrote:

> My connection with the Munich Philharmonic has had one continual snag: the concerts take place in the Gasteig Hall. You know perhaps what nonsense the Munich folk have managed with this tiny cabin for the arts: acoustics that do not let the orchestra play with precision but that also make the soloist's job very difficult; because of the lack of focus, he cannot find a spot where more than half the hall can hear anything.

An addition to the narrow circle of close friends was the then director of the music section of the (West) Berlin Library (Staatsbibliothek). How curious the beginning of a long, long friendship can be, is clearly shown in this case. Rudolf Elvers found it quite disgraceful that Fischer-Dieskau should have spirited a music-stand (actually belonging to Felix Mendelssohn himself!) from under his very nose—from him, the Mendelssohn specialist. Nevertheless, the relationship had been established, and it proved to be long-lasting. Elvers, a man of vast culture, widely-traveled, yet still a man of the state of Mecklenburg (in the north-east of Germany) at heart, was able to strengthen his friendship with the Fischer-Dieskaus by dint of the particular sense of (slow) humor of the people of that area—a sense of humor that had triumphed over many difficult times. Elvers, a specialist in music and literature, was able to help Fischer-Dieskau's literary research without any fuss or formality; always very frank, his strength, much praised by Fischer-Dieskau, lay in his natural, unassuming form of friendship.

The involuntary hiatus in his operatic work, caused by the car accident, lasted two years nevertheless. His comeback took place in Japan on a tour with the Deutsche Oper Berlin. On 27 March 1970, Fischer-Dieskau played Falstaff again. After six performances in Tokyo, there were Lieder recitals and orchestral concerts in Tokyo itself, then in Fukuoka, Sapporo, and Nagoya. Another twelve years of operatic performances still lay ahead.

From 1966 to 1972, Fischer-Dieskau completed the enormous task of recording almost all the Schubert Lieder for the male voice with Gerald Moore, who accompanied him in masterly fashion, even after his retirement from the concert platform in 1967.[23] In 1969, the first twelve LP records appeared, containing 172 Lieder.

Fischer-Dieskau wrote in his memoirs: "During such continual concentration on one's own precision and purity of voice, one just cannot 'wake up' and enjoy company." This may make strange reading for more gregarious people, but it is also just possible that the growing student unrest may have played its part here, for, regardless of how people felt about it, it did cause deep depression everywhere, since no one could be certain where the frightening, arbitrary actions of the demonstrators would lead. Fischer-Dieskau then wrote of "critical drops that make holes in so many of the stones of traditional conventions,"[24] though with the obvious benefit of hindsight. It was then, at the beginning of the 1970s, whether by pure chance or not, that his own personal—and German society's—crises coincided: his second failure to effect a much desired private union that would reestablish the balance between his own demands for artistic perfection; and the great insecurity of the basis of German society, the seeming *devaluing* of all values by Germany's young people. In any case, together they were grounds enough for the singer to feel, more acutely than ever before, the isolation of the artist, perhaps the isolation to be found also in Schubert's Lieder.

One should not read too much into Fischer-Dieskau's interpretation of Schubert's Lieder, for the moment of great art is different from that of all other times of life, and the personal experiences of an artist can never be directly reflected in his work. Schubert's song *Der Pilgrim* (D794) of 1823 in the complete recordings was described by the critic of the *Salzburger Nachrichten* as "moved by an experience and a passionate plaint." It tells of the pilgrim's experience and *his* "passionate plaint"—Fischer-Dieskau's voice brings it to life.

In the praise of the first set of recordings of Schubert's Lieder, the question of the dramatic and the lyrical interpretation of Lieder was inevitably, and regularly, raised and compared historically with the vocal technique of Schubert's contemporaries, Johann Michael Vogl (1768–1840) (for the dramatic) and Karl, Freiherr von Schönstein (1797–1876). Vogl, a baritone, nearly thirty years older than Schubert, was the singer who, after meeting Schubert in 1819, made his songs popular by performing them wherever and whenever he could, often accompanied at the piano by Schubert himself. Schönstein, a tenor and of Schubert's age, was the dedicatee of Schubert's 1823 song cycle *Die schöne Müllerin*. Max Kaindl-Hönig came to a not unexpected conclusion in his comparison:

> Fischer-Dieskau is neither a successor to Vogl, the "dramatic" singer who only started singing Schubert's Lieder at an advanced age [fifty-one], nor is his style that of the "lyrical" Schönstein. Fischer-Dieskau can do both and moves quite deliberately from one to the other.

Then the reviewer mentions *Der Pilgrim* again, as well as *Das Lied im Grünen* (D917) and *An die Musik* (D547), and defines the scope and range of these Schubert interpretations:

> For example, in the first group (à la Vogl), there is *Der Pilgrim*, moved by an experience and a passionate plaint, treated in declama-

tory fashion with colorations, a stressing of words and syllables within the phrase—and then, in contrast, the other type (à la Schönstein), the wonderfully flowing *Das Lied im Grünen* and *An die Musik*, purely lyrical, sung free of all pointed interventions.

Yet this is hardly about one or the other type of singing, but rather about how the singer treats a song according to his understanding of it, and that, again, is dependent on the mood of the moment. If it depends on Fischer-Dieskau's much-discussed "prior study," the result would always be the same. Indeed, his approach varies very deliberately; it always did, but one cannot deny that there are, and were, times when the abysses were deeper and the cliffs steeper than others.

It was a Friday—and the thirteenth. On this 13 November 1973 was the first rehearsal of Puccini's one-act opera *Il tabarro* (The Cloak), part of his celebrated *trittico* (his triptych, with *Gianni Schicchi*, the main character's name, and *Suor Angelica*). Julia Varady, the soprano, who at that time had only been in Germany for three years and was at the beginning of her career, had come to this rehearsal with some trepidation, for Dietrich Fischer-Dieskau, whom she was to partner in her role of Giorgetta, the wife of Michele, the barge-owner, had long been a model for her. During her studies, she had learned to understand and to sing Schubert's Lieder from his recordings. She related later: "He stood up and grew bigger and bigger. I could hardly believe that such wonderful sounds could come from such a colossus."

During the rehearsals and the performances of the opera, a warm friendship developed between them, which, at first, was just like the understanding that develops between partners on stage when things are going well, an attraction situated somewhere between illusion and reality. Puccini's opera's theme is the game of love and jealousy. Giorgetta provokes her husband Michele by playing up to the barge-hand Luigi before eventually becoming his lover. When Giorgetta looks for Luigi in the dark, Michele has already strangled him and he shows her the corpse under his cloak. Both plot and music are dark, full of great emotion. Puccini comes his closest here to Italian *verismo* (realism). Julia Varady always interpreted Giorgetta's role to show that, in her heart of hearts, she really loved her husband, and that her dallying with Luigi was really meant to make Michele take more notice of her.

In reality, the singer had found in Fischer-Dieskau a man who has never ceased to attract her. From that first performance together in 1973 grew a mutual attraction out of the game, not of jealousy, but of love. From Julia Varady there radiated (and still radiates) a love of life and a warmth that chased away the threatening dark clouds of those difficult days of worry and failure in Fischer-Dieskau's marriages and—to keep to the metaphor— allowed the blue sky to peep through again. Fischer-Dieskau wrote with gentle irony in his memoirs:

> Now, the sly but caring director Günther Rennert thought his own thoughts as Julia Varady and I began to rehearse. My wooing of my blonde partner expressed itself rather more vehemently than Puccini had had in mind, even though that nice story that, during the rehearsal, I proposed to her by means of a little note is pure invention.[25]

Julia Varady grew up in Oradea in Transylvania (today, Romania). Her mother tongue is actually Hungarian, but she also speaks fluent English, French, Romanian, Russian, and Italian—and, naturally, now German, too—all of them with the same lively intensity. Her training as a singer began at the School of Music in Cluj (Romania) and continued at the conservatory there. She had stage experience as well during her studies, and graduated with a teacher's diploma in singing. Once qualified as a singer, she did not stay long under a totalitarian government but left Romania with only her voice as capital. She knew nobody in the West, and no one knew her—but that quickly changed. She won a competition in Italy, and Christoph von Dohnányi, the conductor, engaged her for the Frankfurt Opera. All this happened in 1970. There she sang many of the great roles: Antonia in Offenbach's *The Tales of Hoffmann*, Elisabeth de Valois in Verdi's *Don Carlos*, and Donna Elvira in Mozart's *Don Giovanni*. Yet, at first, her standard of living did not match these glamorous roles. She lived on meager rations in a small furnished room, with white-painted boxes and bookcases as furniture, opposite a huge, constantly flashing advertisement for Coca-Cola. Her Frankfurt colleagues used to help out where they could.

Mozart arias became her favorite domain. In 1971, she was engaged by the Bavarian State Opera and made her debut there as Vitellia in Mozart's late opera *La clemenza di Tito* (The Clemency of Titus) and as Cio-Cio-San in Puccini's *Madame Butterfly*. After her Donna Elvira came the Giorgetta in *Il tabarro*, then Fiordiligi in Mozart's *Così fan tutte* in Istvan Kertesz's Mozart cycle in Cologne in 1972, followed by Donna Elvira in his *Don Giovanni* production.

The change in her personal life also brought her undoubted success. In the same letter in which he had written that Kristina, as he saw it, was not "putting her life to rights," there is also a passage in which Fischer-Dieskau writes of himself as someone "who is very happy with a partner who is not giving up her own personality, is even in the same profession, yet is

First meeting with Julia Varady. As Michele in Puccini's one-act opera *Il tabarro* (The Cloak) in Günther Rennert's Munich production in 1973.

completely part of his life." It could not have been better put. Only a warm-hearted, positively orientated—and very strong—personality can manage to become part of another, without losing its own individuality. What came into being then—and what has remained firm and unchallenged since—is the partnership of two self-willed people who do not tire themselves out in arguments with one another to prove their independence.

Julia Varady showed herself ready and eager to learn. (The film made for Fischer-Dieskau's seventieth birthday celebration in 1995 showed her rehearsing a Verdi role while Fischer-Dieskau "coaches" her from the piano. *Trans.*) Moments of personal happiness were one with moments of artistic happiness when they were together on the stage, as they often were. She arranged her engagements as far as she could so that she could sometimes accompany the singer on his recital tours, and she took over for herself Fischer-Dieskau's long-established practice of not joining the mad jet-setting of the other operatic stars. She also shared the services of Fischer-Dieskau's secretary Diether Warneck until his departure. Munich and Berlin also became her regular opera houses (appropriately enough, since they have houses in both cities), but Vienna and Covent Garden were soon to be added.

Thus 1973 was a very significant year for Fischer-Dieskau and Julia Varady, but it held yet another significance. In February, Fischer-Dieskau had conducted an orchestra for the first time—the New Philharmonia Orchestra of London. There will be more to say about this in later pages.

A month before, the singer had completed an American tour with Schumann Lieder in Cleveland and Chicago, accompanied by Daniel Barenboim, who also conducted the Brahms *German Requiem* in Chicago. There were also recitals of Brahms Lieder, accompanied by Günther Weissenborn, in New York's Carnegie Hall and in the Lincoln Center in Washington, D.C.[26]

Munich saw Fischer-Dieskau as Amfortas in Wagner's *Parsifal*, conducted by Wolfgang Sawallisch. That is history now, yet there are those who still like to compare it with the recording made two years earlier with Georg Solti, in which the singer really did manage to merge his personality with the character of the suffering king. Then he sang Count Almaviva again in Munich, a role that had become so much a part of his repertoire and personality that the Munich intendant Günther Rennert felt justified in beginning his little speech "Carissimo Conte" (My dearest Count)! Again in Munich, Fischer-Dieskau played Barak in Richard Strauss's opera *Die Frau ohne Schatten* (The Woman Without a Shadow) (1919), ten years after his debut in the role at the opening of the Bavarian National Theater in 1963. Had time really passed so quickly? Instead of Joseph Keilberth, Wolfgang Sawallisch was now the conductor. Had Barak's transformation gained depth? There was a straight answer to the question of why Fischer-Dieskau liked this role: "The simplicity, the kindness, and the cantilenas."

On 7 December 1973, *Il tabarro*, Puccini's one-act opera, was premiered at last, with Fischer-Dieskau as Michele and Julia Varady as Giorgetta, his wife. (Fischer-Dieskau sang Gianni Schicchi—in another of the three operas in the triptych—on the same night, a part which needed a quite different vocal timbre from the Michele role.) Later, Julia Varady was his Arabella in Strauss's opera (in 1976, after Lisa della Casa and Gundula Janowitz), his Countess in *The Marriage of Figaro* in 1978, and his Eva in Wagner's *Die Meistersinger* in 1979, among many other roles.

The mention of Wagner's *Die Meistersinger* also signals the conclusion of a long period of deliberation and a crucial decision for Fischer-Dieskau. He had written to Wieland Wagner in Bayreuth, in May 1966:

> My feelings tell me that every year that I can look forward to this divine role is a year gained. . . . So, all that I can say is to wish you, with heartfelt honesty, that you find a suitable Sachs. But am I really one?[27]

According to Montague Haltrecht in his book on Sir David Webster, *The Quiet Showman*, Sir Thomas Beecham had offered Fischer-Dieskau the role in a Covent Garden production for 1950–1951; although that never came to pass, the part had retained an attraction for Fischer-Dieskau, which he almost seemed to feel as a temptation. Twenty-five years later, on 12 March 1976, shortly before his fifty-first birthday, he was to make his debut as Sachs—not in Bayreuth, but in the Deutsche Oper Berlin. Peter Beauvais was the director. He came so well prepared for the preliminary discussions that Fischer-Dieskau, the perfectionist, had to confess with some surprise that he himself was not as advanced in his study of the work as this exceptional director who knew the whole opera by heart. Both Fischer-Dieskaus became very attached to Beauvais, a scrupulous worker but a deliberate thinker who used to call them up at regular intervals—and then fall silent. He sat there in rehearsals, biting his tie, deep in thought, taking his time—but then what he eventually said made sense.

After the Sachs role, he helped Fischer-Dieskau in his first venture into films, as the Emperor in a version of Heinrich von Kleist's 1810 play *Käthchen von Heilbronn* (Cathy of Heilbronn). That was when Fischer-Dieskau learned all about film-making: up at five in the morning in the misty damp of the Fichtel mountains near Bayreuth, only to hear, after waiting for hours, the dreaded words, "No good today!"—and the same thing the next day. The carefully learned part, broken up by "takes," vanished from an indignant memory in take number fourteen. The producer soothed the incipient panic with calming words: "Don't let yourself get annoyed."[28]

The Fischer-Dieskaus's partnership gained new satisfaction from Strauss's *Arabella* in Munich in 1977. Fischer-Dieskau's Mandryka, a part which he had studied into the recesses of its soul and had sung so often,

As Mandryka in Richard Strauss's opera *Arabella* in 1977, with Julia Varady in her first appearance in the title role.

seemed to gain a fresh impetus. Julia Varady sang Arabella and Peter Beauvais directed. The *Meistersinger* production in Berlin has also always remained fresh in Fischer-Dieskau's memory. Just about that time, 1976, the tension had been uncommonly great. Norbert Miller, the Berlin lecturer in music, critic, and later a friend of the singer's, wrote in his review for the *Süddeutsche Zeitung*:

> The event of the evening was naturally expected to be Fischer-Dieskau's debut as Hans Sachs. He did not disappoint these expectations, neither as singer nor as actor. The part could almost have been written for him. Its highly charged earnestness and its resigned good nature, its fits of brooding, and then those gestures with their popular appeal, make it easy to identify the part with the singer.[29]

Had Fischer-Dieskau delayed singing Hans Sachs in order to be able to be "identified" in this way with the part, with its arch humor and, perhaps more so, with its resigned melancholy? "Highly charged earnestness" had always been one of his characteristics; had he perhaps needed time to take

As Hans Sachs in Richard Wagner's *Die Meistersinger* (The Mastersingers of Nürnberg) with Julia Varady as Eva, in Munich in 1979.

on that resigned mood, which Wagner's character seems to know so well? The air of finality that Fischer-Dieskau managed to give to his Sachs is remarkable when seen in that context.

Peter Beauvais, the director of the 1976 production, watched the scene in which Sachs left the Festwiese (the Festival meadow) alone, with admiration:

> The way the philosopher went back into his workshop, that was just him. For me, the end came when he simply disappears from the crowd around him—just as in *The Magic Flute*. There, too, the crowd has to take over. And then, suddenly, in the premiere, he surprised me by going away up the slope and disappearing again—a stroke of genius.

That was not all that there was to admire. Norbert Miller hit the nail on the head in his remarks on Fischer-Dieskau and his Sachs when he wrote in his review:

> He made the singing so unmistakably a heightened medium for the dramatic dialogue. No other singer has been able to bridge the gap between the beautiful passages and the change-over to the recitatives so successfully. He was Sachs for the whole performance.

There are echoes here of Fischer-Dieskau's exhortations to his students to "become the person who is singing." He has done this himself, on the concert platform, in the recording studios and on stage—and a fortiori with this Hans Sachs. The critic H. H. Stuckenschmidt, writing in the *Frankfurter Allgemeine Zeitung*, noted: "Yes, in the course of that long evening, Fischer-Dieskau's personification of the cobbler-poet Hans Sachs becomes a great experience, obliterating everything else." This was his comment on the debut role of a master who represents in the opera the master of all masters. The critic accompanied the singer step for step through the opera, thus doing a service for those who could not attend the performance, and there were many:

> The way in which he enters the Singschule, greets the masters with a friendly reserve, and watches the proceedings thoughtfully from his stool, creates a wonderful atmosphere. Slowly, but obviously, the knight [Walther von Stolzing] gains his sympathy and the new way of singing his approval. The voice is in top form. Yet Fischer-Dieskau holds himself back, a master of irony, too, in the burgeoning argument with Beckmesser. The Fliedermonolog (The Monologue Under the Elder Tree) in Act II receives new resonances—a quiet passion and a lyrical resignation, which give a

matchless expression to the "süsse Not" (the "sweet demand" of
Walther's song). The scene with Eva, with the music in the bari-
tonal high register, is the first joyous moment of the performance.
When Beckmesser comes on the scene, then come the roguishly
acted nuances.[30]

Does it not appear therefore that the reviewer has given a picture of an
ideal interpretation of this role instead of a description of the performance?
Nevertheless, it was the truth, and the word "perfection" appeared, as it were,
involuntarily, in the critic's review—and he was not the only one to feel this.
When, three years later, in 1979, the opera was given in a different production but with the same Sachs in Munich's National Theater, Hans Mayer,
the Germanist and Wagner specialist and expositor, a refugee from the then
GDR, attended the dress rehearsal. He wrote to Fischer-Dieskau: "This is
the first Sachs for decades for me who can match, in a very professional way,
the Masters of my memories." He also had a word for Sachs's Eva:

> I was very taken too with the Evchen. This is a very difficult role.
> Thomas Mann spoke once in a rather unkind way of "dear little Eva,
> that simpleton." She *is* that from time to time and that has to be
> brought out in the characterization. She is also a quarrelsome
> teenager, then, again, a clever and sympathetic woman for whom art
> and love are indivisible. When she sings at the end: "Keiner wie du
> so hold zu werben weiss!" (There is no one who can woo like you!),
> the music reminds us of the moment on the bench under the elder
> tree. Frau Varady sang that with heartfelt beauty, and the little trill
> on the last phrase was just right. . . . Please send my sincere
> compliments to "Fräulein Pogner."[31]

The Sachs debut was a triumph for Fischer-Dieskau, as all had expected
it would be. Had he waited unnecessarily long to sing it, or had the long wait
been the prerequisite for the ultimate fulfillment? He had not refused to sing
it without good reasons—despite the "siren calls." Six years before his great
triumph, he had forced himself to what had sounded like a definitive "No,"
and had said at the time:

> After several trial runs measured by a stop-watch (it is two hours, five
> minutes of singing), with its bass coloring and continual demands
> for a broad vocal quality—Sachs is not for me. I shall have to resist
> all the siren calls from my mother, my teacher, and so many maestri,
> for this grape really does hang too high for me to reach, although it
> certainly looks shiny and tasty. I have sung through the part once
> again (how often have I done that already!), and even with the most
> generous holding-back on the part of the orchestra, and using

Sprechgesang (spoken recitative) as often as possible, I cannot see how I could manage it without damaging my voice.[32]

(Other voices in other countries had wondered whether his singing in Wagnerian operas at this time had not slightly coarsened his voice anyway, and he had noted to one interlocutor how tiring the Sachs role was: "I'm on the stage for five or six hours and only sing for two." *Trans.*)[33]

In 1976, had all his doubts vanished? It would not have been in Fischer-Dieskau's character for him to throw *all* doubts overboard—and decades later, one can hear him say that such a role really belongs to a true bass-baritone like his friend Hans Hotter (b. 1909). If he had nevertheless become a "perfect" Sachs (to repeat the compliment), that is surely part of the development, the process of maturing, that he had gone through since that "No" of 1970; yet, quite clearly, awareness of the right moment is all-important, too.

Can one speak here of "genius"? Many have used the word in connection with the art of Dietrich Fischer-Dieskau, and that is perhaps justified in the eighteenth-century German philosopher Immanuel Kant's definition: "Genius is the talent for doing what cannot be learned." The question of what "creative" means for an interpretative artist goes far beyond the question of "talent." When the singer changes himself into the "person who is singing," he is following, with all faithfulness to the words and the music, not only the poet and the composer, he is singing also from the depths of his own soul. That is why his mastery of the score distinguishes a musician like Fischer-Dieskau, yet it does not hinder his creative impulse. In his work with accompanists, conductors, and lately with his students, one hears him ask time and time again: "Is that really in the score?" The score is the *terra firma* on which he walks and moves and has his being, and when he does manage to soar above it—without leaving it behind—this seemingly rather absurd formulation is the justification for talking about "genius." The capacity for genius in an interpreter is not expressed in that desire for change for which conductors and directors (under that catchword "deconstruction") like to take credit. [Think of poor Anton Bruckner's fate. His works have often been shortened and "improved."]

Fischer-Dieskau felt good in Peter Beauvais's *Meistersinger* production, which had remained faithful to tradition.[34] Fischer-Dieskau has never shied away from new ideas in the theater, since, for him, "grease-paint and stage-dust belonged to the necessities of life—part of what I love," but there was a "but . . . ."

But new ideas should abide by what is sensible—and not what is sense-*less*. The great works can bear so many visual and interpretative innovations that one does not need to distort their meaning.

That has nothing to do with my love of the theater and my involvement, up to complete exhaustion, in the role of the moment.[35]

This was in 1985, two years after he had retired from the operatic stage. Such
devotion to his interpretation, to the character that he had to reincarnate, was
hardly compatible with what he had called (to his intimate friends) "director
fetishism." Still:

The directors, like Max Reinhardt (1873–1943) (the Austrian director in Salzburg and Berlin), who would accept an idea from an actor
and then extend it in his (and the actor's) conception, belong to the
past. The diverse dictators among the directors have also left their
traces behind them. . . . You'll be beginning to think: "They are
always at war with their directors," but, as I say, this *is* in the air, and
the plague of autocracy attacks everyone, despite all this touching
talk of "co-determination."[36]

It certainly was "in the air," and here was a singer who, after all, had himself
determined the production of many operas by trying to get to the heart of the
true musical meaning of the work, and was giving vent to his feelings. Was a
work of art not being underestimated, if directors tried to "make it relevant"?
Was the attempt to mirror recent history in the operas of the nineteenth
century by adding externalities to the work not degrading art to a mere means
to an end? On the other hand, was not too much being asked of the work?
Fischer-Dieskau had no doubts on that score:

Where the subject is the barbarism of the Third Reich and its
catastrophic consequences and a normal fictional plot and the cor-
responding style are used to depict it, it turns me off, for it is
inevitable that trivialities will be worked into any plot that is freely
narrated or produced on stage.[37]

The crude allusions and the down-to-earthness of so many modern operatic productions could not interest him. Yet where was the modern relevance
of a work of art for him? How were his audiences faced with reality in *his* performances? He asked his friend Heinz Friedrich once, rather skeptically:

Have I shaped reality creatively? Perhaps you have to ask a creative
artist that question so that he can become aware of it. For to exclude
the "rauhen Odem der Wirklichkeit" (the rough breath of reality)
seemed to me always to create a fresh need to bring about a revolution from within—and that I see as my sort of Romanticism.

"A revolution from within" could well be Fischer-Dieskau's artistic
credo. It is also an echo of the adolescent's own world, the world that the

mature and privileged adult had never really thought of leaving. Should one keep to one's self what was really so difficult to pass on? This letter to Heinz Friedrich, written when Fischer-Dieskau was fifty, seeks the truth in actuality. He went on: "Truth must always be perpetually reestablished; it requires patience and an untiring curiosity, but never accommodation." This also applied to his relationship with his sons, who "question everything that has come down to them, and yet find answers for themselves that lie handily close to their own experiences."[38]

The three sons had all looked for, and found, jobs in artistic professions. Their father's example did, of course, strengthen and encourage their resolve, yet that very example gave grounds for mutual irritations and tensions between the two generations. All four tried to overcome these tensions. In the father's letters, the hope always gleams of establishing a mutuality of interests that would bridge the gap between them. The narrator that he is makes the arrival of a letter into a *scena*. He wrote to his son Martin from Munich on 2 April 1979, when he was rehearsing Béla Bartók's opera *Duke Bluebeard's Castle* with Julia Varady:

> Dearest Martin,
> Our letters crossed in the post. When, after a particularly stressful and nerve-wracking opening session of *Bluebeard* for DG (Deutsche Grammophon) under Sawallisch, Julia came running into the room, waving your wonderful long letter wildly in the air because she knew how much I had been longing for a letter from you, our joy knew no bounds.

Who else but Julia could have been able to find so much joy in "wildly waving" good news? The father, in turn, answered his son with a similarly long letter, telling him of the rehearsals that were taking place, as well as of new events, such as the impression that the recently completed opera *Lulu* (of Alban Berg) had made at its premiere in Paris:

> Cerha's added orchestration really only confirmed the opera's basic weaknesses, that is, that the Berg-Wedekind marriage was something of a misalliance: an unctuous Tristan vis-à-vis withering sarcasm.

Even here, admiration for artistic achievement is not lacking, despite the criticism—perhaps an example of the "singers' trade union"? "Stratas's all-out performance had to be admired." Yet his summing-up did remain critical:

> My nostalgia for the torso-like version grew—the additions only offered "reminiscences," not like the many dramatic climaxes found in so many other places in the work.[39]

In Berlin, with his three sons, Manuel, Mathias, and Martin.

His attempts always to keep in touch with his sons by drawing them into his own work can be seen in the above excerpts. Here, too, the artistic profession they shared is seen to be the desired arena for mutual understanding, but again, the very similarity of their artistic interests complicated, even obstructed, their relationships. Arguments between fathers and sons have a long literary and psychological history behind them, not to mention the many psychoanalytical exegeses, particularly in German-speaking countries. The sons of famous and important men contribute significantly to this history, which may also be connected with the fact that contemporaries, and posterity, show so much interest in them. Sons of less important men often suffer no less, and many suffer much more immediately under their fathers. Two things condition the relationship with a famous father: first, the desire to get away from under his shadow, and that must encourage the young man to set himself up against his father, or, if things go well for him, to prove himself independent in his own field; second, the justified ambition to make the famous name, which, wherever he looks, seems to belong only to the father, his own.

Even in the 1980s, Fischer-Dieskau could write to Detlev Jürges, the pianist and a friend of his POW days: "My children have become independent men, too, each to be admired in his own way, bravely combating the difficulties that arise, in part, from their well-known name." But would one not expect the well-known name to have opened doors for them, given them confidence? Alas, we live in an age that mistrusts rather than trusts, and the fear of seeming to be protected out of kindness is great. Could society—and its outriders, the press—not be happy about the doings of an artistic family, could it not take pleasure in a father and his artistic sons? Seemingly not. When there was to be a family performance at the Schubertiade in Hohenems in Austria—Martin Fischer-Dieskau was to conduct, Mathias Fischer-Dieskau was to do the décor, Julia Varady-Fischer-Dieskau was to sing (and Dietrich Fischer-Dieskau was not to take part at all)—a section of the press complained loudly about "nepotism." Fischer-Dieskau would just not let himself be exposed to such imputations.

The composer and conductor Antal Dorati spoke very frankly about the burden that an inherited, famous name can become, after he had decided to appoint Martin Fischer-Dieskau as his assistant:

> The burden of a father's name is best shown by the fact that I nearly didn't appoint him as my assistant, even though he was better in the conducting audition than the other candidates, for it would "look" as if I had appointed him because of you. I really had to be firm with myself and give Martin the position and his just deserts, which he had honestly earned from the audition.[40]

To have to make one's own name first of all proves to be an unusual challenge for most people. The example that Fischer-Dieskau gave to his sons by his own self-discipline, his concentration on the work in hand, his obvious delight in music (all of which must not be forgotten when reading all these stern commandments) as in his work on the stage, in operas, and in the shaping of characters—this example could only mean that the sons soon found that the profession they chose had to be an artistic one. So, burden and encouragement, both together, still accompany them today after they have long since founded their careers: Mathias as a stage designer and composer of electronic music for the stage; Martin as a conductor who, just as Antal Dorati advised him, combines operatic and concert work and is also a professor in Bremen; and Manuel as a cellist who was able to gain fame with the Cherubini-Quartet and works now with Bavarian Radio and will shortly appear as soloist with the Berlin Philharmonic.

It is rare to see all three sons with the father, but these are wonderful occasions when they can make music together, for it is in music that their most obvious common denominator can be found. It is a *sine qua non* for Fischer-Dieskau that his sons' independence should be welcomed and supported, although the consequential separation remains as painful now as at the beginning, when his engagements took him away from home so often — and yet not so frequently as seems to be lodged in his sons' memories. All this moves, and moved, him much more than it would have done many other fathers who perhaps do not have his background and resolution that make him long to be a true *pater familias.*

His professional life (which certainly did not embrace only work and duty but also those consistently new and tempting engagements in whose great moments there is pure fulfillment, not just a drug) was always his first priority. With that came the knowledge, confirmed times without number, that his art made so many people happy that they waited for him, and that he then had to (and wanted to) go on singing for them, for his and for their sake. So his life has remained irregular, but of course, accompanied and watched over by his beloved wife Julia Varady.

In the 1970s, the much-traveled singer began to think of a place of his own amid lovely scenery, a refuge between engagements and perhaps even a place for his retirement, although it must be said that the house in Berlin always gives the impression of an island of peace in the middle of the noisy German capital. In 1974, the Fischer-Dieskaus found the place just outside Munich — not quite the expected place for the reserved "townee" from Berlin, yet under this bright sky whose light over the lakes of the Alpine foothills has attracted so many painters — well, perhaps it would be just livable here! Munich, their place of work, had been the starting point of their search for a house. So, in the midst of beautiful scenery and not far from Lake Starnberg (where, reputedly, the Munich millionaires live), they built their house, inspired by the singer-painter's imagination and, at least as strongly, by that of the future lady of the house, who, a keen gardener, took over the planning of the grounds and the garden herself — and that is not just meant in the metaphorical sense. Now, as then, she loves to work in the garden, plants shrubs and bushes, and prunes trees — all with a professional touch and under the amazed admiration of the man of the house, who uses the paths to din words and music into his head while he walks. The central focus of the house is the music room: you look up to the ceiling, which is like a little cupola making the room at once large and cheerful, because it does not seem too ponderous among the other rooms. The house seems large, but it is not "stately" in a negative sense. It is a place for living and working in, but there is room for guests too. Fischer-Dieskau loves meeting and talking to friends, although the conversations must be on sensible topics and guests

Julia Varady and Dietrich Fischer-Dieskau, accompanied by Wolfgang Sawallisch, sing duets by Robert Schumann.

must take their share of the discussions. Making music with his guests is one of his favored activities, but also listening to music, for his enormous collection of recordings, including rare records of long ago, enables the company to make comparisons of interpreters and interpretations. Literature also has a major role to play. Fischer-Dieskau has been an avid reader from his earliest days, and classic and modern literature often form topics of conversation. As the conversation ranges over many authors, such as Adalbert Stifter (1805–1868), Martin Walser (b. 1927), and the Austrian Peter Handke (b. 1942), the guest finds himself being invited to take part in the reading of bits of correspondence, to everyone's delight. It is a social intercourse far removed from small talk and based on a seemingly vanished social culture, but which is nevertheless seen to be both illuminating and topical.

It would seem that the room in which all these activities take place had been tailor-made for them, the production of a familiar play in a new stage-set, as it were, for the same sort of occasions had been held in the very different ambience of the rooms in the house in Berlin in the early years. They were much less private, of course, but still with record evenings, well-prepared with music, slides, and texts, but later for much more restricted groups.

Strangely, the house in Berlin now seems quieter, and, no doubt because of that (and what is probably the reason for the quietness), it seems more cut-off, too. The light is different, it falls gently through and is filtered by the white curtains. There seems to be an even larger collection of books, as well as pictures, mostly in smallish format, but everything is connected with music, the dominating factor of his professional career. Sometimes, as in the house near Munich, there will be one of his own paintings among the others; their positions are changed from time to time, as if the painter were trying to find their proper place in the house. The Berlin house could be the house of an academic, although an academic with a concert grand.

The building of the Munich house aroused great interest among the fans of the two famous married singers, who were both loved by the public but abhorred publicity. It is truly remarkable that even as late as the 1970s, the cult of stardom could still be celebrated as in days of yore, and that there were still people who would take a handful of earth from their idols' building-site!

The music-loving public treasured their great singer who had opened their minds and hearts—and obviously their ears too—to the German Lied and, on the stage, had shown them people, not just figures and vocal automata. But the public's love always demands something more than just "great art," however human and warm it might be. All great artists are bathed in the public's enthusiastic glare, but Fischer-Dieskau does not relish this public enthusiasm, for therein lies a temptation that, if yielded to, awakens a new, even stronger desire for familiarity. He drew back as far as he could from such embraces, and the respect he gained thereby proved him to have been right. Can he not be compared then to Hans Sachs whom everybody loves (apart from Beckmesser, of course, and in Fischer-Dieskau's case there are a handful of Beckmessers!) but who distances himself from his fans, albeit at the price of a temporary loneliness? "The philosopher returns to his workshop." That is why Hans Sachs is one of the major roles of Fischer-Dieskau's career, even if he did not devote as much time to it as he did to others in his long stage career.

One role still awaited him—one that he had had in mind for a long time. The idea of an opera on Shakespeare's King Lear had not materialized with Benjamin Britten, but Fischer-Dieskau had never forgotten the planned project. One could say that the composer for his *Lear* had literally been made for him. Aribert Reimann (b. 1936), a Berliner like Dietrich Fischer-Dieskau, had met the singer while studying with Boris Blacher (1903–1975), the composer of free contrapuntal music. He became very important for Fischer-Dieskau, both as composer and accompanist. They first worked together during the preparatory work for Hans Werner Henze's opera *Elegy for Young Lovers*, which had its premiere in Schwetzingen near Heidelberg in May 1961. At that time, the young Reimann used to come to Fischer-Dieskau's house in Berlin to help him as a singing coach for the role of Gregor Mittenhofer, the eccentric poet, but their relationship did not stop there. On 29 August 1961, Fischer-Dieskau gave the first performance of Reimann's *Totentanz-Suite* (Suite of the Dance of Death) for baritone and chamber orchestra, with the Berlin Philharmonic, conducted by Werner Egk, and there was no doubt for whose voice the suite had been written.

It is always comforting to see a great talent being recognized and acknowledged in our own times. Perhaps this just proves that the present is actually more reliable than the so-called "good old days" of the past. Fischer-Dieskau has accompanied the younger man with friendship on his chosen path, has urged him on, given him encouragement, and shown him new paths as an accompanist to Lieder, but most importantly, he put the idea of an opera on King Lear into his head, and he never failed to return to the idea whenever the opportunity presented itself. A certain impatience that lies in the character of this most active of men did not fail to have its effect and reward.

One day, quite on his own impulse, Fischer-Dieskau sketched out a libretto. On 6 February 1972, he wrote to Reimann:

> Dear Aribert,
> In the middle of, I must admit, very boring rehearsals for [Richard Strauss's opera] *Die Frau ohne Schatten* (The Woman Without a Shadow), I sat down to the *Lear*, and just wrote away. It is rather more a five-fingered exercise than a finished piece of work, and the first half of the opera would certainly only look a little like the enclosed. Do you think that I should go ahead with this sketch? At any rate, the snags and the language difficulties have been revealed, and I now know where the main accents have to lie.

That sketch was certainly much more than a mere draft. Fischer-Dieskau had worked out the most concrete details. He went on:

> You can cheerfully put a question mark over the passages for the chorus. I find that an opera on a subject like this cannot be managed without a sort of "speech chorus," with crescendi and decrescendi, particularly at the beginning and the end. The passages that are to be sung simultaneously (mostly at irregular intervals) are also marked, but, of course, they can be thrown out at any time.

Of course, it did not all work out like that, but Fischer-Dieskau's practical sketch did help eventually to get the whole undertaking moving. He loves to play down his part in the creation of Reimann's opera. He was not thinking only of the uniting of drama and opera; because of his practical familiarity as a singer with Reimann's principles of composition, he had also discovered musical points of departure. In the book produced to accompany the opera, Fischer-Dieskau wrote:

> Shortly after talking to Aribert Reimann came the second performances of vocal works with orchestra. Above all in the *Wolkenloses Christfest* (A Cloudless Christmas), a requiem on a text by Otfried Büthe, there sounded a note of melismatic stress of dark colorations and despairing outbursts, of blocks of frictional, orchestral dialogues with the soloists that foreshadowed the *Lear* opera. This was an internal approach to the theme of the later work.[41]

Claus H. Henneberg, who wrote himself into operatic history as the librettist of Reimann's *Lear* (and could be thus compared, and not unjustly, with Arrigo Boito, Verdi's librettist for his Shakespearean operas, *Otello* and *Falstaff*), wrote with some feeling in that same book that he felt at first that

With the composer Aribert Reimann at the recording of his song cycle *Shine and Dark* in 1990.

the play could never be set to music but nonetheless then delivered the sketch of a libretto. He also described the role that Fischer-Dieskau played in its further development. Henneberg found his meetings with Reimann and Fischer-Dieskau "very painful and difficult operations":

> I don't know how many opera libretti and Lieder texts Fischer-Dieskau knows, but his ability to make connections is unlimited. All the more amazing, since, unlike so many actors, he doesn't just speak in quotations. After we had eliminated all the various connections and associations, I could hardly find my way through the original typescript, so I started work on a fourth version.

The composer, on the other hand, loved those meetings, in which everything was discussed. He said that Fischer-Dieskau had been fabulous and had

With the producer Jean-Pierre Ponnelle and Julia Varady during a rehearsal of Aribert Reimann's opera *Lear* in 1978.

always queried the necessity of each passage—"a superb Beckmesser in the best sense of the term."[42]

When the plan had first been accepted, and first Reimann and then Henneberg had become enthusiastic about it, Fischer-Dieskau's musical and literary knowledge became enormously important for the developing libretto. There was something else, more important and more decisive: it was Fischer-Dieskau's voice that the composer had in his head. For a composer to have to write for a particular voice is always a great advantage. The history of music is full of such examples, from Mozart via Verdi up to the present day. How many composers have written for this voice and have become very bold with their ideas? Ernst Křenek (1900–1991), the "grand old man" of modern music, wrote about Fischer-Dieskau: "I certainly thought of giving the interpreter plenty of room in the planning of my work, but I also knew what interpreter I was thinking of at the time."[43]

Aribert Reimann, with confidence in this voice, was heaping up mountains of challenges for the first, but also for all subsequent interpreters of the difficult role of King Lear. That is how Fischer-Dieskau saw it, too. He wrote to the composer on 12 October 1976:

> Dear Aribert,
> The first pages of *Lear* have arrived and I grabbed them up hungrily, as you can imagine. Wonderfully promising, superb orchestral effects, great dramatic possibilities (you should have been the director as well!), and, from my point of view, favorable registers. . . . I imagine that you will insert the dynamic signs later (for the solo voices), e.g. from the 5/1 measure, page 1 for 3 measures *piano*! My only fear is that a good deal will be lost because of the simultaneity and will go unheard. But that is obviously intended at times . . . so what! At the first outburst of anger, at "so, so," I should opt for undefined noises from inside my stomach, don't you think?

Thus, after the positive reaction—down to the details. Later, summing up, his memory registers his slight shock nevertheless:

> I was bowled over when I had the first pages of the score. Not only did I have to sing the beginning a capella, that is, on my own, but, despite all my work with modern music, I was terrified by the feeling of utter helplessness that overcomes the singer in front of an orchestra that is offering no support at all and that, in addition, is often playing quarter-tones in the general sound pattern.

That meant that the singer, over long passages, had to remember his own note instead of being able to find it again in the orchestral accompaniment. Fischer-Dieskau continued:

> Since then, we *Lear* interpreters have become accustomed to this style and have managed, more or less, to master it, but at the time the mountain seemed too high to climb. Aribert Reimann must be given the credit for having, on the one hand, written impeccable, declamatory music such as had never before been written in the history of vocal music interspersed with recitatives (there are long passages in which the length of the note is not precisely indicated) and, on the other hand, for not robbing the music of its autonomous rights.

Rehearsal and performance: as King Lear, with Julia Varady as Cordelia, in the premiere production by Jean-Pierre Ponelle in Munich in 1978.

How great are the physical demands in this opera on singers, musicians, and conductor was described most vividly by the conductor of the premiere on 9 July 1978, "the specialist for difficult works" Gerd Albrecht:

> *Lear*—that meant for me going into the intermission after Part I with a pulse rate of 190 and, after twenty-five minutes, still feeling it beat at 180. . . . When I went to see Dietrich Fischer-Dieskau after Part II to discuss a tiny musical detail, he was lying in all his royal splendor on the floor, and he said to me: "My pulse won't go below 200—I think I'm going to die!"

Fischer-Dieskau has often praised Aribert Reimann's *Lear* for its expressive musical and dramatic power, but now and then with a sigh: "Shakespeare didn't have to bother with counting the beats or with searching for the notes." On the other hand, we can see how strongly he identified with the character by the way King Lear continually recurs in Fischer-Dieskau's paintings. This is not a characterization, but a Lear of the imagination. "That must be a wonderful role, just made for you," wrote Jörg Demus in

November 1978, and since the singer had caught one of the colds that circulate at that time of the year, he added sympathetically and humorously:

> It's an irony of Fate that someone like you, who would much prefer to be communing with the most intimate and great thoughts of the great masters, with the poets and all the images that they express, with the great figures of literature and the theater, should have to think of nothing else for days on end than his nose or his vocal chords.

> The day-to-day life of a singer is prone to misfortunes that his admirers can scarcely imagine but that irritate them nonetheless, as when he is not always prepared to shake their hand or embrace them every time, for these people all too often carry infections.

From the premiere during the Munich Opera Festival of 1978, *Lear* continued to be a great success story for the composer, for Fischer-Dieskau,

With the conductor Kurt Masur and the composer Siegfried Matthus during the rehearsal of the latter's opera *Porträt des Holofernes* (Portrait of Holofernes) in the Leipzig Gewandhaus in 1981.

and also for the singer of the role of Lear's daughter Cordelia, Julia Varady, who in 1977 had become Frau Fischer-Dieskau, officially, by civil law.[44]

The eponymous main character in the opera remains indisputably at its center, and Fischer-Dieskau filled the spot completely. H. H. Stuckenschmidt wrote:

> The evening centered round the achievement of this extraordinary singer, musician, and author, almost without a break. In physical terms alone, the measure of the characterization is gigantic. What this beautiful baritone voice gives us so dynamically, from an almost whispered *pianissimo* to those volcanic outbursts of anger and hatred, is the audible expression of histrionic perfection. When he carries Cordelia in and breaks down over her dead body, the world seems to come to an end.[45]

That was Fischer-Dieskau's last operatic premiere, but it was by no means the last premiere altogether. On the contrary, in the years that followed, there was a veritable avalanche of performances of contemporary works. It seemed as though he wanted to give modern music a fresh impulse, something that he had always been doing anyway, ever since his appeal to Paul Hindemith when he was a young singer hungry for new music. That hunger had never left him. The stage and the rostrum should never become a museum, however lively. What is being thought out and composed today should also be heard today. The list of his premieres is imposing. It begins with Boris Blacher's *Drei Psalmen* (Three Psalms) in the early 1950s, followed by the Lieder of his brother Klaus Fischer-Dieskau, accompanied on the cello by his first wife, Irmgard Poppen, and on to Wolfgang Fortner's *The Creation* (1955) and Henze's *Fünf Neapolitanische Gesänge* (Five Neapolitan Songs) of 1956. Then came works by Hermann Reutter, Hans Chemin-Petit, Horst Günther Scholz, Gerhard Kastner, Karl Amadeus Hartmann, Friedhelm Döhl, and Sir Michael Tippett's *The Vision of St. Augustine,* premiered in the Royal Festival Hall in London on 12 January 1966. (The German premiere was in Berlin on 5 October 1966, but Fischer-Dieskau has not sung the work since.) Names occur regularly, like Henze: *Fünf Neapolitanische Gesänge, Elegie für junge Liebende* (Elegy for Young Lovers) (1961), the cantata *Novae de infinito laudes* (1962), *Ein Landarzt* (A Country Doctor) after Franz Kafka's tale (in the solo version of the 1964 premiere), and *Das Floss der Medusa* (1968); then Aribert Reimann: *Totentanz-Suite* (1960), *Fünf Lieder nach Paul Celan* (Five Songs to Poems by Paul Celan) (1962) and *Zyklus* (Cycle) (1971), *Wolkenloses Christfest* (A Cloudless Christmas) (1974), the opera *Lear* (1978), *Lear-Fragmente* (1980), *Requiem* (1982), *Nunc dimittis* (Let Us Depart in Peace) (1983),

Drei Michelangelo-Lieder (Three Songs to Poems by Michelangelo) (1985), and the Joycean *Shine and Dark* (1991). Benjamin Britten would come next with A *War Requiem* (1962), *Cantata misericordium* (1963), *Songs and Proverbs* of William Blake (1965); and, finally, the Austrian Gottfried von Einem (born 1918): *Rosa mystica* (1973), *An die Nachgeborenen* (To Those Who Came After) (1975), and *Hesse-Lieder* [settings of poems by Hermann Hesse (1877–1962), 1977]. In addition, there were premieres in the 1970s of works by Siegfried Matthus (b. 1934) and Wolfgang Rihm (b. 1952). Often, great patience was needed before the fruits of the encouragement Fischer-Dieskau gave to these works could be garnered.

In October 1973 Fischer-Dieskau met the Polish composer Witold Lutoslawski (b. 1913) after a Hugo Wolf recital with Sviatoslav Richter in Warsaw. Two years later, toward the end of November 1975, a letter arrived from Poland asking the singer whether he still remembered their conversation, "during which you asked me about a work for a baritone." The suggestion had become a reality, Lutoslawski wrote; he had put other work aside in order to write a piece for baritone and orchestra. After eighteen months' work, it was now ready and in the mail to Fischer-Dieskau. Eager, but also anxious to learn whether Fischer-Dieskau wanted to sing it, he said that he was grateful for the encouragement to compose something that he now considered to be an important part of his *oeuvre*. Of course, Fischer-Dieskau remembered the conversation: "In truth, I have been curious about whether, and when, something would come to me out of it all," and one can readily believe that, despite all his many engagements, new works can never come soon enough to suit him. Nevertheless, this (happy) impatience can clash with many already firm commitments. As always, his engagement diary was bursting at the seams: "I cannot see a chance of singing it before 1978. If you should prefer to have the work performed in the meantime, I could well understand that, even though it would pain me."

Witold Lutoslawski agreed: "I shall wait patiently. I would not think of having it performed before then." After eighteen months' work on a composition, having to wait at least as long again for a performance is not easy for any composer—but for this singer . . . . On 12 April 1978, it came to pass. *Les espaces du sommeil* (Spaces of Sleep) was premiered in the Berlin Philharmonie, conducted by the composer. Fischer-Dieskau thought highly of the work, because he could see that Lutoslawski had been so considerate of the human voice, "which is always a particular blessing for the tormented interpreter of contemporary music."

He continued to bear this burden of "torment." Nothing could stop him from seeking out and experimenting with new works, even when that brought moans and groans. Yet things could move more swiftly than they did with *Les espaces du sommeil*, albeit again under very different circumstances. The composer Siegfried Matthus wrote to Fischer-Dieskau on 18 December 1980: "It was a happy shock for me to hear from Herr Masur that you would like to sing the premiere of one of my works in a concert in the [Leipzig] Gewandhaus on 25 November 1981." It would certainly be the fulfillment of one of his most secret longings, he added, if Fischer-Dieskau were to sing something of his, but (and this was the cause of the "shock") "it doesn't give me much time to write a new work, and, apart from that, I'm in the middle of work on an opera."[46]

Matthus, a pupil of Rudolf Wagner-Régeny and Hanns Eisler, had thought of something that might do, however. The role of Holofernes in his opera *Judith* on which he was working had been written for a baritone: "When we looked over the completed parts of the *Judith* score (along with Herr Masur) for a concert performance, we found some very attractive possibilities." He then detailed his suggestions, but Fischer-Dieskau rejected the idea of taking single passages out of the context of the opera. Matthus guessed that it would be sensible "to use the text and the music of *Judith* with which I am familiar at the moment. Could we not compose a musical portrait of Holofernes?"—and that is what came about. A new, independent composition was born. Fischer-Dieskau wrote to the composer on Easter Sunday 1981: "The score for the portrait has arrived—and behold, all is well!"

The premiere took place as planned on 25 November 1981 in the Leipzig Gewandhaus. The composer was amazed as he sat listening. He wrote Fischer-Dieskau on 24 December 1981:

> I just cannot explain to myself all the strange things that have happened to you, and because of you, between the final rehearsal and the performance. At any rate, on that evening, a Holofernes leapt out at me whose unpredictable demonic power would terrify anyone. It is difficult for me at my premieres to concentrate absolutely on the work. Uppermost in my thoughts is the careful, critical, yet helpless awareness as to how my new young child is behaving for, and being accepted by, the audience. Quite different with the *Holofernes*. Even after the first few bars, I was so swept up in your interpretation that I completely forgot that tiresome "aware-ness," and could give myself up entirely to the pleasure of listening. I have to tell you, with enormous gratitude, that the rehearsals and the performances with you were among the most valuable, the hap-piest, and the most beautiful hours of my artistic career to date.

So, there it is again—and this time from the pen of a composer after the interpretation of his own work by Dietrich Fischer-Dieskau—that feeling of joy that almost all those who have worked with him experience during the period of hard toil together, a joy that of course is then communicated to the audience. Another leitmotif of this artistic phenomenon Fischer-Dieskau can be heard in the composer's admiration for the changes that had taken place between the final rehearsal and the performance. That is the secret of a great stage or concert platform performer: that everything leading up to the performance (all "pre-knowledge," too) has to be forgotten, and that everybody else, the audience, and in this case the composer as well, worried about his "new young child," have to forget the outside world for this one moment of great art.

Just to speak of the premieres in which Fischer-Dieskau sang does not do justice to his ceaseless support of contemporary music—and here "contemporary" means the music of our century. He sang the classical works of modern music—Schoenberg, Webern, and Berg—and found in Berg's opera *Wozzeck* (1925) a role that was quite different from Mozart's or Verdi's baritone parts, that is, the role of a suffering man, but a sufferer "with a great need to express it all" (Fischer-Dieskau). He wrote in his memoirs:

> Berg's music naturally led me much more deeply into the style of contemporary opera. To reveal such raw suffering, one had to develop fully all possible powers of dramatic expression in one's singing and acting, perhaps precisely because Wozzeck, vocally, psychologically, and musically, took one to the very limits of one's abilities.[47]

A certain solicitude, perhaps even a predilection, made the singer also promote the works of more traditionally minded composers—Ferruccio Busoni (1866–1924), for example, whose *Doktor Faust* (1925), in the version completed by Philipp Jarnach, he rescued from oblivion. When the 1969 recording of the opera was published in 1970, the journal *Musica* wrote with some justification that "one of the most influential, perhaps even *the* most significant, Busoni work of all" had been made generally available. Fischer-Dieskau had made his interpretation of the role a very personal one, as had always been the case. Nor must it be forgotten that it was Fischer-Dieskau who had made these rediscoveries possible—if only because his name on the record sleeve considerably reduced the producers' financial risks.

Among the composers of whose qualities Fischer-Dieskau reminded the swiftly moving world of music was, for example, Reinhard Schwarz-Schilling

(1904–1987), about whom he wrote to a record company: "This composer would deserve another chance for his music, even if he does not belong to the avant-garde or the ever-topical." That was in 1970. Fischer-Dieskau felt close to the composer, even though he was twenty years older than himself, and after hearing one of his symphonies, he wrote to him:

> My main impression is that, amazingly, there are still possibilities of doing new things in tonal music. This is one of the features of complete sincerity in your music, which captures and convinces the listener. And this "joy in your work," despite all your experiences of suffering, awakens kindred feelings in me.

From the very beginning of his career as a singer, Fischer-Dieskau has taken a great interest in the work of another modern composer, the Swiss Othmar Schoeck (1886–1957). He sang the composer's cycle *Lebendig begraben* (Buried Alive) to fourteen poems of the Swiss writer Gottfried Keller (1819–1890) in Zurich's Tonhalle for the first time on 2 February 1955, thus acceding to the "ardent wish" of the composer to hear his work sung by Fischer-Dieskau, even if (as usual) the singer was rather doubtful of his own competence to sing them. By his own admission, singing Schoeck became a must for him, and by singing the cycle, he gave the Swiss composer the joy of a lifetime, for he had only a few more years to live. He died in 1957. (Fischer-Dieskau recorded the cycle with the Radio Symphony Orchestra of Berlin, conducted by Fritz Rieger, in 1962. *Trans.*)

When Schoeck heard, in 1956, that Fischer-Dieskau planned to sing his *Notturno*, his reaction was grateful joy. He wrote:

> Oh, you cannot quite guess perhaps what it will mean to me if *you* sing the *Notturno*. After the immense experience of your *Lebendig begraben,* to hear the *Notturno* sung by *you*, will be a gift from the gods. I feel newly born, just thinking of it.

What attracted Fischer-Dieskau to Schoeck's works, which he continued to sing long after the composer's death, was Schoeck's extraordinarily subtle and conscientious handling of the poems being set, on the one hand (one could sense here a master of the relationship of poem to music), and, on the other hand, that his works demonstrated an attempt at a sort of contemporary Romanticism, based on the great predecessors but working with his own means toward a modern form of contemporaneity. Schoeck, a great admirer of the Viennese composer Hugo Wolf, who died in 1903, carried on from where Wolf had left off. The gulf was great enough to allow him to compose in a contemporary style, but his distancing from the music that had been developed in the tradition of Schoenberg's Second Viennese School (as clearly seen in Aribert Reimann's music, for example) was nevertheless considerable. [Fischer-Dieskau kept up a friendly connection with the composer's wife, Hilde, and was able to commemorate Schoeck's centenary birthday celebrations by singing his cycle *Unter Sternen* (Under Stars) in 1986. *Trans.*]

After Fischer-Dieskau had put all his musical and acting energies into his *Lear* characterization, as he did for every stage role, and had thus fulfilled one of his most ardent wishes (and that had played no small part in it all), a certain "opera-fatigue" began to creep over him. Again and again, he was forced to think of returning—not indeed this time to that "philosopher's workshop" of Hans Sachs—but to what had first set him on his path as a singer: the German Lied. He wrote to a young colleague in 1979: "When I began, there was no work in opera houses to rely on; there was simply a long period of silence and reflection, which made people come to Lieder recitals in droves," but, he added, only a small section of the audiences was really interested in the work being performed; the greater part was made up of fans of vocal music and the wider opera-going public. He was always concerned with that smaller section who came because of the work, even when he was well aware that many were coming just to hear him, no matter what he sang. And there is a point that even the most purist of singers must recognize when interpreting a work.

Fischer-Dieskau had never neglected the Lied during his long operatic career. When a decision had to be made toward the end of the 1970s between stage and concert platform, he had no doubt about that decision. The peripheral state of chamber music in the world of music was bound to appear quite attractive to him, even if one senses a certain regret in his words:

> Just like chamber music generally, the Lied will only be able to eke out a living on the periphery; indeed, if there are no creative reinforcements in the future, it could well disappear.

That additional remark expresses Fischer-Dieskau's personal concern, for he did not really need to worry about the state of the German Romantic Lied; he had awakened what Professor S. S. Prawer of the University of Oxford had called the "Sleeping Beauty" out of its half-sleep, and whenever he sang, he had moved it from the periphery to the center of musical life.[48] Yet could an art form that took so little from the contemporary age remain alive in the long run in its traditional and conventional form? Never just by chance are all artists happiest when they see young people in their audiences. Of course, this has to do with a general human love of youth as well, and perhaps also with a pedagogical impulse, but also with the hope for a future for their own art form. If the concert halls in a city like Munich are filled, evening after evening (and it is no different in Berlin, Frankfurt, or Vienna) and with patrons under thirty, one can conclude that the Classical-Romantic music of the eighteenth and nineteenth centuries, including the Romantic Lied and chamber music, is fulfilling a need, now as always. One cannot deny, however, that the contemporary music that is played in concert halls makes only a bare living, and needs to be animated and inspired and made attractive by performances by well-known artists who can bring in an audience. Few enough bother to make that effort. In many countries, the lure of Westernized pop music has proved too strong and is seen as the alternative to Classical-Romantic music, pushing contemporary music even farther into the background. If the majority of young people feel more attracted by today's pop music, that tendency is more a turning toward a new form of music than a turning away from an old, traditional one. Whether the German art song will have a place in the musical landscape of the future will be decided by the composers, who will, in turn, be guided by the market—something Schubert would hardly have thought of—and by opportunities for performances of their works. And these are certainly hard to come by. Interpreters with a reputation could help here. Fischer-Dieskau, not alone but as one of the leading interpreters, has set an excellent example.

More and more regularly one could hear him say that there was so much to do and yet the year was always too short. He had done his bit on the operatic stage; the gradual wearying with opera was shown first of all by his canceling several much-loved projects. He wrote to Wolfgang Sawallisch in November 1979 that, on doctor's orders, he had to take a two-months' break to "set his constitution to rights," which the much too packed engagement diary of the last few years had probably overburdened. He went on:

> That means that I shall have to give up the Borromeo part. You know how much I think of the man and the composer [Hans] Pfitzner, and how much working on *Palestrina* meant to me—but it is not to be.

One can easily understand how the constitution of a singer who is always busy, always giving one hundred percent, could go on strike after the enormous exertions of the years 1976 to 1978. Yet now came the characteristic voice of a man who needed to spare himself, for at the end of the same letter we read: "By the way, I did agree to do the Brahms in London."

As Amonasro in Verdi's opera *Aida* with Julia Varady in the title role, Deutsche Oper Berlin, 1982.

In February 1980, *Lear* was to be produced again at the Munich Opera, and repeated in July. In August 1981, he sang one of his major roles, the Count in *The Marriage of Figaro*, with his wife Julia Varady as the Countess, in the Deutsche Oper Berlin. Yet the grand plan to do a *Don Giovanni* with Daniel Barenboim was canceled as a precaution. Now one can hear new notes in his letters, and they sound the decision to concentrate on Lieder:

> and now this role (conceived by Mozart for a young singer) where the climax arrives only after three and a half hours. I have sung through it all again and find that I cannot meet my own standards, so I'll have to give it up. When I said "Yes" to you after a long hesitation, you had talked me into it. It's a rogue who gives more than he has.[49]

These "own standards," set naturally at a very high level, had determined all his actions from the very beginning of his career. They had often, too, caused him to hesitate to choose or to accept engagements that he thought might be beyond his capabilities and made him, if not immune, at least unresponsive to well-meaning or even to snide criticism; above all, however, they held him firmly in their grasp and demanded absolute obedience from the whole man.

In 1982, he sang Amonasro in Verdi's *Aida* once again with Julia Varady as Aida and Luciano Pavarotti (b. 1935) as Radames. Once more, eyes and ears were opened by an interpretation that broke with all conventions—this from a singer who, as the critic Norbert Miller wrote, "recreated this ambiguous, lacerated figure, with every gesture, every note, every movement, as if it were a fully developed operatic character."

At the same time, the same critic wrote about Pavarotti that he *sang* Radames, he recreated Verdi's hero as a bel canto role. Julia Varady's Aida was also perfectly described:

> Aida was interpreted by Julia Varady as a woman doomed to death, fragile, easily wounded, sinking back into pain after every outburst of domineering passion, yet completely free of hysteria or the ecstasy of suffering. Managing every dramatic climax, taking over the lead in an ensemble almost casually (even in that welter of sound in the triumphant finale to Act II), she directed her musical interpretation toward these inspired moments before she gives herself up to her fate. She sings with an incomparable shading of nuances and alters her registers with a refined and breath-taking finesse that never becomes mere virtuosity.

Fischer-Dieskau reads such praise of his wife with quiet pleasure—it cannot be great enough for him—and Julia Varady knows very well herself, and enjoys telling people, how much her artistic career owes to his example and to their study together. That may sound too good to be true, but it is nothing but the truth about a really unusual partnership. Other artistic events prove it, too. In that same year, 1982, they made a deeply impressive contribution to a performance of Shostakovich's Symphony No. 14. A critic who was present, Karl Schumann, wrote:

> Dietrich Fischer-Dieskau went down to the realms of the bass register to show that there are no limits to his vocal abilities and capacity for expressiveness. Julia Varady's impulsive intensity lent excitement to the lyrical as well as to the dramatic passages. Out of it all came a performance in which musical bravura was made subservient to thoughtful interpretation.

That was (and is) an essential characteristic of Fischer-Dieskau's approach to music. One could just add a little more on the almost tangible bond that unites those two artists in such solo works, and, particular, in this work. "An example of a truly committed art," added Schumann. (They had already recorded Symphony No. 14 in 1981 in a performance with the Concertgebouw Orchestra of Amsterdam, conducted by Bernard Haitink. *Trans.*)

The Munich Opera Festival of 1982 witnessed more productions of Reimann's *Lear* and Strauss's *Die Frau ohne Schatten*. With these, Dietrich Fischer-Dieskau closed his operatic career. It had lasted thirty-five years and had included a list of roles that had become his life: Posa, Wolfram von Eschenbach, Count Almaviva, Don Giovanni, Amfortas, Mathis der Maler, Cardillac, Gregor Mittenhofer, Mandryka, Falstaff, Hans Sachs, and Lear. Also, there were Jochanaan (John the Baptist), Don Alfonso, Wozzeck, Dr. Faust, Dr. Schön, Macbeth, Renato, Germont, Danton, Onegin, Barak, and Wotan in *Das Rheingold*. Nor can one forget his Gianni Schicchi and his poor Michele in Puccini's *Il tabarro* (a character who did bring him luck, however, it will be remembered), or those important minor roles: the King's Herald in Wagner's *Lohengrin* and the Speaker in Mozart's *The Magic Flute*—enough for the whole lifetime of a singer, yet only a selection of the roles that this singer of Lieder presented to the public. The number of roles, and the innovative power Fischer-Dieskau brought to them all, is impressive, particularly when one considers that his name all around the world is primarily that of a "king among Lieder singers." If the Lied were his mother tongue, so to speak, then musically speaking he had grown up bilingual; neither genre was thought of as a foreign tongue—a not unknown state of affairs to music lovers.

He made no great brouhaha about his departure from the operatic stage—it was just as if he had left a room and silently closed the door behind him. If one looks in his engagement diary, one will not find a gap. He had always seen his operatic work and his work on the concert platform as a continuum. He had been a singer and an actor in both spheres. Thus, leaving the stage caused him no particular heartache—he had chosen it for himself—and the future meant going on singing, and, as we know, not only that and not only Lieder.

Return to the World of Lieder

The international appeal of Dietrich Fischer-Dieskau's art can hardly be overemphasized. His first appearance (on 7 June 1951) in the Albert Hall in London in Frederick Delius's *A Mass of Life* (a setting of words from the nineteenth-century German philosopher Friedrich Nietzsche's *Thus Spake Zarathustra*) was followed by his first Lieder recital in Great Britain, in the Kingsway Hall in London on 31 January 1952: Schubert's song-cycle *Die schöne Müllerin*.[1] On 6 October 1952, he sang a Beethoven Lieder recital in the Old Assembly Rooms in Newcastle in northeast England (for the first and only time in that area). So it went on for decades, no differently in other European towns and countries—in the north, up to as far as Reykjavik, the capital of Iceland, in 1953, and in the south to Rome (for the first time in 1954). He first sang in Paris in February 1955—the Mörike Lieder of Hugo Wolf—and in the same year came his first tour of North America.[2]

In the 1980s, after thirty years of touring, during which the world had changed so much and a new generation of musicians and audiences had grown up, the rapport between a singer who had first appeared on platforms as a young man in his mid-twenties, and his audiences, never weakened. Despite all the changes that the singer, too, has lived through, and suffered, his appearances on the world's concert platforms have never changed; they have also displayed their constancy in turning out to be something quite new, from time to time, rather than what was expected. Jean Cocteau, the French author, once said to him: "You sing as though you were composing while you are singing."

Less than a week after that last performance of *Lear* in Munich on 3 August 1982, Fischer-Dieskau was singing again, and again with Julia Varady, in the *Lyrische Sinfonie* (Lyrical Symphony) by the Austrian composer Alexander von Zemlinsky (1872–1942) in Salzburg. Jörg Demus accompanied him in Lieder by Othmar Schoeck in Lucerne, and Alfred Brendel was at the piano for his recital of the Heine Lieder by Schubert and Schumann in Salzburg. There were many more recitals—all to prove that this was not the beginning of retirement but a time to reap the fruits after decades of the hard grind—only that did not stop either.

The world lay at his feet, open as always, and could not be disappointed. Next came a grand tour of Germany with Jörg Demus in October and

November 1982 with performances of Wolf's Mörike Lieder, which, once again, reinforced the old rapport with his audiences and had the critics saying that this was a new Fischer-Dieskau that they were hearing—but they really meant the "old" Fischer-Dieskau, or rather the *young* Fischer-Dieskau!

The international scene began once again in 1983 at the Salle Pleyel in Paris.[3] Fischer-Dieskau's accompanist on this occasion was the very young Hartmut Höll, who soon became a regular partner. Once again, it was this ever-ready willingness to take on a new partner that reveals the Fischer-Dieskau paradox: constancy and change, or rather, constancy *in* change.

There were also people in Germany who believed that they could detect fresh nuances in the voice; for example, in the Brahms Lieder, which the pair performed in Paris, then in Amsterdam and Munich, and finally at the Salzburg Festival. Karl Schumann wrote:

> Since the appearance of the two complete recordings of the Brahms Lieder and of the vocal ensembles, one should have been prepared to expect something more substantial than a pleasant morning recital confirming the accepted image of Brahms.

The critic then painted a rather sober picture of the composer—"powerfully arching melodies, straightforward emotions, reminders of Brahms's folk music style, a rough piano accompaniment, a few manly tears, a little anger"—to emphasize more effectively the extraordinary side of this new interpretation. His words made the Fischer-Dieskau–Höll interpretation very vivid:

> The Brahms Lieder were shown to be a very intimate art form, deli-cate realizations of a poetic-musical vision, bordering now and then on the mood-pictures of the [French] Impressionists. The gentle falling-away of the final syllables, the passages up into the head register, and the beautifully articulated breathing of many sections, seemed to be legitimate means of intensifying Brahms's basic note of resignation.

Hartmut Höll was described as a

> sensitive partner, comparable to Daniel Barenboim, who had first tried out with Fischer-Dieskau this idea of a completely sensitized interpretation. The sound was more oriented on the late Intermezzi rather than on the massive power of early or middle Brahms.[4]

Many observers believe that the choice of the young Hartmut Höll rejuvenated the singer. It is certainly true that a musical partner with whom one has to undertake so many, and sometimes such long, journeys will become a close friend, and this must have an influence on one's physical well-being. In his letter of congratulations for Fischer-Dieskau's sixtieth birthday, Höll recalls "the walks in the Imperial Gardens in Tokyo, visits to the Wagner-Nietzsche house in Tribschen, to Van Gogh's works in Amsterdam, and leisure hours on the grass under the rare trees in Edinburgh's Botanical Gardens." The pair lay on the wonderful lawns there gazing up at the sky, just as in Mörike's poem "Im Frühling" (In Spring), set by Hugo Wolf, the poet lies on his Frühlingshügel (spring hill) gazing into the beautiful heavens. The unobtrusive words of the self-confident young pianist betray little sign of shyness. Fischer-Dieskau knew exactly why he had chosen him—and why he has retained him for so long. Perhaps the truth is that Hartmut Höll was the right person to confirm that streak of youthfulness that has always been part of the singer's personality, but Höll was also the colorful, technically brilliant pianist that Fischer-Dieskau had been looking for.[5]

Yet what do the words "old" and "young" mean in art? The reviewer of a Lieder recital in Frankfurt on 29 September 1985, illustrated the point very neatly when he wrote:

> The almost imperishable voice became fresher with each song, the shimmer of its *piano* carried uniquely into the farthest corners of the hall and restored the magic of art as a cry for a life worthy of human beings. If people expected the "wisdom of age" here, they were reminded of Friedrich Schiller's words that "youth is old and age is young." Dietrich Fischer-Dieskau was the Lied interpreter richest in hope.[6]

The musician's youthfulness was not just to be noted in his voice, or simply in his looks, although the sixty-year-old belied his age then in a remarkable way. In fact, he had never looked better than at that time. Yet that ever-nagging curiosity, his never-ceasing work with music and poetry, which demanded an exaggerated sensitivity and subjectivity, the closest examination of the most intimate turns of phrase, of their very inner soul—all that is probably the true source of an inexhaustible youthfulness. It is not really surprising that words like "innocence" (despite granting all his knowledge) and "inwardness," after which his Lieder singing strives, come to the critics' minds. The female reviewer of his *Winterreise* in February 1986 wrote:

> Fischer-Dieskau's singing was innocently invulnerable to all that materialism and sentimentality that one connects with Lieder singing. . . . With all its contrasting tones, it was an intimate conversation directed to his own, and the listeners', inner con-

sciousness—the quietest notes could be heard everywhere in the huge hall.[7]

How many times had Fischer-Dieskau sung *Winterreise* before this one, which he, knowingly and "innocently invulnerable," had offered his audience? It was nearly forty years since he had broadcast that first *Winterreise* for the RIAS station in West Berlin. However disturbed, exhausting, restless his career had been, contentment had been his since he had found Julia Varady for his down-to-earth partner. Even short absences made him unhappy. He noted at the beginning of 1987:

> Julia has just disappeared through the garden gate en route to the airport, and I won't see her for the next three weeks. So, I'll worry, and I'll be on my own, and then there will be all that work, which doesn't mean much to me without Julia's criticism and encouragement.

His sons' personal and professional emancipation from their father also brought a sigh of relief. The two older ones had established professional careers by the 1980s—Matthias worked as a stage designer, Martin was a conductor—and the youngest, Manuel, was on the right path by 1982. Fischer-Dieskau's old friend Hans Erich Riebensahm wrote about "Manuel's concert at the Warnecks' [Fischer-Dieskau's secretary]. A man made music with wonderful concentration and an impressive assurance. 'He'll become something, Karl,' as Uncle Bräsig said."[8] ["Uncle Bräsig" was a character in a novel by the writer, Fritz Reuter (1810–1874), who wrote in north German dialect. *Trans.*] Indeed, Manuel has "become something": a well-known cellist. Also, from him and his charming French wife, Fischer-Dieskau and Julia now have three grandchildren.

On the occasion of his sixtieth birthday on 28 May 1985, various people summed up their memories of Dietrich Fischer-Dieskau. That meant that journalists who took their journalistic work even half seriously could not avoid writing about him, but had to express their personal feelings about man and musician, whether they wanted to or not. Joachim Fest, just such a journalist, was attracted by the idea of "double vision":

> People speak of the "double vision" of Romanticism, simplicity paired with extreme awareness, conventionality with the most extreme artistic refinement—in that sense, Dietrich Fischer-Dieskau is the Romantic singer par excellence. That has less to do with his choice of program, which is, of course, just the result of the Lied being a Romantic genre. Rather it is because whatever he sings, with all the vocal richness of the coloration, all the abrupt changes

of mood and register, it seems to be the absolute immediate inspiration of the moment. Yet, at the same time, he presents the Lied also as a work of art, with an almost imperceptible hint of calculation.

So, what is his secret? "It is transformation and interpretation at one and the same time."

Joachim Fest has described what many feel, or rather, have said or heard, and also what annoys others who detect in that quality the real schism in Fischer-Dieskau's "personal style." Realizing that is also part of following a musician's career. Ivan Nagel seized on the word *life* in his birthday article:

> Many of us have spent half our lives with Dietrich Fischer-Dieskau. We would know a lot less without him, and we would have experienced a lot less. No—we would have *lived* a lot less.

At the time, all this sounded more like a farewell, but the "farewell" only came some seven years later, and that was a big enough surprise. In 1985, Sabine Dultz of the *Münchner Theaterzeitung* asked him: "You are about to celebrate your sixtieth birthday and are already something of a legend. Are you actually aware of that?" His answer was: "Yes, I know, and I find it terrible. But I may get my own back on all these people who've made me into a legend—simply by continuing to give recitals."

He did not spare himself, hardly reducing the number of performances. He was now able to indulge his preference, however, for certain venues and certain countries. In the 1980s, for example, he gave only one recital in New York, whereas Japan, with its attentive audiences, welcomed him in 1981, 1983, 1987, 1989, and, finally, in 1992. He had always had a soft spot for Japan and the Japanese. He loves their finesse and their friendliness, the heritage of an ancient culture that even today lends its modern business world an aura of gentleness and perfection of form. The choice horticultural artistry of the Japanese attracted him as much as the absolute technical perfection of the stage crews during his performances in Japanese opera houses. When Verdi's *Falstaff* was produced in Tokyo, they only needed one technical rehearsal, and the whole stage set was made up without a single mistake. In the evening, the Japanese translation of the Italian text being sung appeared as a synchronized supertitle above the stage. Fischer-Dieskau sings the praises of the Japanese concert-halls too; no German town has anything to touch them. Nonetheless, all that was overshadowed by the musical open-mindedness and the air of expectation that is so typical of Japanese audiences.

Paris, London, Salzburg, Berlin, and Munich were never absent from his itinerary. Amsterdam and Zurich were also favored venues. Among the

Attitudes of a singer: at the Schubertiade in Feldkirch, Austria, 1991.

Festival towns, the Schubertiade in Feldkirch in the Vorarlberg region of Austria was paid a regular visit: in 1983 and 1984 in the nearby Bregenz Festival Hall; and 1985, 1986, 1988, 1989, 1990, 1991, and 1992 in Feldkirch. There were nine recitals of Schubert Lieder, two of Schumann's, two of Wolf's, and others devoted to Mozart and Beethoven. Besides Hartmut Höll, who accompanied him eight times, Alfred Brendel, Christoph Eschenbach, Norman Shetler, and András Schiff partnered him also.

1985 was a very special year for Feldkirch, for on four separate evenings, Fischer-Dieskau sang song-cycles by one composer: Schubert, Schumann, Mahler, and Wolf, respectively, programs that were then repeated in Berlin, Frankfurt, and Munich. The initiator of these was the director of the Feldkirch Schubertiade, Gerd Nachbauer, who then promptly engaged the singer after his retirement in 1992 for the 1995 Schubertiade to celebrate his seventieth birthday. (The main attraction that year was a Jubilee Schubert program on 17 June when Fischer-Dieskau conducted a performance of Schubert's *Lazarus* with soloists from among his own students at the Berlin Academy, and then later played four-handed piano duets with András Schiff. He hoped to be appearing at the 1996 Schubertiade again, among other things conducting the Radio Symphony Orchestra of Stuttgart in Schubert's seventh symphony and Mahler's *Das Lied von der Erde*, again with one of his own students, Christian Elsner, as a soloist. *Trans.*)

Fischer-Dieskau has also sung at the Schleswig-Holstein Festival in north Germany (since its second year, in fact), but he felt that the halls in which he sang were more architecturally charming than acoustically suitable.

The singer's thirst for work effectively excluded any reduction in his artistic activities. That went, too, for his readiness to travel and to perform, as well as for his choice of programs, which he could easily have lightened, and for the expenditure of his total energies and of his voice—always at full volume.

Fischer-Dieskau did not particularly like hearing admiring comments on how amazingly well his voice had kept, how "balsamic" its sound was, now that he was between sixty and seventy. That the voice of a sixty-year-old did not sound like the voice of a thirty-year-old was a simple and natural fact of life, after all, he used to say. How to make his voice sound "young" when the music demanded it, was part of the secret of his vocal genius. Many observers of his art at this time thought that they could detect a fresh naturalness in the singer, which is not, however, discernible from the recordings on the forty CDs that document all the phases of the singer's career, since these recordings were all made under different conditions to accord with the particular nature of the musical work being recorded. To judge a singer and the nature of his interpretations has never been just a question of his singing but, equally, of the listener's listening. Ideally, both concert-goers and critics should have the chance of attending a school in the art of listening.

The singer's life was always a very full one with little time for leisure, for, as everyone knows, there were other artistic interests with claims on his time behind the scenes, as it were. Or so it seemed: "I keep my eyes fixed on the mountains yet to be climbed (like an explorer does), while my momentary successes just flit by—they seem unimportant," he wrote to Heinz Friedrich in 1975.[9] That statement would also have accurately described his life ten or fifteen years later. His inner springs were still coiled, his restlessness unsatisfied, his love of singing greater than the oppressive drudgery of a life of traveling, the quickening of the pulse and the tension before a recital—everything was connected with his profession. Yet what enthusiasm, what love greeted him in every town and in every country. And how much there still was to sing!

Reviews of recitals can give little notion of the wealth of impressions, the spirit of the music, the moments in which his artistry had changed people's lives. The critic Professor Joachim Kaiser examined the expectations that the world had of Fischer-Dieskau and discovered, as he put it, "den Fluch der guten Tat" (the curse of the good deed). After a Wolf recital on 13 October 1986, he wrote:

> Dietrich Fischer-Dieskau has accustomed his huge following throughout the world, and above all in his second home, Munich, to expect, not just polished performances, but revelations. We go to his recitals as if they were pronouncements, religious services of Lieder, and with the avowed intent to allow ourselves to be shattered, "purified." And for decades now, we have never been disappointed.

It is true that this description, which undoubtedly holds true for the majority of concert-goers, contains echoes of that "High Priest of the Lied," a tag that Gerald Moore used but that Fischer-Dieskau detests, yet the tension between the expectation and his clearly understood duty of not disappointing that expectation remains one of Fischer-Dieskau's essential driving forces. After such a long career, comparisons between past and present performances were inevitable, even in his interpretations of modern music, let alone that of the Classical-Romantic repertoire. In 1986, he sang Karl Amadeus Hartmann's *Gesangsszene* (Song Scene) (1963), which he himself had premiered in Frankfurt in 1964. Instead of the "still the same" type of comment, the critic Karl Schumann employed the more elegant "now as before":

> Just as then, here is that thundering and whispering interpreter, climbing up into tenorial heights and conquering these as well as the operatic aspects of this vision of doom. In the great sweeps in the recitatives, hardly ever, or at times, not accompanied, and in the spoken words of the finale ("Es ist ein Ende der Welt! Das traurigste von allen") (This is one end to the world. The saddest of all), he maintains a simply breath-taking tension, and, where Hartmann's passionate music demands it, he offers the extreme in espressivo.[10]

In 1988, Fischer-Dieskau sang Hanns Eisler's *Exil-Lieder* (Songs of Exile). Wolfgang Schreiber, a critic who because of the general adulation of Fischer-Dieskau had been rather more reserved in his praise, paid him, not

With the pianist and conductor Daniel Barenboim at a rehearsal in Berlin in 1980 of Gustav Mahler's Lieder.

grudgingly but rather out of compulsion, his respects. He wrote of Eisler's various states of emotion and levels of expression, and added: "It is clear that this range of emotions is particularly acceptable to an interpretative artist such as Dietrich Fischer-Dieskau."

Apart from the fact that the phrase "interpretative artist" can be taken several ways, the critic came to the convincing conclusion: "Poetic insight alternated with epic exhibitionism, lyrical excesses, factual reporting, sarcastic blusterings—a masterly performance."

In 1989, in what was rather more than an act of fond remembrance, Fischer-Dieskau sang the part of Amfortas in a concert performance of Wagner's *Parsifal*. How many memories must have welled up within him? He had sung the role in Bayreuth in 1956 under Hans Knappertsbusch, a conductor very different from Daniel Barenboim, who directed this concert performance and who was so very much nearer the singer in his modern view of music than the old "war-horse" of "holy" Bayreuth. The critics wrote of an unrestrainedly expressive Amfortas "absolutely secure in a role that has been his province for decades—and no hint of a 'vocal crisis'!"

In May 1990 Horst Koegler reminisced: "Can we imagine the musical landscape (and not only Germany's) after the great caesura of 1945 without this man who is celebrating his sixty-fifth birthday today?" Once again, the theme is the fusion of word and music:

> When he sings Lieder, the concert platform becomes an imaginary stage. No other interpreter has mastered this art as perfectly as Dietrich Fischer-Dieskau, the singer who sings softly and intimately in our age, so afflicted by the noise of the mass media.

In that year, 1990, on 20 September, Fischer-Dieskau ended a recital of Schumann's song-cycle *Dichterliebe* (A Poet's Love) in the Deutsche Oper Berlin, accompanied by Vladimir Ashkenazy, after only the eighth song, "Und wüssten's die Blumen, die kleinen" (If the Little Flowers Knew). Nobody had noticed anything amiss before he decided to break off. Was this a sign? Not at all—or so it seemed at the time. In October 1990, there was a performance of Shostakovich's Symphony No. 14 with Julia Varady and Dietrich Fischer-Dieskau as soloists, which, as Baldur Brockhoff wrote, "was admirable, beyond praise."

Could he have gone on like this? The law of supply and demand proved, as always, the deciding factor. In 1993, after a 1992 filled as ever with engagements, Dietrich Fischer-Dieskau drew a line under his career as a singer. 1992 had begun with a concert performance at the Deutsche Oper Berlin of Berlioz's *Damnation de Faust*; then came a whole series of *Die schöne Müllerin* recitals, and once again, he recorded the song cycle *Das holde*

Bescheiden (Divine Modesty) in honor of the composer Othmar Schoeck, whom he holds in such high esteem. Then Lieder by Richard Strauss and many recitals of Schubert, Schumann, Wolf, Dvořák, and Brahms Lieder. Once again he sang Aribert Reimann's "Shine and Dark" as well as his "Unrevealed." Then, in November, for the last time, he sang in Brahms's *German Requiem* with Lucia Popp (who was to die so tragically in 1993 at the age of 54). Mahler's *Lieder eines fahrenden Gesellen* in Berlin; and Shostakovich's *Michelangelo-Suite* in December 1992 in Stuttgart, were his last Lieder recitals.

On 31 December 1992, Fischer-Dieskau sang Count Almaviva's aria from *The Marriage of Figaro* at an evening concert in the Bavarian State Opera in honor of Wolfgang Sawallisch's retirement. He then took part, as Don Alfonso, in the finale of Act I of Mozart's *Così fan tutte*, followed by the first scene from Verdi's *Falstaff*. The end of the evening, and of a great singer's career, was crowned with the great fugato from the finale: "Tutto nel mondo è burla. L'uom è nato buffone." (Jesting is man's vocation. Man is born a jester).

The Author

Dietrich Fischer-Dieskau

*Fern
die Klage
des Fauns*

Claude Debussy und seine Welt

DVA

"For a Singer,
the Fusion of Words and Music
Is a Joy for Life"

It was obvious that Dietrich Fischer-Dieskau, after having worked with, tested out, and enjoyed to the full on myriad occasions that wonderful fusion of words and music in the German Lied, would one day want to write about the music himself. The comprehensive preparation for his interpretations of Lieder and operatic roles had taught him to work like a literary scholar; that, and the often-mentioned desire to express himself, had led him to explore the backgrounds to these works—the results of which, of course, his audiences only heard and experienced in the concert hall or opera house.

There had been youthful attempts at writing—dramas, naturally enough from a young lad madly keen on theater and with a father who wrote operettas; then a few childish attempts at a novel and some sentimental poems—but nothing that could be taken as hints of later ambitions to become an author. These were just the natural effusions to be expected from a child from such a cultured background. Yet there was something there, more important than the scribblings: there was the example, or perhaps more accurately, the vision, of his father, sitting at his desk working devotedly away at his books, be they dramatic or scholarly. The schoolboy had little or no hand in the writing of the headmaster's plays or articles, but the very act of the writing, the working habits of the author, excited the child irresistibly to imitation.

Yet this was not the only motive for Fischer-Dieskau's later work as an author. There was always a positive leaning toward authorship, created probably by the father's example, all the more so when we remember the picture that the twelve-year-old boy had of his father after the latter's death: he was the man who was always writing.

The fusion of words and music also made him conscious of something else, namely, how quickly music vanishes, whereas the written word seems to promise permanence. The word can await the hour when it will be recognized, used, and treasured: the singer's song is something quite different. The musician almost envied the permanence of the written word (which in truth, however, is often very limited). From childhood on, Fischer-Dieskau had always had a great respect for what had been written and printed. Those who grow up with books pick up a book, even when they are adults, quite differently from any other object. Books do not just have a destiny as a book, each book has its own life. People who read understand this—and Dietrich Fischer-Dieskau was one of these from his earliest childhood. The books in his house can be numbered in thousands (as can his records), and he is always reading them. Just as anyone wanting to be an author has never been frightened that so many books have already been written, neither was he intimidated by the number of books on his shelves or by the wealth of printed matter. All the same, just as when he was asked to take on a new stage role, he needed to be talked into becoming an author when he was first approached.

It was not very difficult to convince him, however, and the person who encouraged him to write also came up with a concrete proposal. This is part of the midwife's role of a publisher. The publisher of the Munich Deutscher Taschenbuchverlag or DTV (The German Pocketbook Press), Heinz Friedrich, himself a well-known essayist, was able to bring the right author together with the right subject. He used what his author had himself created: a public for the Lieder of German Romanticism. What could be more obvious than that Fischer-Dieskau should gather together the poems that he had studied, whose settings he had sung so often?

Dietrich Fischer-Dieskau and Heinz Friedrich had first met in 1965 in Ruth Leuwerik's Munich house during one of those parties that Fischer-

With the publisher Heinz Friedrich.

Dieskau found rather too elegant for his tastes. In 1968, the little paperback *Texte deutscher Lieder* (Texts of German Lieder) came out, and, having proved so popular, has continued to appear in new editions.[1]

The author has always wanted to publish an extended edition, for there is so much to discover and to add, but the original book seems to meet all the wishes of concert-goers. Also important for Fischer-Dieskau's career as an author was that, apart from the task of selecting and arranging the poems, he also provided an introductory essay explaining the rationale behind the settings of these poems to music and, indeed, for the very existence of this particular German art form of song with a piano accompaniment.

This was not the first time that Fischer-Dieskau had written on the German Lied, however. He had often contributed essays on single works, the relationship of words to music, the interpretation of Lieder, and so on in magazines, on record sleeves, and in recital programs. The extended essay in this book demanded a more systematic approach, which the author found in the history of music itself. His major premise was the definition of the time-span of the German art song, not limited, of course, to the period of German Romanticism. Has the Lied had its day? In 1968, Fischer-Dieskau wrote:

> It would need a composer as optimistic as Hans Werner Henze, who refuses to echo Gustav Mahler's feelings about the terminal fate of the symphony, to create anything of validity in this area for the future.

Almost twenty years later, he returned to these and other questionable areas in the history of music, when he came to consider the present and future position of the Lied. The question about its future status was really only a rhetorical one in this case; the past history of the Lied was the subject of this essay in a book that also served as an evaluation of the present situation. The development of the art song out of the eighteenth-century Singspiel was, in Fischer-Dieskau's opinion, due to a great need for "self-expression" after "the previous, mere technical brilliance." How deeply he himself must have felt this, and how much he must have appreciated, above all, Beethoven's decision to make the Lied a medium for the most personal of confessions.[2] Fischer-Dieskau then trawled through the history of the Lied, and his path led to his central themes: contemporaneity and what might be called "distancing." The nearer the Lied approaches our present day, the further back it reaches into history. Fischer-Dieskau writes:

> If one looks back, the settings of eighteenth-century composers (such as those of the young Beethoven) are of poets such as Friedrich von Matthisson (1761–1831), Ludwig Hölty (1748–1776),

J. W. L. Gleim (1719–1803), and Gottfried Bürger (1747–1794), all contemporary writers. But with Schubert and Brahms, we feel that their poets are no longer contemporaneous; then, when Richard Strauss sets Klopstock's "Das Rosenband" (The Rose-colored Ribbon; 1897–1898), the result is charming but, stylistically speaking, rather questionable.

The fondness of modern musicians for the poems of the ailing poet Friedrich Hölderlin (1770–1843) is relevant here. The treatment of side issues in the history of the Lied, such as the number of dilettante composers, illustrates Fischer-Dieskau's knowledge of the whole development of the problem and even then demanded more space than was available. He let twenty years pass before returning to the theme in a larger work, his *Töne sprechen, Worte klingen* (Music Speaks, Words Resound) of 1985, a book dedicated in the main to the art of interpretation, which was only touched upon in that introductory essay.

The *Texte deutscher Lieder* of 1968 was Fischer-Dieskau's first publication, and, of course, we know that he continued to write. Where, with all his singing commitments, did he find the time to do the research and to write? An above-average energy and the disciplined division of the hours of his working day provide one answer, but, in truth, he felt compelled to write.

"On the Trail of Schubert's Lieder"

"To Heinz Friedrich, in gratitude" reads the dedication of Dietrich Fischer-Dieskau's book on Schubert, *Auf den Spuren der Schubert-Lieder*.[1] That was no empty gesture of friendship, for the publisher had not been sparing with advice on the writing of this second publication, Fischer-Dieskau's first real book. Parts of the manuscript had gone back and forth several times, for Fischer-Dieskau was seeking the know-how of the essayist, and this the "young" author received in full measure (although a book like this was never actually meant to be published in paperback format). The communal work deepened their friendship.

The theme, Schubert and his Lieder, was of course very much part of the singer's professional work, particularly since Gerald Moore and he had just recorded for Deutsche Grammophon all the Schubert Lieder for the male voice.[2] Thus, one task was combined with another, and in this, his first book on a composer, one also finds the key to Fischer-Dieskau's working practices and how he shapes his interpretation of a Schubert Lied.

Readers can follow this process for themselves by playing a recording of the song while reading the description in the book. This is one advantage of having such a book. Fischer-Dieskau follows this practice himself when reading books on music by other authors. How much this two-way process of reading and listening can contribute to the appreciation of a work is shown by the example of his book.

We also find here, in a rather roundabout way, a rehabilitation of biographical literature, although Fischer-Dieskau has certainly not written a biography of Franz Schubert. His original idea, to follow "the trail of the Lieder," was conscientiously observed. What sort of "trails" were these? They were musical, literary, but also psychological ones—pointers to Schubert's life. The author wrote succinctly and somewhat apodictically: "There is really little to tell about Schubert's life; he lived it from within under the compulsion of composition, which was his attempt to impose a form on his life."

Fischer-Dieskau meets Schubert where he prefers to find himself: at work. "With no other composer were life and work so completely one," Fischer-Dieskau continued. "His life is a mere shadow; it is not surprising that the world around him was of little significance."[3]

The singer's life, on the other hand, was never lived in the shadows but under the most glaring spotlights, yet it is very plain how strongly he identifies with the inner world of the creation of the music that he interprets. Where should one find an artist? "Bent, hunched over his work!" had been Hans Werner Henze's answer once. The author Fischer-Dieskau follows the trail of the Schubert Lieder chronologically, so that the songs are followed by a description of Schubert's life at the time of their composition, and not the other way round. Here, the life stands *behind* the songs, not before the songs.

Whoever writes a book, writes about himself, so they say. Motifs from the singer's professional life were bound to impose themselves and did not need to be scared away—an echo of that age-long, endless argument about the dramatic expression of a Lied and its interpretation. We are reading here about Schubert, but also about Fischer-Dieskau:

> The early works show us clearly: Schubert, in most of his songs, used a small format not because he could not master or fill out the larger canvas, but because the small format was large enough for him to cover the whole gamut of human emotions. So it is really a misunderstanding to see the Lied as simply a musical miniature with a lyrical basis.

Now comes the conviction from his own experience and perspective: "A Schubert Lied contains within itself the essence of all drama and the depth of emotion of the cosmic view."

"Here, the almost incalculable cosmos of Schubert's Lieder is examined," wrote Karl Schumann in the *Süddeutsche Zeitung* after the publication of the book, "and is seen as part of the composer's autobiography, a self-confession and a self-definition." It was not just the scope of the scholarship that impressed the reviewer; it was also the debunking of the legend of "literary illiterate" Franz Schubert, "who was carried away by a melody as soon as he saw rhyming words." Fischer-Dieskau showed that Schubert was well-informed about world literature, old and new. Where Schubert's sensitivity to quality supposedly deserted him, he was still moved by the emotional relationships, by the physical feelings in the words of the poem. "An artistic and creative personality such as Fischer-Dieskau's," wrote Karl Schumann, "could perceive those relationships more clearly that many an academic, and his judgments, like his readings between the lines, have retained their validity." The same reviewer could also go too far, however:

> We have hardly ever had such a description of practical performance methods; the remarks on *Die schöne Müllerin* or "An die Leyer" could replace a master class on the Lied.

So, once again, it is the singer's way of interpreting Lieder that is under discussion: "Fischer-Dieskau legitimizes his much-criticized over-emphasis on the words by showing that he simply produces what Schubert asked for."

Fischer-Dieskau's authorial interpretation of "An die Leyer," a poem by the now forgotten poet, Franz von Bruchmann (1798–1867), one of Schubert's closest friends, might serve as a fine example of the author's working practices in this book, and it can be taken as typical. Bruchmann borrowed his poem from the Greek poet, Anacreon. Before he begins his treatment of the song, Fischer-Dieskau writes of the German Anacreontic poets of the eighteenth century—Johann Peter Uz (1720–1796), Joseph Götz (1721–1781), J. W. L. Gleim (1719–1803), and Friedrich von Hagedorn (1708–1754)—and of the zest for living and loving of the sixth-century B.C. Greek poet, Anacreon, a zest that was found again in Klopstock, Hölty, and Goethe.

> "An die Leyer" (To the Lyre) is divided into rhythmic-dramatic and hymn-like arioso passages, which are purposely not homogeneous, so as to make clear Anacreon's humorous accentuation of the reversion to the lyrical from the strongly dramatic. This version of the Greek original actually gains from such a structural change, which, after two dramatic surges, allows the lyrical tone to reassert itself—it was also typical of Schubert's own state of mind at the time [1822–1823]. After periods of excitement, he liked to subside again into a state of calm. In songs like this, it becomes very evident that a good Schubert singer must be able to command both harshness and softness of tone. This is meant to be an heroic song, and the listener's experience is to be both a poetical and a musical one. The song begins with great energy, the piano strews chords energetically about, sixteenth notes scuttle around, the second time in octaves, and there are defiant dotted diminished sevenths, above which the singer proudly proclaims his "Ich will" (I will) for the whole world to hear. The piano is just beginning to develop its motif, when the musical idea eludes us and wanders off in a different direction—and the tense pause following reveals that it is "only" a love song after all. Schubert's show of strength is not equal to his original idea. However beautiful the E-flat major melody is, it disappoints our hero, who, after all, wants to be heroic and to be driven to his limits. So, it is understandable that after failing with the first attempt, he should try again. His mistake is to believe that he has only chosen the wrong mode of expression—so he calls for a different instrument, more energy, a more powerful presentation, the most sublime themes. He seems to be succeeding. "Alcides Siegesschreiten"

(Alcides' Victory March) sounds indeed like a triumphal march, but once again, the music slips over into a love story. The singer is not resigned, however. He looks into his heart, renounces the heroic song, and returns to the love story he sings so well. As the trill on the low G on "drohen" (threaten) proves, he still feels some resentment, but it cannot dampen his optimism.[4]

Can one do anything else but want to go off and listen to the song again and again?—but with the knowledge from, and the interpretative remarks of, that narrative passage.

There were also obvious interactions between the written and the sung interpretations of the Lieder. A character such as the Schubert singer Johann Michael Vogl interests the author as it did the singer. And there were also chance stimuli. On 18 July 1971, he wrote in answer to a question:

> Your discussion of Vogl's *embellissements* arrived while I was in the middle of my book on Schubert, which I hope will be published (by Brockhaus) next Christmas. My view of this insoluble problem is very like yours. Diabelli's edition of the *Schöne Müllerin* songs really does show that Vogl's additional intermissions and declamatory supports were not part of the "Italianization" of the Friedlaender edition, but had rather to do with the veracity of expression. It is certain that his aging voice could well have been responsible for the alterations, but the altered passages are not really accounted for by that. I vote for the version freed of the modish cadenzas and interpretative arbitrarinesses, and believe that that one is nearest to Schubert's concept. It has also been reported after all how the composer tried to defend himself against Vogl when the latter's dictation went too far. Then, as you know, most of the alterations were approved by the publishers after Schubert's death [in 1828]—and they were not all Vogl's. Brahms's support for the printing of the original version speaks volumes too!

This letter allows us to appreciate both the singer's technical knowledge and his efforts to get as near to the composer as possible. It also tells us something of the joy with which Fischer-Dieskau undertakes such historico-critical work, which compares editions and leads to conclusions. Yet his goal was always to turn these into portrayals—in words, in music, or in both.

Another episode from the singer's life is relevant here, too: the story that the manuscript of the first version of his Schubert book disappeared from his London hotel in 1970, and was never seen again. "We were paralyzed for a few days," he wrote to his stepbrother Achim, "then, after having lost eighteen months' work, I sat down to work on the second version."[5]

"Life Without Music
Is Just a Mistake,
a Drudgery, an Exile!"

Friedrich Nietzsche, the German philosopher (1844–1900), wrote these words to his friend Peter Gast on 15 January 1888, and Dietrich Fischer-Dieskau used this confession to sum up his remarks on Nietzsche in his book *Wagner und Nietzsche* on the relationship between Nietzsche and the composer Richard Wagner: "The artistic and philosophical creative processes became one in Nietzsche's persona, for he had begun his career as a musician."[1]

It seemed somehow typical for the musician and author Dietrich Fischer-Dieskau to exchange what was for him the secure terrain of Schubert and his life for the slippery ice of Nietzsche-Wagner scholarship. Such change is his element. There was no external reason, no particular commemoration of either of the great men in the offing, nor any ongoing study of a particular Wagnerian operatic role when he sketched the plan for the book. Nonetheless, the project matured slowly. He wrote in his memoirs:

> I had always been fascinated by the thought of writing a monograph about these incongruous friends, Wagner and Nietzsche, ever since reading those curious remarks of Nietzsche's sister, Elisabeth Förster-Nietzsche, on the subject. I was seventeen at the time.[2]

Some years after the publication of this book (in 1974), Fischer-Dieskau wrote to the author of another book on Nietzsche:

> Your point of view is not quite confirmed by the two people you are dealing with. The imposing power of the musician made the possibility of a fair judgment of the philosopher difficult, even at that time. Little has altered today. After the "re-evaluation of all values," we can only really understand nowadays what Nietzsche's *Über-mensch* (superman) was: a man with the ability to realize his whole potential. No more, no less. In colloquial language: only a man who has ensured the state of health of his ego can become his equal. It is interesting that the biologically orientated anthropologist (Carl) von

Weizsäcker comes to the same conclusion in his *Garten des Menschlichen* (The Garden of Humanness).

There is a melancholy irony in these words. Then, the writer becomes more concrete:

> I think that it was only possible to start working on this material because from my earliest days I had been fascinated by the antinomy of the two figures, and because some essential features of that antinomy had become part of my own professional life.

Therein lies the particular reason for writing for this musician; it provides a direct connection with his own artistic work via the study of documents and the contemplation of inter-relationships.

The author never overestimated Nietzsche's forays into music; he considered them professionally, that is, by singing them. He wrote:

> Nietzsche's unpublished musical work shows how deeply anchored the bond with music was in the philosopher's whole being. Yet one cannot allow any misunderstandings to arise: Friedrich Nietzsche did not write any music that even vaguely approaches the originality, the depth of meaning, the stylistic brilliance of his literary and philosophical writings. One also has to realize that almost all of his compositions fall into the early period of his career, that is, before the time that his enthusiasm for Wagner colored his judgments. As far as the later works are concerned, these are marked by a clearly visible inability to master the "Wagnerian" harmonies.

Fischer-Dieskau treats not only Nietzsche's amateurish musical language, but also the discrepancy between the two men's views of art. That began with their understanding, or rather misunderstanding, of the Romantic philosopher Arthur Schopenhauer (1788–1860). The two men had one thing in common—their view of Schopenhauer corresponded to their own mode of thinking. In his book, Fischer-Dieskau promulgated a thesis from the very beginning, which he eventually formulates provocatively: "So the question for us is not how Nietzsche could become an enemy of Bayreuth, but rather: How did Nietzsche not realize from the outset how little he had in common with Wagner?"[3]

Fischer-Dieskau describes Nietzsche's secret opposition to the composer, showing that Nietzsche could not understand Wagner's nationalistic views and loathed his anti-Semitism, but he emphasizes the incompatibility of their basic conceptions of art and music. How long was it before Nietzsche realized that Wagner was not on the way to "the greatest of all symphonies," and that *Tristan and Isolde*, the work over which he had most enthused, and which was not in vain the least theatrical of Wagner's works, was not the first step to their breaking-up? Fischer-Dieskau wrote that Nietzsche's decided antipathy to all that was "theatrical" was most characteristic of his view of art.

The dispute "Wagner contra Nietzsche," which had raged furiously in the nineteenth century and can still arouse emotions today, is dealt with here in quiet language, a cautious judgment that nevertheless, according to the Bern paper *Der Bund*, reveals an "energetic, summarizing mind."

Fischer-Dieskau, then near fifty, made not only friends with this book, however. The critics were soon on the warpath. Yet why should there not have been divergent views? It would have been very surprising had it been otherwise on this subject. The argument about whether a thesis is valid or not is legitimate. Only when envy seeps through the reviewer's words, when it is clear that there is resentment that the famous singer is writing books as well, does the prejudice become annoying. Undeserved criticism is never easy to dismiss, yet just as Fischer-Dieskau was exposed to criticism on stage or concert platform evening after evening, so too he continued to be subjected to it as an author.

"To Crown the Head of a True Poet with a Wreath of Music"

The title of Fischer-Dieskau's next book, *Robert Schumann, Wort und Musik. Das Vokalwerk* (Robert Schumann, Word and Music: The Vocal Compositions) does sound rather severe, but since his book on Schubert, his authorial technique had veered even more toward the narrative.[1] Much of this book reads like a biography, accompanied by analyses of the songs. The author is much more ambitious here than in the Schubert book, although, once again, it is the description of the Lieder and the other vocal works that makes the book such an attractive, musically inspired read. Thus, from a Lied like "Mondnacht" (from the poem by Joseph von Eichendorff, 1788–1857), which is "one of Schumann's most celebrated songs and which every lover of Lieder thinks he knows well," he extracts the possibility of a fresh way of listening:

> Eichendorff's words "still" (still), "sternklar" (starry clear), and "träumen" (dreaming) gave the composer the stimulus for the mood of the song. Thus, his directions read: "Zart, heimlich" (gentle and secretively), which do not say anything very precise about the required tempo but all the more about the character of the interpretation. The melodic material appears to be very simple; five of the six couplets of the poem are set to the same eight-measure phrase. Variety, and consolidation, are provided by the prelude, which returns to separate the verses.

He deals with the passage "und meine Seele spannte—weit ihre Flügel aus" (And my soul spread / out wide its wings) thus:

> It is not meant to be a caesura, but rather an extension of the basic idea such as was introduced by Romantic poetry. It is not a drop in pitch, as was common in the poetry and music of the eighteenth century, but rather an intake of breath, as it were, as if to extend the space of the song into infinity. This is also the significance of the final suspended fifths, which play such an important role in "Mondnacht." At this point, the melody and the harmony part company, yet without losing their cohesion. The rhythm in the

218

accompaniment remains unchanged too, and the piano prelude is woven into the accompaniment. Right to the end there is a single, basic melodic motif. The continuous accompaniment, the gentle "Flügelrauschen" (rustling of wings) in the interludes, the furtive, independent life of the middle voice, the piety of the conclusion, which becomes more and more lineal—all that reveals Schumann's art of combining the language of the soul with that of nature.[2]

That is surely a demand for the song to be heard!

Fischer-Dieskau illustrates his book with many musical examples and describes the lives of the various poets; the poems themselves are reproduced in their entirety in an appendix. All of this almost makes the book into a reference work, yet, as mentioned above, the biographical element is stronger here than in the Schubert book, and that is explained, of course, by the very different private and creative lives of the two composers.

Fischer-Dieskau is absolutely fascinated by Schumann's obsession with the theme of the Doppelgänger (the double, the Jekyll-and-Hyde type of character, celebrated later in R. L. Stevenson's story of 1886). This was a central theme of late German Romantics such as "Jean Paul" (Jean-Paul Richter, 1763–1825) and E. T. A. Hoffmann (1776–1822), who were clearly models for Schumann. In the introductory chapter to his book, Fischer-Dieskau writes:

> The idea of instrumental music as "original" corresponds exactly to Hoffmann's esthetic of the sublime in a work of art. That was of course contrary to the expectations that Schumann shared with many during the Vormärz [the period in Germany between 1815 and the 1848 revolution]: the view that creative writing would have a fresh and redemptive influence on the development of art. This view also underlines Schumann's heightened sensitivity to those hidden interactions between words and music, and also explains the extremely hypersensitive behavior that drove him in 1828 (under the influence of Jean Paul) to a theme that obsessed him from that date on: the theme of the Doppelgänger.

Fischer-Dieskau knew this theme only too well. His life had been lived between words and music, and just as Schumann saw it in the middle of the nineteenth century, Fischer-Dieskau saw, too, in our century "the vacuity and sickness of our society as the cause of a lasting melancholy." Does he, like Schumann, see this "as a call for arms against the philistine"?[3] All the same, he asked himself as he paused for a moment during all his time-consuming activities:

Is it really enough to lose one's self in the contemplation of a genius [he was thinking here of Schubert, but it could have been relevant for Schumann, too] who, from today's standpoint, made himself a sort of spiritual refuge, without taking sides, without inviting any rectification, . . . an artist who shares Beethoven's view of the revelation of religiosity in art? His musical language cradles us in fantastic dreams, but it is all about the possibility of dreaming, and that leads us, of course, back to ourselves.

These were Fischer-Dieskau's final conciliatory words on the subject in this letter to his friend, Heinz Friedrich, on 12 February 1978.

"To find one's way to one's self," the eternal theme of Doppelgängerism, the longing for the undivided existence of the simple man, those were Schumann's leitmotifs. This book keeps returning to them, and the biographical account portrays Schumann loving and suffering, writing and composing, reasoning—and, unfortunately, also getting drunk.

Schumann's illness is also considered by Fischer-Dieskau, of course, as it was by all previous writers, but he postulates a thesis that radically contradicts the usual portrayal of the "Verfallserscheinungen" (signs of deterioration) that can be found in Schumann's works:

The erratic graph of qualitative differences in Schumann's later works corresponds to the seismographical effects of his experiments with his musical language rather than to his clinical condition.[4]

But Fischer-Dieskau does not leave the matter there. He analyzes the late vocal works up to the *Szenen aus Faust* (Scenes from Faust, 1853). He knows the strengths and weaknesses of that work very well, having worked on it in 1972 with Benjamin Britten as conductor. Britten then produced it in Aldeburgh (on 8 June, and performed and recorded it for Decca in September, with Fischer-Dieskau, Peter Pears, Elizabeth Harwood, and John Shirley-Quirk as soloists, *Trans.*). Britten wrote to the singer: "I am enjoying working on the *Faust*, and my admiration and affection for it grow steadily." So it was no late work of an expiring composer that was brought back to life in Aldeburgh that year. As was to be expected, however, Schumann supporters disagreed with a thesis that questioned not only the composer's creative abilities, but also touched on Schumann's alcoholism. Fischer-Dieskau tried to justify his argument:

In this book I have attempted, above all, to correct the impression that the mature Schumann was mad with the consequent dismissal of his later works based on that impression. That could, in all honesty, only be granted if the really unproven charge of schizophrenia were to yield to the much more probable one of alcoholism (with some completely clear phases of withdrawal and its tragic consequences), which, I am convinced, tallies better with the well-proven care and attention given to him up to the end, as well as his despairing attempts to free himself from his addiction.[5]

The medical testimony of Franz Richarz, the doctor in the clinic at Endenich in Bonn, which was released from Aribert Reimann's family papers in 1994, confirms that Schumann was neither a manic depressive nor a schizophrenic but that his fatal illness was caused by a syphilitic infection.

Must we now therefore regard Schumann's alcoholism as having been less damaging? Fischer-Dieskau was concerned with revising the negative assessment of Schumann's later works. He wrote a preface on these lines to some Schumann recordings by Jörg Demus, who thanked him for his efforts:

> For I have found some real pearls just among these later things, and it is perhaps not the least important part of such a task that we discover wonderful pieces among unknown and rejected things.

"He Gave Poetry Music and Music Words"

The Austrian poet and dramatist Franz Grillparzer (1791–1872) composed the above epitaph for the tombstone of his friend Franz Schubert, although another version, "Music buried here a rich possession, but many more beautiful hopes," eventually appeared on it in the summer of 1830.

Yet that first epitaph could be thought of as more relevant to Dietrich Fischer-Dieskau, and he varied it slightly for the title of his next book, *Töne sprechen, Worte klingen* (Music Speaks, Words Resound).[1] The book is a sort of balance sheet, a summary of his life, his work, and his times. Was it just by chance that he wrote it in the three years before his sixtieth birthday in 1985? Even in a busy life such as his, that date has its often accepted, and just as often denied, significance. A singer will probably not be able to avoid the thought that in the following decade, his instrument, the voice, might one day not be able to do what is asked of it. Fischer-Dieskau was not surprised by this thought as he approached this particular time of life. He had been thinking about it for a decade or so, had questioned and examined himself, and could thank heaven and his own worrying consciousness that his voice was still allowing him to realize all his creative interpretations of Lieder, yet this consideration had also made him decide to end his stage career in 1982. The knowledge of the finiteness of those physical, interpretative abilities, always being renewed and modified, could not be denied. The unavoidable question then arose: Would the inevitable silencing of his voice not herald more than just the end of a single, personal career?

Fischer-Dieskau had never voiced this openly himself. Yet in this new book, we can hear the melody of an Abgesang (the last verse of a *Minnesänger's* song):

> Even if the genre Kunstlied (art song) seems, for many reasons, to have become outdated (also because of the nature of the poetry in the mass production of the last forty years, of which only a few poems, mostly philosophical in nature, have claimed general interest), then it is still only fair to give credit where credit is due. The Lied touches an area of the emotions that has little relevance these days.[2]

Although Fischer-Dieskau claimed at the same time that the percentage of young people attending his recitals was growing, the resigned tone of the passage above does speak volumes. It was indeed rather surprising that he used a favorite phrase of those 1968 "revolutionaries," that is, "mass production," but, contrary to its use in those days, he gave it not a positive connotation but rather one of futility, as the sentence following it confirms. Although it is a word to be used with caution, it *is* rather "tragic" that this musician, who has supported contemporary vocal music as no other and has encouraged so many modern composers to write Lieder, can write, after a career as a singer spanning forty years, of the need to "give credit where credit is due." While watching the waves of the river Traun follow and flow into one another, the aging Brahms is supposed to have told Gustav Mahler, after the Austrian had tried to prove to him that symphonic music was bound to have a future: "Look, there goes the last wave!" Fischer-Dieskau would never make such an apodictic judgment, but he feels nevertheless that it does seem rather improbable that a new great age of the Lied, of the contemporary, creative Lied, lies before us.

Yet the symphony, too, as an all-embracing musical form, was disintegrating after Brahms. So it is not surprising that Fischer-Dieskau follows, quite deliberately, a systematic classification in this book, with its subtitle *The History and Interpretation of Songs*, and he divides up the genres to provide an overview, although the interlocking of genres has always been part of his basic musical credo. Here, however, he uses the categorizing method to suit the needs of the learner. As the book's title suggests, the author's theme is the old one of "Wort-Ton" (Words and Music), his own major theme since he began singing. There is no doubt that he "explains the mutual workings of text and music" in the Lieder of Schubert, above all, and of Schumann, Brahms, and Wolf, "in such a way," wrote Hans Jürgen Fröhlich, "that the old question of whether the music had to match the poem, or the poem the music, becomes, in effect, meaningless." The singer had already witnessed that a thousand times on the concert platform.

He had no fear that the precise and comprehensive study of the connections, and the differences between poetry and music could take away his naiveté as a musician. But could such a book, which presents information drawn from knowledge, facts, and artistic workaday practice, rob the reader of his or her "naive" appreciation of a work of art?

No, the opposite is the case. In describing the historical place of a composer in the detailed examination of a Lied, the author is aiding not only the listener's understanding but also his or her ability to empathize. Yet Fischer-Dieskau himself did not seem to have been quite clear about how much a listener should know when he wrote:

The great public is often unaware (and should not become aware) of how intensively an interpreting singer has to listen to the language and its sounds to make them the intellectual and technical core of his interpretation. Singers can neglect this, especially with Brahms and his orchestral-like piano accompaniments . . . . So it cannot be taken for granted that the singer who is studying Brahms's song "Wie Melodien zieht es mir" (Like Melodies, a Feeling Steals) will make the difference between the first and second part of this through-composed, strophic song perfectly clear. Soft consonants, legato singing, vocal control at "Wie Melodien"—these are replaced in the second verse by the graphic pronunciation of the words, for here the poem says: "Doch kommt das Wort und fasst es / und führt es vor das Aug' / Wie Nebelgrau erblasst es" (But words come and grasp it / And bring it before your eye / and it pales like the graying mist).[3]

Will the reader of that passage not hear Klaus Groth's poem in Brahms's setting differently from before, and be more responsive to the "Duft" (perfume) that reposes "im Reim verborgen" (hidden in the rhyme)? Was that not the case already, in the concert hall, when Fischer-Dieskau's knowledge aroused an answering echo in the listeners, so that they better understood the language of the emotion that the song evoked? Fischer-Dieskau claims that this language leads, in the ideal case, from thinking "with language" to thinking "without language."

When Schubert in "Die Nebensonnen" [The Mock Suns—the twenty-third song of his *Winterreise*] composes music to the notion of "drei Sonnen" [three suns, i.e., the girl's two eyes and the real sun], which can only be understood from the text of the poem, he has to use generalized musical categories and thus gives the song just a generalized meaning. He employs a triplet rhythm that is found neither in the lines nor in the verses of the poem. A piano part that imitates wind instruments alters what is in the poem to something that everyone who knows how to listen can understand, because they will imagine what the word *stier* (staring) means without being able to explain it. So when Schubert leads the music back from thinking with language to thinking without it, he attains the true goal of the experience. All attempts to imitate music in speech, or to turn music into speech (onomatopoeic poems, meaningless prose), show that speech cannot afford to be a serious competitor here.[4]

In that passage, indeed in the whole book, one finds the affirmative credo of this great singer—so often both praised and criticized for his feeling for words, his purity of enunciation based firmly on his desire to be understood—and that means, in the last analysis, everything must have been turned back into music. The *melos* (the music) must remain the fundament of what is sung, he tells the composers, and he mistrusts the directors and producers of operas who have only "a very peripheral idea" of the music, so that a work "whose intentions have been very clearly indicated by the music" is only imperfectly understood—a point he makes even more firmly in the 1995 film mentioned above.[5]

He had just ended his operatic career in 1982 when he delivered this judgment. He was to dedicate himself now entirely to Lieder, as he said and as the facts, in one way, proved. On the other hand, the then cult of producing opera in a manner that was inimical to the music had probably also contributed to his decision. In his discussion of opera production, he asked:

> After all, what is left? A destruction of that deeply felt art form fashioned by man which our age has been fortunate enough to experience. An interpretation that is independent of the music— and thus ceases to be an interpretation—is a phenomenon of our times, in which, in general, characterization has become more important and more emphasized than the work itself.[6]

Yet opera, or what the Germans call "das neue Musiktheater" (the new music-theater), had been given many new opportunities by the new young generation of composers, so Fischer-Dieskau looks now to the future:

> Perhaps it is actually only through opera and its ability to shape words that the exhaustion of musical material can be combated, an exhaustion that lames musical inspiration so much and that has allowed this movement to profit at the expense of purely musical phenomena. And one more thing: the words of the poet, in the original, and not worked up into an operatic libretto, pervade the music scene today as never before. With "literary opera," a new tree has grown from old soil.[7]

Were it but so, one is tempted to add. It would not be Fischer-Dieskau speaking if there were not a "light at the end of the tunnel" of his taking stock, if he were not looking to the future according to a favorite line from Schubert's *Der Wanderer* (The Wanderer) (D649): "I climb up bravely, sing with joy, and the world appears good to me."

This very personal attitude pervades the book. The author was consciously avoiding a mere supplying of information when he wrote of a "report of his experiences over forty years as a singer." It is true that the chapters "Gesang und Poesie" (Song and Poetry), "Gesang oratorisch" (Music for Oratorios), "Gesang ohne Sänger" (Song Without Singers), and "Gesang und Theater" (Song and Theater) each follow a chronological pattern, but the connection with the present and the author's personal attitude toward composition and interpretation is always bravely maintained.

What comes out of all this is the abandonment of all apparent objectivity. The last chapter, "Gesang in der Werkstatt" (Song in the Workshop), gives a very concentrated picture of the musician Dietrich Fischer-Dieskau himself. What puzzles critics and audiences alike after his recitals, what everyone asks about—namely, the secret of his art—is certainly not completely revealed here, yet one can find some clues to the basic principles of how he thinks and works. These principles are often so simple that they do not seem to tally with the miracle of those perfect interpretations. Though they seem so simple to put into practice, many of these remarks are not; for example, this very significant one: "What lies between the notes should be set free, and what is in the notes should not be violated."[8] This refers, of course, to the duty, and the license, of the interpreter to direct his powers of expressiveness to the work in order to give those listening a similar experience. According to Fischer-Dieskau, there is no such thing as a completely authentic interpretation:

> Again and again, one is deluded into thinking that one has reached perfection, but to deduce from that that the result will endure unchanged for ever, is quite unjustifiable—still less, to use one's interpretation as a refutation of another. No two voices are alike, still less, two talents. . . . Apart from the difference in the nature of the voice, the one more cantabile, the other more declamatory, the beginnings of an artistic talent are probably to be found in an attitude that has been formed by childhood disposition and influences.

This from a man who knows only too well the fleeting nature of such beautiful delusions—and there was more, too. On the biographical point of departure:

> Such an attitude creates an obsession and a readiness to sacrifice oneself to the realities of an artist's life. That is in contrast to the far greater number of people who remain trapped in the real world.[9]

Artistic reality and the real world as opposite poles, to be seen as two possibilities of choice, remain the twin concepts that have determined Fischer-Dieskau's life. No one need puzzle over which pole he chose, or what rules his life. Here, in this last, modestly titled chapter, "Song in the Workshop," he enunciates it and reveals himself to the world.

At the same time, there is plenty to be read here about tonal intensities, nuances of coloration, and the psychology and the technique of singing, but also about the "self-creative act which no re-creative activity can do without."[10]

"My Heart Feels Every Echo"

My heart feels every echo
of sad and happy times.
I walk 'twixt pain and joyfulness
In these lonely climes.

This verse from Johann Wolfgang von Goethe's poem "An den Mond" (To the Moon) lends the title of Fischer-Dieskau's book of memoirs *Nachklang* (Echoes) (1987) a peculiar mixture of dark and light tones.[1] The poem was written between 1776 and 1778 and was found among the poet's letters to his married friend in Weimar, Charlotte von Stein [whom Goethe left in 1786 to undertake his *Italienische Reise* (Journey to Italy) (1786–1788)]. This verse only appeared in the second version of the poem (that of 1789), when the original reason for the poem (Goethe's deep love for Charlotte) was only a memory: thus *Echoes*. Such is the title that Fischer-Dieskau gave to a description of his life in which he allowed himself much greater freedom than in his previous books, in that he did not write to a systematic, chronological plan but allowed himself to be led by association, wandering from theme to theme, thus avoiding the additive nature of "memoirs." Instead, we have a weft of personal stories that, together, give us a picture of his life. One could even call it a "book of encounters." The people whom the singer met during his long career are all there, described mostly in short, graphic characterizations: the composers, his singer colleagues, conductors, accompanists. Nor does he spare his private life: the happy and the sad hours are sketched with honesty, seriousness, and a clearly visible pleasure in depicting them. The overwhelming impression given by the narrative style is of a cheerful, very positive attitude toward life, a sort of serenity in looking back, encompassing more than what is in the book, which, as the balance-sheet of a musician's life, allows one to guess what an enormous stone this Sisyphus had to push upwards to the summit. Here is a man to whom everything seemed to, and, in a certain sense, actually did come easily, because of his enormous talents. More of that, even if only between the lines, can be read in his 1985 book *Töne sprechen, Worte klingen* (Music Speaks, Words Resound), which is much more a contribution to the whole history of music.

Fischer-Dieskau's memoirs reveal a man who is very wary of pronouncing judgments upon others—a rare case! He looks back in a friendly manner; the basic intellectual approach is sympathy with those "others," an approach that found a resonance with people of like mind. From the United States, the conductor Thomas Baldner wrote in 1989:

There is so much friendship, warmth, almost brotherliness in your book that I could not lay it down for days on end. It was as if I were reading my own life story, with this difference—that you have become the bard of our times, whereas I have become what, in my very early days, an Italian woman called me, a *maestrino.* . . . We have never met (I was possibly even more shy than you are) but I

With Julia Varady after a reading at the Schubertiade in Feldkirch, Austria, 1993.

remember your *Four Serious Songs* of Brahms, with Ludwig Hoffmann at the piano in the shabby lecture hall of the Berlin Academy of Music, probably in 1946. And it goes on and on—to the moon over Manhattan. I had almost the same feeling as you when I came out of my first musical in 1949 and did not want to believe that the moon was not an advertisement. I have often heard and admired you, particularly one evening in Frankfurt, many, many years ago, when, perhaps because of an indisposition, you practically had to whisper your whole program—to the breathless fascination of your audience. I knew then what a masterly performance that was, and I appreciate it much more today.

Reminiscences awake reminiscences. Thomas Baldner spoke for many people: "This is to thank you for *Nachklang*, and also for the wonderful music which you have given us throughout your life." [2]

If this book created such echoes for its readers, if it freed such emotions, that was due also to its form of free-association narration that gave Fischer-Dieskau himself time to remember. Fischer-Dieskau wrote in a letter in 1982:

Memory plays a different, deepening role altogether in one's life. Perhaps it is one of the loveliest and most enriching things about growing older—and a compensation for much that had to be sacrificed.

"If Music Be the Food of Love"

There has been a good deal of scholarly debate about the meaning of the first sentence of Shakespeare's play *Twelfth Night* (1623). The speaker, Orsino, has been disappointed in love and he wants—or does not want—an excess of it, that "the appetite may sicken, and so die." If music can therefore be only a substitute for love for him, then one can say with certainty that music is here taken as a synonym for love. Dietrich Fischer-Dieskau chose *If Music Be the Food of Love* as title for a book in which music and love are inextricably mingled.[1] That is also the theme of the relationship between Pauline Viardot (1821–1910), the French mezzo-soprano of Spanish parentage, and the Russian writer Ivan Turgenev (1818–1883), in much the same way that the love affairs of the contralto Maria Felicita Malibran (1808–1836), Viardot's sister, overshadowed *her* life. Those who had expected that after the formal experiment of *Nachklang* Fischer-Dieskau would return to writing another monograph-type book, were most surprised by a book that, behind the rather indecisive subtitle *Artistic Destinies in the Nineteenth Century*, took the full-blooded life story of the singer Pauline Viardot as its major theme and connected it with a description of some of the basic modes of life typical of creative artists of the nineteenth century.

The author's portrayals of Schubert and Schumann were quite obviously products of his life-long acquaintanceship with their works, which, in turn, influenced the reference-book nature of these studies. The Nietzsche-Wagner book was really a long essay, but here, in his new book, the narrative form was needed to show the mores of an age via the story of the life of a family and its friends. The need to tell a story, and to incorporate historical references into its flow, attracted the author, who was thus able to avoid the reference-book style of those earlier works. But the field he had chosen to cultivate was not an easy one to till.

Nevertheless, the effort was rewarded. Fischer-Dieskau had a secret helper in this, though hardly a hidden one, for it was a writer whom the material—or perhaps rather, the destiny of his protagonists—presented to him: "In 1843, after a performance of Rossini's *The Barber of Seville* in the St. Petersburg opera, Ivan Turgenev stood in Pauline's dressing room."[2]

The Russian writer became the singer's lover and, for the author, a source of inspiration as well as a stimulus. Fischer-Dieskau's sources were

Turgenev's letters and diaries, so he was able to create narrative passages such as this:

> Turgenev had been twice in Paris already. One day, during his third visit, he noticed how Pauline moved through the crowds on the shopping boulevards with an amazing lightness of step. She let herself be carried along through the throng of people without touching any one. Turgenev does not speak to her, fearful of spoiling her pleasure, and embarrassed too, because he himself is not a very skillful shopper. He sees her through a shop window as she tries on a dress of printed silk, he sees her laugh as she looks at herself in the mirror, dressed as a Spaniard with a comb and a fan painted with flowers.
>
> Turgenev spies on her, utterly bewitched, follows her breathlessly. Once he goes so near to her that her perfume wafts over him. Yet she has not seen him, probably because she is walking along so majestically as she always does when she thinks that she is being observed.
>
> He does not dare approach her, for fear of destroying the spell. When he loses her in the crowd, he realizes that he has nearly forfeited a meeting for which he has been longing for ages.[3]

Even when Fischer-Dieskau writes as narrator, the historical picture carries tints of the present, traces of his own experiences. Who could have involved himself so deeply in the life of a famous operatic singer with such extensive cultural interests better than this man, who has always had a keen interest in the social and cultural life of the nineteenth century—a life of letter-writers, of educated conversation, and reading? What scenes were revealed, what a galaxy of personalities involved! Wagner and Berlioz, Clara Schumann and Rubinstein, Meyerbeer and George Sand, Turgenev and Theodor Storm, Vincenzo Bellini, Chopin, Liszt, Rossini, the singer and Brahms's friend Julius Stockhausen, and Tolstoy—all of them moved in the Garcia family circle of musicians, and thus in Pauline Viardot's, too.

The author turns Pauline's crises into his own and allows the heroine to pronounce his own beliefs:

> If you only sing with your voice, you are soon finished. If, however, you possess the fire of poetry, if each poem seems to you to be spontaneously spoken as if by one who is creating a fantasy, with exact contours and the space around them, then you may certainly show virtuosity, but you will use it to express the idea, the character, the thoughts of a work or a role.[4]

Stylistically speaking, Fischer-Dieskau transformed the authorial technique of association of *Echoes* into a perspective by means of which he described the political, social, and artistic aspects of the nineteenth century, as well as those affecting his characters' private lives.

When he published this book about Pauline Viardot-Garcia in 1990, he had already been following a new profession for some years, that of a professor of singing in Berlin, a career that had also helped Viardot to a second period of fame when she became a professor at the Paris Conservatoire in 1871. The young Fischer-Dieskau's career as a singer began with a study of the vocal theories of Manuel Garcia (1805–1906), Pauline's brother, whose pupils included Jenny Lind and Julius Stockhausen. Now, toward the end of his career, the teacher Dietrich Fischer-Dieskau wrote this book on the Garcia family. Klaus Geitel wrote in *Die Welt*:

> One is once again amazed, as so often before, at his almost inexhaustible range of talents—besides singing, rehearsing, painting, traveling, teaching, also the ability to write weighty books. This is one of the most astonishing feats to date.

"Because Not All
My Blossoming Dreams Ripened?"

Do you think then, that I should hate life,
flee into the wilderness,
because not all
my blossoming dreams ripened?

For his next book, Fischer-Dieskau's authorial technique changed again from that of his previous book. Here he was attempting a biography in the more precise sense of the term. *Weil nicht alle Blütenträume reiften* (Because Not All My Blossoming Dreams Ripened?), the story of the Kapellmeister Johann Friedrich Reichardt (1752–1814), one of the early masters of Lieder composition, is correctly encompassed by a title that is almost ironical—perhaps even a little against the author's own wishes. Fischer-Dieskau attempts to win some sympathy for this distressed man, who one day, almost by mistake, fell in love with the French Revolution and then was surprised by the anger that this aroused at the Prussian court.[1]

In Fischer-Dieskau's portrayal, Reichardt is shown to have been far in advance of his contemporaries in his love of music yet unable to fulfill that love in his work or in his life, for he lacked both the courage of the great personality and the strength of an exceptional talent. Thus, he was a man whose almost self-imposed misfortunes made him attractive for an author. What attracted Fischer-Dieskau to him? Fired by Reichardt's contribution to the birth of the German Lied, Fischer-Dieskau presented his man as the representative of a changing age, one whom the waves of the river of Time raised up and then cast down, one who tried, by a little "maneuvering," to escape the elements. Reichardt's influence on poets and composers on into the Age of Romanticism, his efforts to found a contemporary kind of musical theater, his friendship with Goethe—everything in his favor is illuminated by Fischer-Dieskau's sympathetic treatment. The narration, along with quotations from Reichardt, enlarge the book in the usual manner, although Reichardt's letters do not possess the literary quality of Turgenev's. Since it is one of Fischer-Dieskau's predilections—as singer as well as author—to announce discoveries, we willingly follow the route he maps out and the iridescent character that traverses it.

Reichardt, a most versatile musician who nevertheless never became one of the really great personalities of his day, developed a rare talent to its greatest extent because it corresponded to a deep need in his character: he had to make friends, easily and quickly. He managed to bring people together, often people who seemed just to have been waiting to meet each other. As time went by, the whole circle of the young German Romantics seemed to come together in the house and garden of Giebichenstein. Ludwig Tieck (1773–1853), Novalis (Friedrich von Hardenberg) (1772–1801), W. H. Wackenroder (1773–1798), even Jean Paul (1763–1825), visited Reichardt's idyllic home. In the good times, the house became a musical country estate. Reichardt's daughter Luise used to sing folksongs there, too.

Perhaps Fischer-Dieskau looked so benevolently on his subject because of Reichardt's ability continually to widen his circle of friends. Perhaps Reichardt's tireless need to be active reminded him of his own irresistible need to express himself—only, with this difference, that his "blossoming dreams" did "ripen"![2]

Having just mentioned a "circle of friends," it is perhaps relevant to take another look at the friends of the author, musician, and painter Dietrich Fischer-Dieskau. The book about Reichardt affords this opportunity because of a book title in the extensive bibliography at the back: Gersdorff, Dagmar von. 1984. *Dich zu lieben, kann ich nicht verlernen. Das Leben der Sophie Brentano-Mereau* (I Cannot Stop Loving You. The Life of Sophie Brentano-Mereau). Frankfurt.

It can only be a peripheral *aperçu* that the Gersdorffs and the Fischer-Dieskaus are closely related as regards Sophie Mereau. The connection between Bernd and Dagmar von Gersdorff and the Fischer-Dieskaus began with a question to the Schubert singer and editor of the *Texte deutscher Lieder* (The Fischer-Dieskau Book of Lieder) whether there were settings of George Philipp Schmidt von Lübeck's poems other than "Der Wanderer" (The Wanderer) (set by Schubert in 1816). That was in 1986. Out of question and answer grew conversation, out of conversation, friendship. The constellation could not have been more fortunate, since both the Gersdorffs were authors. Bernd, who was an engineer by profession, had an important position in an industrial firm, and was also a professor at the Technical University in Brunswick, had shown that he was also a knowledgeable student of German history. He had used this knowledge to make films about, for example, the "Grossen Kurfürsten," the Great Elector, Friedrich

Wilhelm von Brandenburg (1620–1688), and about the old German imperial roads. Dagmar von Gersdorff, whose biography of the German writer Marie Luise Kaschnitz (1901–1974) underlined her knowledge of contemporary literature, has concentrated mainly on the literature of the nineteenth century, however, and her links with the literary and musical trends that Fischer-Dieskau has written about are obvious.

Fischer-Dieskau relates how they encouraged each other to write books. He, as well as his wife Julia Varady, can well appreciate how Dagmar von Gersdorff has managed to organize a house, almost a salon, one could say, that connects to the old Berlin tradition of Jewish literary salons in the nineteenth century run by women such as Henriette Herz (1764–1847) and Rahel Levin (1771–1833). This common bond cannot be underestimated.

Now as then, Berlin is the city where most of Fischer-Dieskau's literary and musical friends are to be found. Elmar Budde is one of them. After their work together on the new Schubert Edition, which was published in 1985, Budde continued to work with Fischer-Dieskau on the preparation of his other books, and also played four-handed piano pieces with him — even once in public. Among Berlin's musicologists, Fischer-Dieskau mentions Rudolf Stephan as the most "unprofessorial" professor that he knows. At the same time he is frequently amazed by his friend's profound knowledge of music and the history of music. Stephan was able to give, quite extemporarily, the entire history of the life and the music of the French composer Paul Dukas (1865–1935) when Fischer-Dieskau was about to give that composer a major role in his next book, *Fern die Klage des Fauns: Claude Debussy und seine Welt* (From Afar, the Plaint of the Faun: Claude Debussy and His World).

"From Afar, the Plaint of the Faun"

The title of Dietrich Fischer-Dieskau's next book, *Fern die Klage des Fauns* (La plainte, au loin, du faune), which was published in 1993, immediately evokes the name of the composer whose life, work, and circle of friends were its subject.[1] Once again, the author turned to a famous composer, but this time not for a monographical study. The technique employed for his book on Pauline Viardot-Garcia (*If Music Be the Food of Love*), a biographical study covering her times and her social milieu, is employed again here. As partner for the French composer Claude Debussy (1862–1918) (and for himself, as author), he found a very competent personality, a much-neglected figure in the history of music in Fischer-Dieskau's opinion, the composer Paul Dukas (1865–1935). In a manner that might almost be called "refined," Fischer-Dieskau gives, in effect, a double biography of the two composers, allowing half of it to be related by Dukas himself. This book proved how assured Fischer-Dieskau now was in the handling of his writing technique, that of a "narrated documentation." The musician-cum-author is still amazed by the subject of his research. He had written in a letter in February 1988:

> In the last few days, I have been so taken up with Debussy that I have not been able to think of anything else. [Just at that time, he had also recorded some Debussy *mélodies* with Hartmut Höll and had called the period his Abenteuertage (Days of Adventure).] This was a composer seduced by his intellect, whose friendship and feelings for Stravinsky I can only now really appreciate. How anyone can manage to compose music that is conceived absolutely to the last surges of emotion, and also with the most subtle touch, this is indeed the mystery of the complete artist.
>
> The interpreter who wants to follow, and to help him, must do more than just keep his eyes and his mind open if he wants to do him justice.
>
> Then there is the French language, that idiom of restful loquacity, with poems by [Stéphane] Mallarmé, [Charles] Baudelaire, or [Paul] Verlaine—one's hair really stands on end when one senses that feeling of responsibility.

Nothing had changed when he was planning his book two years later; when the time for writing it arrived, version after version of the manuscript appeared before that "feeling of responsibility" was at least halfway assuaged—and his hair could be smoothed down again!

Despite the authorial technique of the double biography, Debussy and his music remain the subjects of the book, which also sketches the epoch in which music was most intimately entwined with painting and poetry, the period of French Impressionism at the end of the nineteenth century. What a theme for a Lieder singer who was also a painter! Fischer-Dieskau is able to show where the two arts blend, and where each goes its own way. But artists of that period did not all write about, or compose, or paint in terms of states of mind, as Fischer-Dieskau writes of Debussy:

> Behind Debussy's music, there are no impressions of nature, rather states of mind. He expresses not so much pictures as memories and emotions, reduced in the hope of attaining the essentials by means of extreme simplification.
>
> Debussy's physical realms are the wind, the clouds, the flowing air, the endless stretches of ocean and the sea as the stage for music that unfolds almost scenically. [He has] an artistic technique like [Wassily] Kandinsky's: theatrical, but without characters or plot, far removed from the naiads and sirens of Art Deco, no arabesques from mermaids, no woman as the danger and the threat of ruination—rather, colors and sounds that give satisfaction in themselves.[2]

Fischer-Dieskau rejects energetically the labeling of Debussy as "the eternal Impressionist." By so doing, he shows the composer to have been in a constant state of motion, the most drastic expression of which was his breaking-away from Richard Wagner or, at least, from "Wagnerism"—what Debussy called "that corpse."

Symbolism is the key word for Debussy's music:

> Is symbolism not just the victory of sensitivity in art? Does it not concern itself exclusively with the concrete and nervous reactions that things, and people, release in us? To retain such subjectivity, poetry, for example, had to free itself from the strict bonds of syntax in which it isolated each word from the mass of images. Painting had abandoned its subservience to line and portraiture in order to study the subtlest refractions of light. But as long as conventional associations had to help to create the effect, painters did not seem to have reached their ideal goal. Thus, it was the task of music, with its absolute subjectivity and immense power of suggestibility, to realize the dream of the Symbolists. It was Debussy who took music furthest along this path.[3]

Theories of art were part of the cultural mores of that age. The examples given show how consciously Fischer-Dieskau immersed himself in the thinking of the period to be able to illuminate it so well from within. Music theory, the classification and association of the various art forms, is one thing—the personal relationships, the prejudices, and the pronouncements of the main players, another. It is these that Fischer-Dieskau has examined, considerately but also determinedly. Here, too, he succeeds in dispelling clichés by presenting Debussy, Dukas, and the others against the background of their times, thus making them comprehensible to himself and therefore to his readers—a process in which the tension hardly slackens over the book's 494 pages. The very last illustration (on page 471) shows a bust of Debussy by the hand of Dietrich Fischer-Dieskau.

The Painter

Pauline, 1989 (dispersion/gouache/110 x 80 cm).

"A Resounding Play of Colors"

The relationship between music and color has often been examined and has been found to be a subjective one; when a musician paints, the connection becomes more obvious.

Goethe's poem "Wiederfinden" (Reunited) about the creation of the world, from the *Buch Suleika* (Book for Suleika) in his set of poems *West-östlicher Divan* (Poems from West and East) (1814 ff.), has a line about the "resounding play of colors"; it describes how the division between darkness and the light vanishes with the dawn, the symbol of love:

> It [the dawn] revealed to the gloomy man
> A resounding play of colors;
> And now we could love again
> After having drifted apart.

This "resounding play of colors" has possibly more to do with Goethe's old idea of the song of the planets (in his *Faust*) than with this immediate relationship of color and sound, as, for example, the composer Alexander Scriabin (1872–1915) postulated with his "mystic chord" (a series of ascending fourths), to which he gave precise values of colors and symbols. The theory that the world was born of musical concord and that Heaven then returned the basic melody to Earth, is as old as mankind. The ancients believed that music depended on the harmony between Heaven and Earth, on the accord between gloom and light. Herein lie the roots of the banishing of the division through this "resounding play of colors" that Goethe had in mind.

Fischer-Dieskau did not become a painter to translate music into colors. Nevertheless, it is quite certain that his paintings do have to do with the uniting of the two art forms.

For a painter, finding images means getting close to nature, to an object, or to a person. If all goes well, a relationship arises that overcomes that which separates. In a world based on a division of labor, which most certainly leads to a feeling of alienation, in a world where men are in danger of becoming strangers to themselves, the simple fact of being creative, of being able to shape something from one's own strengths and abilities, from immediate and independent contact with the natural world, makes clear sense.

In his memoirs, Fischer-Dieskau wrote:

> The age of reproduction has not yet managed to render invalid the
> originality of a work of art. There is a deep and lasting need within
> us to see ourselves in art, a sort of challenge, but also a confirmation
> that cannot be imitated or replaced by any other reality.[1]

This strong desire for self-expression, which must always be seen as an integral part of Fischer-Dieskau's personality if one wishes to comprehend the
range of his activities, is always seeking new outlets.

Yet one could ask: Has not his undeniably creative art of interpretation
already united several art forms? For who else, if not Dietrich Fischer-
Dieskau, has made the music of a Schubert—to give but one, albeit the
supreme, example—his own? Was it not then, when he sang Schubert's
Lieder, that all divisions vanished?

Still, he would never ignore another art form in which he could express
what cried out for expression, especially as it had always held such an
attraction for him. He wrote once to a questioner:

> Painting fascinated me from early on. I was encouraged by the father
> of my first piano teacher, Friedrich Seyer, whose huge Botticelli
> copies looked down on me during my lessons, and he enticed me to
> imitate them.

The elderly painter's remark when he saw the sketch of a portrait made by
the young man, "You could become a painter," stuck in his memory.

The immediate translation of his own ideas into symbolical form proved
at last to be irresistible. The decision came after visiting an exhibition of
works by Paul Klee, the Swiss painter (1879–1940), in Berlin in 1960. The
"play of colors" there exercised an enormous spell on him. Just as he tells
young singers that the most important lesson is to "learn by listening," so he
too began to "learn by looking." It seems remarkable that Fischer-Dieskau,
whenever he writes or speaks about painting, tries, like every outside observer,
to build first of all a bridge between his profession as a singer and that
of a painter.

In the catalog to one exhibition of his works, *Bilder aus drei Jahrzehnten*
(Pictures from Three Decades), held in 1985, he tells us that he began with
portraits:

> a genre that, since the all-persuasive influence of photography on
> our way of seeing things, has unfortunately lost its importance. But
> since my way of singing Lieder is also concentrated on the art of
> "portrayal," it seemed only right to make this the main platform
> of my second "profession." I longed to express that unconscious
> emotion within me in a figurative way.[2]

How else could we understand (that is, "portray") him? As always, as banishing divisions.

This determination to "learn by looking," and its subsequent realization, can be easily seen in his portraits. Elmar Budde, a music historian with an art background, said in an interview:

> Seen from a technical point of view, his portraits are distinguished by a very precise awareness of line, so that they retain the action of movement and gestures, just as if they were frozen movement. . . . This propensity for line has perhaps really got something to do with music.

Again, the connection between painter and singer.

Fischer-Dieskau has never ceased painting portraits, always using different techniques. A few have become very well known and can be found reproduced in books on art, often because of the fame of the sitter: Richard Löwenthal (1961), Sviatoslav Richter (1982) (according to his youngest son Manuel, one of the best), Alfred Brendel (1983), and, again and again, his wife Julia Varady. There are also a few self-portraits (from 1985, for example), and these were done, not from postcards but from looking at himself in the mirror. (As Elmar Budde remarked about one of them: "It's the wrong way round!")

The Lear portrait of 1979, painted the year after the premiere of the Aribert Reimann opera, is not a portrait of the role. Hans Neubauer, in the introduction to that 1985 catalog wrote:

> Here, he has continued to examine his relationship with the figure of the aging king. Lear is just outlined, touched up in white, in a portrait dominated by blue tones. The two violent red patches are not meant to represent naturalistically created wounds, but rather the fatally wounded soul of the broken old man. Isolated eyes surround the tear-blinded king—and one must remember what he said to the blinded Gloucester: "If thou wilt weep my fortunes, take my eyes" (Act IV, Scene 6).

The Lear portrait (another appeared at the 1995 exhibition in Feldkirch in Austria) belongs to the few works that tempt an immediate exegesis. With most, the secret is more deeply hidden; with others, it is the play of colors and form that is the principal attraction. "I love color and I am its servant," wrote the painter in his introduction, "for it can best make the inner world outwardly visible."

There were not only portraits. Fischer-Dieskau also treated objects in nature. Many sketches were made out in the open. Chalk, pencil, and water-colors (including a miniature watercolor kit) help him to make his "notes," as he calls them, and they change on the canvas, under the paint (or rather, under the paints). When he was asked once what was his favorite color, he replied: "Since I've been painting, and that's thirty years now, I have no longer one favorite color—they all work together, each has its own special place."

The type of paints used is also important: acrylic, oil, tempera, India ink, dispersion. It is a regular battle with these various media—the slipperiness of oils, the quickly drying colors of dispersion, the fading of the watercolors.

The art historian and exhibition organizer Werner Spies spoke at an exhibition arranged for Fischer-Dieskau's sixtieth birthday at the Bavarian Academy of Fine Arts in Munich in 1985. His speech was later published:

> These are largely expressive works in which a shy, introverted force is trying to find its way. Woods with no egress, internal forests that make one think of the psychic and physical labyrinth in which Golaud has become trapped at the beginning of [Debussy's] *Pelléas et Mélisande*, "Je ne pourrai plus sortir de cette forêt" (I cannot get out of this forest), he cries.

Indeed, pictures of forests are a recurring motif. In these we find once again the stark line drawing of the portraits with an emphasis on the wood of the trees; but there are also airy forests where light and shade show the trees in relief. In a few pictures and particularly in the sketches with only a suggestion of color or form or line, one only sees the pictorial motif after long and careful observation. Often, a person suddenly appears from out of the dense background. In some pictures, it is expressly named as *Der Einzelgänger* (The Lone Wolf). In others, this solitary figure seems to appear hesitatingly from the labyrinth of his night. Frequently, just the sight of *Nature* wakes the painter's own world of experience.

And his forerunners? Fischer-Dieskau has not based his technique on any one past figure, but as one who has lived his entire life with and among paintings, he knows them all, yet will not deny that his preference is for the moderns. He tries to find a fresh concept for each picture, not just the same "handwriting," as it were, for each one, but rather his own rationale for each individual picture. He says, however, that among the artists of the past, the French school is nearest to his heart (and that for a very secret reason). He always likes to mention a forerunner of the Surrealists and Symbolists, Gustave Moreau (1826–1898), particularly his "spontaneous" works with which he experimented, trying out the various effects of color and form. These experiments inspired Fischer-Dieskau, and whenever he was due to sing in the famous Salle Pleyel in Paris, he always found time for a visit to the tiny Musée Moreau.

Schneise (Forest path), 1993 (Chalk, 21 x 28 cm).

Incidental byproducts, such as Victor Hugo's pictures of tobacco or cigarette ash or coffee grounds, fascinated him too, for his curiosity about such metamorphoses has never left him.

He is always interested in transitional stages. The Parisian artists demonstrate that, one day, the heavy Romanticism of Jean Auguste Dominique Ingres (1780–1867) or Eugène Delacroix (1798–1863) had to be overthrown, just as Claude Debussy got rid of Wagner and raised music to a high degree of abstraction without sacrificing its content.

Fischer-Dieskau wants his pictures to be artistic and sensuous, with a degree of abstraction that will vary according to the subject, the thought behind it, and the experiment with the form. But he is also continually aware of what has already been done by other artists, and the question of whether everything has not been said already—which he has never ceased to ask of music, too—hangs over him in his studio as well.

He feels, however, that we must be watchful that we do not just accept the way others see objects; all his pictures underline this. Nor can he be a friend of what is called in German "Installationen" (mounting). He sees in the artistic "over-paintings" of an Arnulf Rainer, for example, painting that is far removed from its dialogue with reality. He knows full well that such an art form is also a reaction to the over-weighty past, which he himself always feels on his back; yet he approaches every new artwork in the hope that it will be his own, something that will be, in the last analysis, quite distinctive.

Fischer-Dieskau's motto is "Keep Working." "I actually do some painting every day," he says. Each time, he is putting together a piece of the world and a piece of himself, and so he is banishing solitude. Over thirty years he has painted hundreds of pictures. A 1986 collage of colors, forms, and figures evokes the labyrinth; the title is *Wohin?* (Where to?). In his paintings, the way is once again the goal. The composer Siegfried Matthus wrote to him in 1981:

> I often think of the conversation with you about the stylistic change in your pictures that I noticed in the Bamberg exhibition. In my opera *Judith*, something similar happened, quite different from my earlier work. I have re-discovered rhythm that relates to meter, harmonic connections fascinate me, lapidary forms are the result of complicated considerations of structure—all things that were different in my earlier music. Looking at your pictures makes me hope that the changes I have made in my *Judith* score are going in the right direction.[3]

This parallel between music and painting is remarkable, because this is in no way a symbiosis of the arts of music and painting, but rather it is a case of an independent development following the initial insight. "Re-discovery" is what it is all about: "lapidary forms arise from complicated considerations of structure." Paintings develop from the other, so familiar, art form.

Only a catalog of his works could demonstrate the paths that Fischer-Dieskau has taken as a painter. It would probably just show that the paths, different though they seem, run not away from but into one another, to unite what had been separated.

Now and then, Fischer-Dieskau has company in his studio in his house above Lake Starnberg, south of Munich. Ulrike ("Uschi") Fischer-Fabian and her husband, Dr. Siegfried Fischer-Fabian, are almost immediate neighbors and friends of the Fischer-Dieskaus. She often works in the same studio at her own paintings. Even when the subjects of their paintings are completely different, the similarity of their work brings a feeling of mutual creativity.

A friendly sociability unites both couples. Dr. Fischer-Fabian once described it humorously:

The number eight is his ideal number for a dinner party; everyone can have his say without usurping that of others. Conversation, that long-forgotten art of talking to one another, has, we know, been degraded to "party talk" or "name dropping," but Fischer-Dieskau still holds conversations, and I have long since accustomed myself to the fact that he doesn't really care about what he is eating, or worse still, what he is drinking. It is all, alas, the same to him!

The Conductor

"There Are
Two Sorts of Blessings in Breathing"

Josef Krips, the conductor of many famous orchestras and still known today for his fine recordings of Mozart, told his "distinguished colleague" a year before Fischer-Dieskau's first conducting engagement: "A conductor who knows that the main thing about conducting is breathing, is destined to be a conductor."

Breathing to music, or rather, making music breathe, had been Fischer-Dieskau's daily bread and butter, after all. To look a little ahead, the reaction of the orchestras that he conducted was similar. "He's made me play the second theme exactly as he might have sung it."[1] A British eye- (and ear-) witness and at the same time the initiator of Fischer-Dieskau's first recording as a conductor, Suvi Raj Grubb, heard the same thing from Daniel Barenboim: "The son of a gun, he makes them play exactly as he sings." How this phase in Fischer-Dieskau's career came about is related in the book by Mr. Grubb. Grubb had been in Berlin in 1972 to record Brahms's Lieder with Fischer-Dieskau.

> I had seen in Fischer-Dieskau's study books on orchestration, on the horn and other instruments, on the history of the orchestra, and the gradual evolution of the modern conductor. Barenboim and I had teased him, asking him was he considering a new career as a horn player or a bassoonist, or perhaps as both! Fischer-Dieskau took this in good part, explaining that his voice was still in fine shape, but the time would surely come when he would have to give up singing. It was unthinkable that he should give up music-making altogether. He was too old to seriously take up the piano, the only completely self-sufficient instrument. The field which seemed to offer the widest possibilities was conducting.[2]

Fischer-Dieskau was then forty-seven; he was famed both as a Lieder and as an operatic singer, and was due to make a tour of the United States in 1972, which eventually became a triumph. The Edinburgh, Salzburg, and Munich Festivals earned him unqualified adulation—and yet, the singer's fear of losing his voice never left him. To repeat, however: Who could have guessed then that the time for retirement was really so far off?[3]

Certainly, another factor came into consideration: that old spur behind all his artistic achievements, his inexhaustible desire to express himself. It would be too negative to say that singing was no longer enough for him—that, one can say with almost complete certainty, was not the case. Mixed with his concern about what would happen after he had stopped singing was his curiosity about whether he could succeed (albeit in a very different field) in still "reigning in the empire of music," as Robert Schumann had described his own will to perform, a formulation that Fischer-Dieskau incidentally would never have chosen, preferring a rather more modest way of putting things.

Yet he is absolutely convinced that he must get as close as possible to the heart of a work in order to communicate to others his own view and emotions, and that means making composition and interpretation one and the same thing. The notion of uniting differences as the meaning of interpretation is realized, above all, in conducting. In the lines from Goethe's proverb-like poems titled "Talismane" (Talismans) in the collection *West-östlicher Divan*, the poet uses the example of breathing and makes this clear:

> *There are two sorts of blessings in breathing:*
> *Breathing in and breathing out,*
> *The first is a worry, the second a relief;*
> *Thus life is a mixed blessing.*
> *So, thank God when He presses you,*
> *And thank Him again when he releases you.*

The singer of the *Divan* talks of a "connection," which he illustrates by the image of breathing, a connection between man and the world.

> He connects it with the image of the *systole*, that is, a contraction (into the ego), and *diastole*, that is, an extension (into the world), as the basic concept of life (Erich Trunz).[4]

For the practicing artist, bringing the ego and the world together remains a constant challenge.

Thus, when the serious invitation from London arrived to take over Otto Klemperer's engagement because he was gravely ill, Fischer-Dieskau was not unprepared. Nevertheless, he went off to see an experienced practitioner, one Harold Byrns, who, according to Fischer-Dieskau's memoirs, had left Germany as Hans Bernstein and returned later, becoming one of Klemperer's successors at the Komische Oper in Berlin (when there was still an East Berlin). "The veteran of a post-Schoenberg group in Los Angeles was extremely kind to me and, later, to my son Martin."[5] (To digress for a moment, here we have another "succession" situation—father and son both conducting at the same time, a variant of that old "father-son-problem" that has occupied the psychologists and scholars of German literature so much.)

Fischer-Dieskau was not to take over Klemperer's planned production of Mozart's *Entführung* (The Abduction from the Serail), but, at Suvi Raj Grubb's request, an orchestral concert on one of the dates set aside for the recording of the opera.

Improvisation has been, and always will be, needed in the hard commercial world of recording. At any rate Grubb phoned Fischer-Dieskau in Berlin:

> Without stopping to weigh the pros and cons, I phoned him in Berlin and asked what he felt about the possibility of making his debut on record as a conductor in two months' time. There was a slight pause, and he asked what works might I have in mind. I had not given the matter any thought—in fact, between the arrival of the idea and my talking to him, less than ten minutes had passed—but replied instantly "Schubert—five and eight." There was a longer pause this time before he said: "Eight? Suvi, all the great conductors have recorded the work and everyone else as well. Do you really think . . . ?" I cut in: "Dieter, some day you are going to have to conduct a popular work such as the 'Unfinished,' I believe in jumping in at the deep end. Think about it and ring me back in a day or two."[6]

So, once again, Fischer-Dieskau had to be persuaded to do something new, but something that he really wanted to do. Here, too, there were to be no provincial trial runs, and here, too, he showed that experienced ability to comprehend a score at first go. This ability stood him in just as good stead for an orchestral score as it had for a Lied. Aribert Reimann described once in an interview how Fischer-Dieskau could bypass the first learning process of a new Lied if he wanted to, when presented with a new score. An orchestral score, however, with its many parts, and despite Fischer-Dieskau's ability to "comprehend" it quickly, needed a more intensive study. The singer explained:

> I have to have it all in my head before I can even think of the first rehearsal. That means that, even if the score is on the desk, the conductor must really know it by heart. The score can serve as a momentary *aide-mémoire*, but, in a rehearsal, it's there, above all, to communicate with the orchestra about tempo indications and rehearsal numbers or letters. The conductor's attention must be on the orchestra all the time, he must be hearing all the parts and must

make the musicians, who are, of course, ready to play, be prepared to listen. If you can't hear the others, you're playing too loudly.

The answer to the question about "inspirations" is not the same for the conductor as it might be for the singer or the painter. There are many on whom one can model oneself, as there should be, for one can learn from them all. Details can be learned that a newcomer can try out without damaging his own individual conductor's "language." Conducting is very much a matter of technique. Looking back on his early life in Berlin, Fischer-Dieskau described very graphically how, even as a schoolboy, he used to observe the conductors by facing them:

> I slipped into a choir in the old Academy for Vocal Music, whose members were all strangers to me. To the horror of the conductor, Georg Schumann, who had seen me right away, I sang in the *St. Matthew Passion* of Bach because I couldn't get a ticket for the concert. How different was the atmosphere in the old Philharmonie, a former roller-skating rink transformed in 1890 into a concert hall! To sit under the great organ behind the orchestra helped me to discover the works, the tricks of the orchestra and the personalities of the conductors. One of them, Hans Knappertsbusch, would only give the first beat to a symphonic poem, and then, for pages of the score, let the orchestra go on as it pleased. Another conductor, Wilhelm Furtwängler, could draw even those not playing into his magic power, irresistibly, from the very first note. We could look right into the faces of Willem Mengelberg and Oswald Kabasta as they conducted.[7]

With how many conductors did Fischer-Dieskau do that later? He soon learned which one would offer support to a singer or the orchestra, which one was a dedicated rehearser, and which one could move an audience during the performance.

Wilhelm Furtwängler made the greatest impression on the singer. He wrote in 1986 that in the course of the four and a half years that they had worked together, he had gradually realized

> the source from which he perceived the world around him; the great "breath" of the performance of a work. His devotion to this "symphonic" breath led him to a very subjective form of expression, but then [then the singer thought of the new school of conductors] the law of action and re-action came into play and a period of basic conducting, with the side of the hand only, which we are now— thankfully—beginning to get over.

Fischer-Dieskau goes so far as to say about Furtwängler that he was "almost a hostage to his breathing," which was probably due to some trouble in his respiratory system, which Furtwängler (like Fischer-Dieskau himself) had to fight against all his life. More importantly, however:

> He simply could not abide music in which at least the thought of breathing did not play the predominant role. That is why he rejected so much "heavy-handed" modern music—he found it difficult to breathe.[8]

A strange remark to make, but one that should make us think about the reception of at least some contemporary music. Fischer-Dieskau always points out, however, the paucity of opportunities to perform this music. As we have already seen, he himself is always prepared to perform music of our own times. Otherwise, the whole music tradition would die out.

When Fischer-Dieskau is asked from which conductor he has learned most, the first name to come to mind is that of the Austrian, Herbert von Karajan, Furtwängler's heir, at least as conductor of the Berlin Philharmonic. Not the closed eyes, not the truly inimitable beat, but something more basic, his whole manner—he is at ease with himself—"and he always had space under his arms," adds Fischer-Dieskau. "It doesn't matter what you do up there, on the podium, whether it's much or little," said Sir Georg Solti, a man of many gesticulations, "the important thing is how many of your ideas you can get across to your musicians." "But perhaps Richard Strauss was right, after all, when he said that a conductor's left hand should really stay in his trouser pocket," added Fischer-Dieskau (not entirely seriously, although he, too, prefers sparing gestures from conductors).

His own technique did not gain him much respect on his first conducting engagement, with the New Philharmonia Orchestra of London. Suvi Raj Grubb found it "just about adequate," but, "the orchestra sensed that he had a clear conception of (Schubert's) 'Unfinished' Symphony and he was able to transmit it to every member of the orchestra." That was really the important factor.

Whether an orchestra accepts a conductor or not seemed to Grubb to be the essential prerequisite for the success of an artistic enterprise. Fischer-Dieskau was clearly accepted right away. Grubb wrote about that first recording in 1973: "Within a quarter of an hour, I realized just what it meant to have an orchestra on the side of the conductor."[9]

Fischer-Dieskau's first public engagement as a conductor had a sad background. Two years after the death of Bernhard Paumgartner, his orchestra, the Camerata Academica of Salzburg, was still without a regular conductor. The concert in Innsbruck's Stadtsaal (town hall), a little distant from the main center of music-making, was a happy affair, however, as the reviewer in the *Süddeutsche Zeitung* described it on 18 October 1973. Once again, this was their music critic Karl Schumann, the reviewer of so many Lieder recitals by Dietrich Fischer-Dieskau. There was certainly none of the "high priest" about Fischer-Dieskau at the beginning,

> as there usually is at his Lieder recitals (though that is none of Fischer-Dieskau's doing). The baton is one of many opportunities for him to prove himself to be the arch-musician, a way out of the curse of specialization.

That was the first impression. Fischer-Dieskau had burdened himself with an audacious program: "Four times Haydn." But, of course, a Haydn interpretation is even nowadays the touchstone of musicality, since Haydn's work is still dogged by as many false historical traditions as Schubert's once was.

> The evening began with the "Drum Roll" Symphony (No. 103 in E-flat). The debutant did not seem as nervous as the Camerata Academica of Salzburg, who experienced some difficulty with Fischer-Dieskau's fast, dramatic allegri, the well-prepared entries, and the dynamic modulations. This was a Haydn of stormy development sections, sharp contrasts, and full, vibrating tone—quite a contrast to the local custom, whose Haydn is usually cossetted, half like a child, half like an old man.

The concert was repeated in Salzburg's Mozarteum. On this occasion, the Cello Concerto was flanked by two symphonies, and on the next day, it was recorded. The CD has Wolfgang Boettcher, formerly solo cellist with the Berlin Philharmonic, as soloist, and also includes Haydn's Symphony No. 104 in D (The "London"). The recording confirms Karl Schumann's impressions of the Innsbruck concert—the full, vibrant tone, the professional shaping of Haydn's symphonic style, the dramatic unfolding, without the clear lines of the development sections being over-larded with a false sentimentality. One could perhaps think that Fischer-Dieskau was following George Szell's mannerisms, with those great dramatic gestures. In contrast to their first concert together, the Camerata musicians, teachers, and students at Salzburg's Mozarteum had obviously listened carefully to the conductor's very unconventional view of Haydn.

In the same month, October 1973, came concerts with the Scottish National Orchestra in Edinburgh and Glasgow. Professor Kenneth Whitton, Dietrich Fischer-Dieskau's first biographer, had "mixed feelings":

> Having watched Fischer-Dieskau, full-face, as it were, for twenty-five years, it was a shock to see his back only and not to hear

The conductor Dietrich Fischer-Dieskau during a guest appearance with the Israel Philharmonic Orchestra in 1974.

his voice. He seemed to start very fussily, leaping from side to side of the rostrum, pointing here and there, but, as in Innsbruck, he settled down as the nervousness left him, and gave an easy and professional-looking performance.[10]

The word "easy" was used by critics in the first years of Fischer-Dieskau's conducting career. There was no question here of "carelessness" or a disregard for the work being conducted, but it had to do rather with the ease and professionalism of the born musician. In November 1973, Fischer-Dieskau conducted Schumann's Piano Concerto with the English Chamber Orchestra, and Daniel Barenboim as soloist. Both artists then recorded the work with the London Philharmonic Orchestra in June 1974 for Elektra. Fischer-Dieskau wrote in *Nachklang*:

What then followed, four years of conducting engagements along with all my singing engagements, contained all the joys and torments of a new career as a conductor.[11]

(Much later, he was to confide in a friend that conducting had also given him pains in his shoulder!)

These engagements came with a rush at the beginning; Zubin Mehta offered the newcomer the chance to conduct both the Los Angeles

Philharmonic and his own Israel Philharmonic; Fischer-Dieskau conducted the latter in Israel from 20–26 February 1974. Alfred Brendel was the soloist in Mozart's C Major Piano Concerto (K503). This concerto was once the last piece of the very successful, ever-increasing group of works composed for Mozart's Concert Academy in Vienna. It holds the balance between symphonic demands and soloistic brilliance—which means hard work for both conductor and orchestra. Fischer-Dieskau had taken over in a concert series that the American conductor Lukas Foss had abandoned after three concerts. As a result, there was only time for a short, introductory rehearsal with the orchestra and a conversation by the piano with Brendel. After the last concert, Brendel said to Fischer-Dieskau: "I played that concerto today just as you would have wanted it." That is what is called "cooperation." The program of the Israeli tour also included Schubert's Fifth (which he had already conducted in London) and Schumann's Third Symphony ("The Rhenish"), of which there is a 1975 BASF recording with the Bamberg Symphony Orchestra.

It need hardly be added that Fischer-Dieskau had spent many hours in preparation for these programs, which he himself had chosen, before he began work with the orchestras. Peter Gradenwitz reported from Tel Aviv:

> He [Fischer-Dieskau] found Schumann's "Rhenish," even in Mahler's proposed retouched instrumentation, still too swollen and opaque; as one with an intimate knowledge of the Schumann "sound," he retouched a few places himself, and marked all the parts for the orchestra before the performance.[12]

Then he conducted the Schumann Piano Concerto again in Los Angeles in March 1974, with Horace Gutierrez as soloist. (Bernard Soll, writing in the Los Angeles *Herald Examiner* on 6 April had found "the celebrated baritone . . . a visually distracting, aurally disappointing tyro conductor." *Trans.*)

In 1975, a tour with the Bamberg Orchestra ended with a performance of Schumann's Second Symphony. Fischer-Dieskau also stepped in for an indisposed Rafael Kubelik on 4 May 1976 and conducted the same symphony with the orchestra of Bavarian Radio. He had already appeared with Kubelik in a concert performance of Hindemith's *Mathis der Maler*. A reviewer saw in the program that Fischer-Dieskau had chosen Schumann's Second and Berlioz's *Harold in Italy*:

> The conductor's forte is exactly that of the singer: high Romanticism, where form and expression become problematical, where there is an inner struggle and a view of new continents.

Then, instead of the "problematical," or rather, instead of the impression that something is being made into a problem, the critic Karl Schumann began to use that word "easy" already mentioned. The conductor was praised for his "firm position on the rostrum, his minimal beat, sparse movements, no grimaces or emotional gymnastics."

"Typical emotions" were taken to be the basis of Fischer-Dieskau's musicianship; his interpretation of Schumann's Second Symphony was marked as "cantabile," "gentle," "flowing and free of coarse rubato." And finally:

> A fine piece of legato music-making, the central feature of which was the eloquently-sung Adagio movement that sums up the theme of the score: the development of a whole world from a minimum of motifs. The basic theme percolates like a fine gas through the four movements, becomes thicker, then pales, takes on a different shape, and then drives on to a lyrical but never too noisy coda.

The fissured scenery of Berlioz's *Harold in Italy* was not pictured in such "an exaggerated and heated manner as it usually is," but rather, "the conductor replaced those extreme theatricalities with a careful analysis and

The conductor Dietrich Fischer-Dieskau during a concert with the Camerata Academica Salzburg at the Schubertiade in Feldkirch, Austria, in 1994.

a fine polishing of a compact sound that is never coarse."[13] That had been exactly the conductor's intention.

Harold Byrns, his old friend and helpmate and a relative by marriage, was one of the first to learn of Fischer-Dieskau's intention to give up conducting, in a letter in September 1976:

> Dear Hans,
> A sad bit of news for you today. I'll have to give up my conducting—at least temporarily. It is difficult to give up such a great love. It's good for Martin, however, not to have a rival of the same name. But every minute of our work together, every second of that questioning immersion into the secrets of a score, will remain precious to me. And, above all, the few moments of absolute joy when the collaboration with the orchestra really worked.

More than twenty years have passed since then. Fischer-Dieskau ended his career as a singer without any great fuss, and without making too much of it. He has begun to conduct again, probably because he cannot stop making music, speaking, or singing—and perhaps also because of those "moments of absolute joy" with an orchestra.

This is not going to be a new career, but we heard the "song with baton and orchestra" again in 1994 in Schwetzingen, with Schoenberg and Mahler, and at the Feldkirch Schubertiade in Austria with Beethoven and Schubert. Indeed, in Feldkirch in 1995, he conducted a performance of Schubert's *Lazarus* with soloists from among his own students as part of the celebrations for his seventieth birthday—and, of course, it had all begun there.

What was it that he used to say to his accompanist Hartmut Höll before going onto the platform? "Gute Reise!" (Have a good journey!)

The Teacher

"Dear Friend, All Theory Is Gray!"

Dear friend, all theory is gray,
But the golden tree of Life is green.
(Mephistopheles to the student in Goethe's *Faust*)

There seems to be nothing more difficult than handing on experience. That is true for everybody—especially so for a singer. After all, what makes a great singer? Aribert Reimann, asked once about the art of Dietrich Fischer-Dieskau, said, "It was what cannot be learned."[1]

Talent is the prerequisite of all artistic activity, but for a singer, there is a physical factor, too. "You must have been given the voice," wrote Fischer-Dieskau to a young singer, "and a constitution that gives you the feeling that it can be handled flexibly."

He had experienced that himself: as a child, first the discovery of the voice, how it could produce "the beautiful sound," then the beginning of the training that taught him how to treat this gift of nature. But everything was already there in the bud, the natural disposition of the voice, the unconstrained working of the larynx, greeted with such joy by his first teacher, Georg A. Walter. Yet he had to learn to control his instrument, the voice. The beginning of all learning was, once again, breathing. Manuel Garcia's theory of singing begins with just that practical instruction: "Everything begins with the breathing." Like his students today before they come to him, Fischer-Dieskau had learned the technique of singing, rather briefly, as we know. Then in the war and in the POW camps, he had entered on a practical course of "singing engagements" whose dangers—in the absence of a teacher—he had avoided by sheer instinct. In 1947, after he had returned to Berlin, he "took up his studies again at the Academy of Music," as the phrase went, and then, in no time at all was singing Schubert's *Winterreise* in an RIAS broadcast, and in such a way that the listeners could not believe their ears. True, he continued to study now and then with Professor Hermann Weissenborn, who, however, really only exercised a control function over the voice—important enough for any singer, since he hears himself differently from his listeners. Anecdotes from the history of music are legion whereby a teacher recognizes genius in a pupil, lays his hands in his lap and says, "I can't teach him any more." A singer can always use somebody else's ear, and most students of singing need more teaching than those very few with great talent. As a teacher, Fischer-Dieskau regularly remarks how really necessary it is to awaken a student's curiosity to look at what is in the notes and the words.

Fischer-Dieskau—who had been painting for some time, had written books, and conducted orchestras—made the decision to take up teaching as well quite late in life. There had been requests to do so, even many years before, just after he had been released from his POW camp in Italy in 1947 and a "secure" job as lecturer for Lieder in Freiburg was offered him—really something in those days. The Academy in Berlin, too, had to wait a long time for his acceptance of its offer. He wrote in *Nachklang*:

> All the time he was Rector of the Academy, [Boris] Blacher kept asking me in his chatty manner, with his slight Russian accent: "Don't you want to teach here with us?" But I was more put off by what he always added to his question: "You'll only have to look in for a minute or two now and then. An assistant will do the rest."
>
> He saw teaching from his own perspective—as a composer— and perhaps could not appreciate how much time singers need before they feel secure and in harmony with their teachers' idiosyncrasies. The real work can only begin after they have found their feet in this way.[2]

To feel responsible is one of those virtues that other Germans used to term "Prussian," and Fischer-Dieskau certainly has his good share of those. Yet whatever held him back from taking it on was probably not a question of whether or not he would be able to pass on his experience—that came later, when it came down to practical work—or even whether he felt up to the job of teaching. Above all else, he wanted to sing, and did not want to take on yet another responsibility in addition to those he had already willingly accepted —and, more, one with such an uncertain future and such unpredictable chances of success. And yet, just as he had concerned himself with contemporary music because it was the only way for him to ensure the continuation of the performing arts, so too he became more and more concerned about the next generation of singers—and not only the singers. He wrote about his first teaching courses:

> At first, I only had the so-called "repertoire-pianists" as accompanists. As the years went by, I managed to persuade the lecturers in piano to send their best students into my courses, so that I had as many learners as possible with me.[3]

In this way, he was able to bring the two performers who make Lieder together and could give each the same amount of attention: "You have to breathe together!" he would call out in the middle of a phrase. The accompanist must see the singer breathe. And again and again he would look over the pianist's shoulder at the score: "Is that really there? . . . Yes, I thought . . . But he [the composer] hasn't done anything there!"

This is typical of a Fischer-Dieskau lesson. There is a continual reference to the score and, from that, the search for an individual response. Yet the reference to the score is not just to the music, "so that no note is missed," one can hear him add. He explains the scene behind the line of poetry; if necessary, he explains the psychic state of the character who is speaking, the emotion from which not only the work, but also the expression, must come: "Surprise—not fear!" and, again and again: "Sing with understanding!—You don't want to become a singer!—Become the person who is speaking!"

Hints about phonetics are mixed with interpretative ones—correction of vocal coloration with tips from his long experience of singing in public: "Look for a fixed point at the very back of the hall.—Find the idea of distance ('Weite') in the sound of 'ai.'—The 'e' of 'längst' expresses the whole idea of time.—Don't spell out.—Please: all the consonants, all of them.—Open your lips wide.—Movements that help the sound.—Rubato to the middle of the measure, then back."

Fischer-Dieskau himself is in a state of high tension all the time, and he tries to get the learners to feel the same, and he often succeeds: "You cannot really express that anatomically," he says now and then, and when an explanation of something to do with vocal expression is required, he always manages to find a complementary gesture: "Wear your tone like a crown," he says, and shapes it at the same time with his hand. He grasps the singer by the arm and sings along with him either silently or aloud. He sings only odd phrases, however, never insisting that the student should copy him. This was how he demonstrated his art at a one-week master class in the Bavarian Academy of Fine Arts in 1993 at which, incidentally, only Lieder by Hans Pfitzner were discussed.

Fischer-Dieskau has never really worried about whether the example given by a teacher can work to the disadvantage of a student. In 1970, a good ten years before he began his teaching at the Academy in Berlin, he was asked that direct question by a young learner, and he gave him a direct answer: If he had been given a voice, then to imitate another voice at the beginning could do no harm, it would not end up as imitation,

> for your own nature will be striving to get away from the exemplar, and your own body and mind will be the catalysts that will assert themselves and will give your interpretation the stamp of your own personality.

Dietrich Fischer-Dieskau finished this "lecture" with a few comments on the notions of the ideal and individuality, which, so it seemed at the time, underlined his own beliefs as a teacher and his belief in the individuality of the artist. He wrote:

> Nothing has ever come from nothing, and an ideal that an artist strives responsibly to reach (something that seems to be despised these days) can only be a drawback to one's own development if one is lazy enough to be satisfied with a lack of independence. But a good teacher should never allow that to happen. There are no absolute interpretations, no characterizations set in stone. An interpretation can only be brought to life by an individual . . . . Interpretations change not only from decade to decade and epoch to epoch, but also from artist to artist. Since Schubert's death, over 150 singers have striven to give valid interpretations; they were only distinctive when they went their own way. And each one was faithful to the work according to—repeat—his own personality.

He tries to direct his students to adopt an absolutely personal attitude toward singing, characterization, and interpretation. During the master classes, which are sometimes held in public (an additional burden for the teacher, because the lesson itself then must become a performance), this "direction" can be quite clearly seen, and it is not long before a working climate is established (despite the public audience), mainly through the teacher's intense concentration, since he never fails to show quite clearly what he is after.

Just as in his recitals, he exudes something that can perhaps be called "high spirits," expressed in his whole attitude. His sense of humor, which comes over strongly when he is teaching, suits this attitude. His friendliness dispels any nervousness on the part of the student, although he never praises where there is nothing to praise. On the contrary, he is rather sparing with approval and prefers to push the student, to urge him on, to encourage him, and thus try to set free the student's individual talent. One needs to have hope, too, in order to become a good teacher, and hopes are fulfilled often in the most audible and beautiful manner from time to time, even if the daily grind of teaching can be as dull as any other daily grind. Fischer-Dieskau poured out his heart once to the pianist Detlev Jürges on 20 February 1988:

> The Sisyphus work of a teacher can often drive one to distraction, for only in a very few cases can one hope that the student will have a rewarding professional future [then comes the true Fischer-Dieskau, part and parcel of his ever-wakeful feeling of responsibility,

and his motto: Always look ahead], but you mustn't take away the inner strength and courage to go on working from all those others who will remain anonymous.

One of the basic tenets that Fischer-Dieskau tries to communicate to his students is this, put this way in another letter:

> I have always worked and practiced by singing *piano* — and every singer should do that. But, please, no falsetto — that is only allowable in some characterizations. It is the *messa di voce* that should be taken as the base, a *pianissimo* in all registers, which, by closing the vocal chords, will rest neatly on the breath-column, free from nasal or thoracic aids.[4]

Experienced words like these would seem to be transferable — but are they? In his book *Töne sprechen, Worte klingen*, Fischer-Dieskau laid down the essential basics of his method of teaching singing. The fusion of language and music is the central motif of his thesis:

> To shape a voice by clarifying, purifying, and freeing the consonants and vowels, comes very near to phonetics. From the changing relationship of the sounds to one another, the singer realizes where the advantages and disadvantages lie for the nature and quality of the sound.

In a chapter on language as part of the teaching of singing, he combines his own experiences as a singer with the basic premises of the fusion of words and music, and the interdependence of the two. At the same time, he believes that phrasing is absolutely dependent on the meaning of the text: "Just as sentences are pronounced in one breath and in one arching phrase, so too the text determines the phrasing in singing." Then, again, he writes about breathing:

> The breath should be expelled gently, quietly, freely. That can only happen if the larynx is not under pressure when trying to save the breath, for example. Even the slightest muscular tension can harm what is the "passive" rather than an "active" passage of carefully organized breathing. The breath should flow gradually, while singing, and while the body is in a comfortable and flexible position. In singing, breathing and technique are one. The beautiful, gentle flow of the breath produces the right sounds. On the other hand, the sound that is felt to be just right, heard first in the inner ear, and well produced, helps correct breathing.[5]

With the pianist and accompanist Hartmut Höll during a rehearsal of the four-handed accompaniment to Johannes Brahms's *Liebesliederwalzer* (Love-song Waltzes), which students of Fischer-Dieskau's master class sang at a Whitsun concert in Cologne in 1993.

Thoughts on singing and interpretation, not at all generalized but very relevant to practical singing habits on concert platform and stage, follow that: forty-five pages of condensed lectures on singing.

After twelve years of teaching, Fischer-Dieskau clearly loves this profession, despite all the drawbacks. He wrote, "Sometimes it makes me happy to have to formulate my thoughts."

He takes his best students to give concerts, and they prove to be worth hearing. Since he stopped singing in public, he accompanies them now and then at the piano; for example, with Hartmut Höll in the *Liebesliederwalzer mit Klavier zu vier Händen* (the four-handed piano accompaniment to Brahms's Love-song Waltzes).

And next? After a concert appearance as a pianist with Daniel Barenboim in Stuttgart in November 1993, a newspaper reported: "After singing, conducting, painting, writing, and teaching, Dietrich Fischer-Dieskau is now beginning his sixth career: as a pianist." That was not meant seriously, of course, and it was not accurate either. The report went on, more accurately this time:

> It was great fun to see how Fischer-Dieskau and Barenboim got their hands completely entangled for a while and, following Busoni's instructions with fiendish joy, demolished all the rules of art by making fun of the folksong O *du lieber Augustin*.[6]

Dietrich Fischer-Dieskau continues to make music, as a conductor and now and then as an accompanist to his students, along with another pianist when there is a four-handed piece. He also does readings with the actor Gert Westphal, of the correspondence between Goethe and Zelter, for example, or between Richard Strauss and Hugo von Hofmannsthal, or from the memoirs of Hector Berlioz, which are always a joy to hear. He continues to write and paint, led by the same desire to create that enabled him as a singer to plumb all the depths of human emotions, to illuminate all the heights of longing, and to mirror in his Lieder the most beauteous things that Earth has to offer.[7]

Notes

Background and Early Life

1. Refers to Antonio Salieri's (1750–1825) rarely heard opera *Prima la musica, poi le parole*, 1786. Fischer-Dieskau's sons, Mathias and Martin, produced it at Drottningholm in Sweden, July 1975. *Trans.*
2. Fischer-Dieskau, Dietrich. 1988. *Nachklang*. Stuttgart: Deutsche Verlags-Anstalt (DVA). 9. English trans. Ruth Hein, *Echoes of a Lifetime*. London: Macmillan. 1989. (All translations of material in this biography are K. S. Whitton's, however, and refer to the original works. *Trans.*)
3. *Beschreibung des Saalkreises von Dreyhaupt im 16. Jahrhundert* (Description of the Saale District by Dreyhaupt in the Sixteenth Century), with a genealogical table of the Dieskaus up to the eighteenth century. Halle. n.d.
4. Fischer-Dieskau, Dietrich. 1992. *Weil nicht alle Blütenträume reiften: Johann Friedrich Reichardt, Hofkapellmeister dreier Preussenkönige* (Because Not All My Blossoming Dreams Ripened: Johann Friedrich Reichardt, Court Music Master to Three Prussian Kings). Stuttgart: DVA.
5. All the following private quotations from Albert Fischer from the manuscript summary of the family history appear by permission of Dietrich Fischer-Dieskau.
6. This, and other newspaper reviews in the family history, have no source references.
7. Fischer, Albert. 1900. *Das alte Gymnasium und die neue Zeit. Gedanken über Vergangenheit, Gegenwart und Zukunft unseres höheren Schulwesens* (The Old Secondary School in the New Age: Thoughts on the Past, Present, and Future of Our Secondary Schools). Gross-Lichterfelde: Bruno Gebel.
8. Fischer-Dieskau, Dietrich. 1988. *Nachklang*. Stuttgart: DVA. 32.
9. Benn, Gottfried. 1930. "Das Genieproblem" (The Problem of Genius). In *Fazit der Perspektiven* (Facit of Perspectives). Berlin.
10. von Lewinski, Wolf-Eberhard. 1988. *Dietrich Fischer-Dieskau: Tatsachen, Meinungen, Interviews* (. . . Facts, Opinions, Interviews). Mainz / Munich: Piper-Schott.
11. In the Berlin district of Zehlendorf is still to be found a path, the "Fischer-Dieskau-Weg," with a signpost recalling the "founder of the secondary school." Dr. Fischer-Dieskau, his mother, and his two wives are all buried in one grave in the "Onkel Tom" cemetery in Zehlendorf. *Trans.*

The Voice of an Angel

1. Fischer-Dieskau, Dietrich. 1988. *Nachklang*. Stuttgart: DVA. 25.
2. Fischer-Dieskau, Dietrich. 1988. *Nachklang*. Stuttgart: DVA. 33.
3. Fischer-Dieskau, Dietrich. 1988. *Nachklang*. Stuttgart: DVA. 13.
4. Fischer-Dieskau, Dietrich. 1988. *Nachklang*. Stuttgart: DVA. 14.
5. Ernst Rittel was speaking during the broadcast from RIAS, Berlin, on 28 May 1985, on the occasion of Dietrich Fischer-Dieskau's sixtieth birthday.
6. Fischer-Dieskau, Dietrich. 1988. *Nachklang*. Stuttgart: DVA. 41.
7. Fischer-Dieskau, Dietrich. 1988. *Nachklang*. Stuttgart: DVA. 25.
8. Fischer-Dieskau, Dietrich. 1988. *Nachklang*. Stuttgart: DVA. 25.
9. Goethe, Johann Wolfgang von. 1811–1833. *Dichtung und Wahrheit* (Poetry and Truth), Book I.
10. Fischer-Dieskau, Dietrich. 1988. *Nachklang*. Stuttgart: DVA. 30f.
11. Fischer-Dieskau, Dietrich. 1988. *Nachklang*. Stuttgart: DVA. 39.
12. Fischer-Dieskau, Dietrich. 1988. *Nachklang*. Stuttgart: DVA. 36.
13. From a letter to Joachim Fischer-Dieskau dated 21 November 1971. [Jochen Klepper's (1903–1942) diaries describe the horrors of the Third Reich in Berlin where he lived and died with his Jewish wife. *Trans.*]
14. Fischer-Dieskau, Dietrich. 1988. *Nachklang*. Stuttgart: DVA. 19.
15. Manuel Garcia (1805–1906) invented the "laryngoscope," whereby singers could watch their vocal chords as they sang. He taught at the Royal Academy of Music in London from 1848 to 1895. *Trans.*
16. From a letter from Georg A. Walter to Frau Fischer-Dieskau dated 20 March 1950.

War, War Service, POW Camp, and His "Apprenticeship"

1. Fischer-Dieskau, Dietrich. 1988. *Nachklang*. Stuttgart: DVA. 35.
2. Fischer-Dieskau, Dietrich. 1988. *Nachklang*. Stuttgart: DVA. 51.
3. From a letter to Jacques Roth dated 16 April 1982.
4. From a letter from Edith Schmidt dated 3 January 1945.
5. From a letter from Edith Schmidt dated 5 March 1944.
6. From a letter from Edith Schmidt dated 3 January 1945.
7. From a letter from Edith Schmidt dated 31 August 1944.
8. From a letter from Edith Schmidt dated 3 November 1944.
9. Fischer-Dieskau, Dietrich. 1988. *Nachklang*. Stuttgart: DVA. 72.
10. Professor Kenneth S. Whitton relates the anecdote by an "anonymous student" and names the work sung as Schubert's *Winterreise*. The student was wrong here, as Dietrich Fischer-Dieskau has confirmed; he sang *Die schöne Magelone*; cf. Whitton, Kenneth S. 1981. *Dietrich Fischer-Dieskau: Mastersinger*. London: Wolff. 26–27.
11. Fischer-Dieskau, Dietrich. 1988. *Nachklang*. Stuttgart: DVA. 55.
12. Fischer-Dieskau, Dietrich. 1988. *Nachklang*. Stuttgart: DVA. 56.
13. From a letter from Edith Schmidt, dated 2 February 1948.
14. Fischer-Dieskau, Dietrich. 1988. *Nachklang*. Stuttgart: DVA. 58.

The First Postwar Years: Love and Music

1. Letter about Hermann Meinhard Poppen dated 1 August 1984.
2. From the radio broadcast from RIAS Berlin for Fischer-Dieskau's sixtieth birthday on 28 May 1985.
3. From an unpublished speech before the members of the order *Pour le mérite* in May 1994. (The Prussian order "for science and the arts" was created by Frederick the Great in 1740 and ranks as the highest German distinction. *Trans.*)
4. Fischer-Dieskau, Dietrich. 1988. *Nachklang*. Stuttgart: DVA. 80f.
5. Fischer-Dieskau, Dietrich. 1988. *Nachklang*. Stuttgart: DVA. 89.
6. Fischer-Dieskau, Dietrich. 1988. *Nachklang*. Stuttgart: DVA. 81.
7. From a letter by Irmgard Fischer-Dieskau to her parents, dated 15 December 1949.
8. Rodrigo, the Marquis of Posa to Queen Elisabeth in Friedrich Schiller's play *Don Carlos* (1787), Act IV, Scene 21.
9. Fischer-Dieskau, Dietrich. 1988. *Nachklang*. Stuttgart: DVA. 83.
10. From a letter to Hans Wolfgang Wunschel dated 10 May 1949.
11. Similar moving tributes can be heard in the fascinating film made for Fischer-Dieskau's seventieth birthday in 1995 by the French company Idéale Audience. *Trans.*
12. In Herzfeld, Friedrich, ed. 1964. *Ferenc Fricsay Ein Gedenkbuch* (A Book of Tributes). Berlin: Rembrandt.
13. From a letter to Karla Höcker dated 28 September 1978.
14. From a letter from Elisabeth Furtwängler dated 30 October 1976. (See also Fischer-Dieskau, Dietrich. 1988. *Nachklang*. Stuttgart: DVA. 106. *Trans.*)
15. Prey, Hermann. 1981. *Premierenfieber* (First Night Nerves). Munich: Kindler. 97.
16. In the 1995 film mentioned above, this point is demonstrated by showing Dietrich Fischer-Dieskau singing Schubert's "Im Frühling" (In Spring) at various points in his career, accompanied, in turn, by Gerald Moore, Hartmut Höll, Wolfgang Sawallisch, and, finally, with great panache, by Sviatoslav Richter, for whom Fischer-Dieskau has enormous respect. *Trans.*
17. In von Lewinski, Wolf-Eberhard. 1988. *Dietrich Fischer-Dieskau: Tatsachen, Meinungen, Interviews* (. . . Facts, Opinions, Interviews). Mainz / Munich: Piper-Schott. 150.
18. See Fischer-Dieskau, Dietrich. 1988. *Nachklang*. Stuttgart: DVA. 76–79.
19. Letter to Paul Hindemith dated 11 December 1953.
20. From a letter dated 22 January 1971 to a female listener of the radio premiere of "Wenn aber . . ." (But if . . .), nine fragments, after Friedrich Hölderlin (1770–1843), for baritone and piano.
21. Christian Gottlob Neefe (1748–1798), Beethoven's teacher in Bonn, composed *Singspiele*, Lieder and odes. Johann Rudolf Zumsteeg (1760–1802) wrote many Lieder, some of which greatly influenced Franz Schubert. *Trans.*
22. Friedrich Schiller, *Don Carlos*, 1787, Act III, Scene 10.
23. Ivan Nagel (b. 1931) is a theater and music critic who has been a theater director, journalist, and essayist. This article, "Der nicht leblos singen kann" (He Who Cannot Sing Lifelessly), was written for the *Stuttgarter Zeitung* and appeared 28 May 1985, for Fischer-Dieskau's sixtieth birthday.

24. From a letter from Oskar Fritz Schuh dated 1 February 1969.

25. From *Musikblätter. Eine Halbmonatsschrift für alle Gebiete der Musik*, No. 22 / 1948 / 2. November edition.

26. von Lewinski, Wolf-Eberhard. 1988. *Dietrich Fischer-Dieskau: Tatsachen, Meinungen, Interviews* (. . . Facts, Opinions, Interviews). Mainz / Munich: Piper-Schott. 27.

27. Dietrich Fischer-Dieskau in the program of the recital *Lieder nach Gedichten von Johann Wolfgang von Goethe* (Lieder to Poems by Johann Wolfgang von Goethe) at the Munich Festival, 1968.

28. In Höcker, Karla. 1970. *Hauskonzerte in Berlin* (House Concerts in Berlin). Berlin.

29. From a letter to Heinz Tietjen dated 2 July 1954.

30. Goethe to Johann Peter Eckermann on 20 December 1829.

31. The anecdote about Karl Böhm and Wilhelm Furtwängler is taken from the book about the Salzburg Festival: Schneditz, Wolfgang. 1960. *Salzburg*. Das Bergland-Buch.

32. "Het Vaderland" (The Hague, 1 September 1951). In *Resonanz: 50 Jahre Kritik der Salzburger Festspiele* (Resonance: Fifty Years of Reviews of the Salzburg Festival), ed. Max Kaindl-Hönig, 1971. Salzburg: SN-Verlag.

The Joy, and the Price, of Success

1. Founded in 1947, the Festival in the beautiful Scottish capital had quickly established itself as one of the leading international festivals of music and drama. It has welcomed all the leading musicians of the second half of the twentieth century, and in the last ten years has developed its peripheral activities, called "The Fringe," into a paradise for young theater, rock, and pop music groups. Fischer-Dieskau has always loved Edinburgh, which, in turn, reveres his name. *Trans.*

2. From *The Times* review of 8 June 1951. Quoted in Whitton, Kenneth S. 1981. *Dietrich Fischer-Dieskau: Mastersinger*. London: Wolff. 40.

3. Alfred Andersch, born in Munich in 1914, was, like Fischer-Dieskau, captured by the Americans in Italy and spent some years in POW camps there. *Trans.*

4. Herzfeld, Friedrich. 1958. *Dietrich Fischer-Dieskau*. Berlin: Rembrandt Verlag. 1958. 12 ff.

5. Dietrich Fischer-Dieskau took part in a recording of Wagner's opera *The Flying Dutchman* (1843) with the Berlin State Opera orchestra conducted by Franz Konwitschny in 1960. (This was also the recording debut of the tenor Fritz Wunderlich, who died tragically in an accident at the age of thirty-six in 1966. *Trans.*)

6. Quoted in Kosnick, H. 1971. *Busoni: Gestaltung durch Gestalt* (Busoni: Design Through Form). Regensburg: Bosse. 24.

7. When Fischer-Dieskau appeared in *Falstaff* in London in February 1967, the journalistic "hymns of praise" were rather more muted. At fault was not so much Fischer-Dieskau. One critic wrote appreciatively of "a man of charm and of character, a real seducer, if by now a superannuated one" (Stanley Sadie in *The Times*), while another (Peter Heyworth in *The Observer*) granted that much of Fischer-Dieskau's singing was "as distinguished as one might expect." At fault was rather the excessive amount of "stage business" in what was originally Franco Zeffirelli's production for Germany. The pinching of bottoms and the "sicking-up of

sack" was not appreciated in London. Fischer-Dieskau was not amused and has never sung in opera again in London. The recording of the performance in Vienna in March 1966 under Leonard Bernstein gained enormous plaudits, on the other hand; Alec Robertson, doyen of British music critics, hailed it as "the most satisfying [interpretation] that we have ever had." *Trans.*

8. In a speech in the *Berliner Lektionen* (Berlin Lectures) in September 1993.
9. Fischer-Dieskau, Dietrich. 1988. *Nachklang*. Stuttgart: DVA. 75–76.
10. Fischer-Dieskau, Dietrich. 1988. *Nachklang*. Stuttgart: DVA. 76.
11. Letter from Lotte Lehmann dated 16 November 1960. (See also Fischer-Dieskau, Dietrich. 1988. *Nachklang*. Stuttgart: DVA. 113f.)
12. Fischer-Dieskau, Dietrich. 1988. *Nachklang*. Stuttgart: DVA. 256f.
13. From a letter from Irmgard Fischer-Dieskau dated 3 February 1956.
14. From a letter from Gerda Riebensahm to the Fischer-Dieskaus.
15. From a letter from Zenta Maurina-Raudive dated 17 August 1977.
16. From a letter from Greta Busch dated 14 April 1964.

"The Way Out of the Vale of Tears"

1. A quotation from the recitative to Wolfram's aria "To the Evening Star" from Act III of Wagner's *Tannhäuser*. *Trans.*
2. From a letter by Dietrich Fischer-Dieskau to the Salzburg music critic Max Kaindl-Hönig of 17 January 1964.
3. Fischer-Dieskau, Dietrich. 1988. *Nachklang*. Stuttgart: DVA. 225.
4. Demus, Jörg. 1967. *Abenteuer der Interpretation* (The Adventure of Interpretation). Wiesbaden: Brockhaus. 88.
5. From a letter to Gustav-Adolf Trumpff in Darmstadt, March 1964.
6. Oehlmann, Werner. In *Dietrich Fischer-Dieskau*, Jörg Demus, Karla Höcker, Wolf-Eberhard von Lewinski, Werner Oehlmann. 1966. Berlin: Rembrandt Verlag. 27–28. (Fischer-Dieskau has always regretted the jettisoning of EMI's plans to have Maria Callas partner him in a recording of *Macbeth*. Like many others, she had a fear of "the Scottish play." *Trans.*)
7. From the letter to Gustav Adolph Trumpff in Darmstadt, March 1964, quoted above.
8. From a letter to Inge and Torolf Engström (n.d. February 1964).
9. Moore, G. 1962. *Am I Too Loud?* London: Hamilton. 176.
10. Moore, G. 1962. *Am I Too Loud?* London: Hamilton. 178. In another place, Moore wrote about Fischer-Dieskau: "He was, even then (i.e., 1951), the complete musician and a fluent pianist, as much absorbed in the pianoforte's contribution to the song as his partner at the keyboard, and he recognized that the projection of a song's mood-narrative picture was not only the exclusive responsibility of the voice. This was very gratifying to the accompanist who was fortunate enough to be playing for him" (from Gerald Moore's foreword to Whitton, Kenneth S. 1981. *Dietrich Fischer-Dieskau: Mastersinger*. London: Wolff. 11.). *Trans.*
11. Fischer-Dieskau, Dietrich. 1988. *Nachklang*. Stuttgart: DVA. 126.
12. From a letter to a questioner dated 22 July 1978.
13. From a letter to a questioner dated 26 March 1955.
14. "Deutsche Vita printed." *Der Spiegel* 29 (12 July 1961): 54.

15. Frisch, M. 1964. *Mein Name sei Gantenbein.* Translated as *A Wilderness of Mirrors.* London: Eyre Methuen, 1967.
16. Noll, I. 1993. *Der Hahn ist tot.* Zurich: Diogenes. 23.
17. Quoted in Whitton, Kenneth S. 1981. *Dietrich Fischer-Dieskau: Mastersinger.* London: Wolff. 289. [James Felton in the *Evening Bulletin* of Philadelphia also called Fischer-Dieskau "the greatest Lieder singer alive" (on 16 April 1974). *Trans.*]
18. Martin Walser in conversation with Ulf Erdmann Ziegler on 31 August 1985. In Walser, M. 1991. *Auskunft* (Information). Frankfurt: Suhrkamp. 166.
19. From a letter from Edith Picht-Axenfeld dated 2 September 1979.
20. This was a radio broadcast from the Bavarian Radio, reviewed by Ulrich Dibelius on 12 August 1961.
21. From a letter to Fischer-Dieskau from Gérard Souzay dated 28 April 1979.
22. Such criticisms could, of course, be read in every country in which Fischer-Dieskau sang and might be summed up by the title of an article on Fischer-Dieskau in the British music magazine *The Gramophone* in October 1963. Desmond Shawe-Taylor, a fine critic, but one of a generation of British intellectuals more noted for pro-French than pro-German sympathies (caused no doubt by two World Wars waged against Germany), titled his article "The Importance of Not Being Earnest," a playful paraphrase of the title of Oscar Wilde's famous play. In it he stated that Fischer-Dieskau lacked the "life-enhancing spirit" of past singers of Lieder, such as Elena Gerhardt or Lotte Lehmann. *Trans.*
23. A contemporary view of Schubert, communicated in conversation by Wolf-Eberhard von Lewinski.
24. From a letter dated 11 April 1985 to Dr. Ritter, a music critic.
25. From a letter dated 24 September 1984 to the distinguished music critic, Professor Karl Schumann.
26. Joachim Kaiser in the *Süddeutsche Zeitung* of 7 August 1967. [Max Friedlaender (1852–1934) was the editor of the Schubert edition published by Peters in 1886. *Trans.*]
27. From Klaus P. Richter's article in the *Süddeutsche Zeitung* of 18 November 1993.
28. Quoted in *Der Spiegel* of 13 June 1962.
29. In the *Frankfurter Allgemeine Zeitung* of 12 September 1960.
30. Letter to Hans Werner Henze, dated 9 January 1959.

From Gregor Mittenhofer to Hans Sachs and Lear: His Major Operatic Roles

1. From the booklet issued with the two records recorded in the Kingsway Hall, London, on 3–5, 7, 8, and 10 January 1963. *Trans.*
2. Fischer-Dieskau translated the text himself into German with "Ludwig Landgraf," the pseudonym of Britten's friend, Prince Ludwig of Hesse. The British soprano Heather Harper had to sing the soprano part in place of the original choice, the Russian Galina Vishnevskaya, who was "indisposed." Vishnevskaya (the wife of the celebrated cellist, Mstislav Rostropovich), did sing in the recording issued in 1963, however. In the film made by Idéale Audience, Fischer-Dieskau hints that the Soviet

authorities did not wish Miss Vishnevskaya to appear beside a "West German baritone"! *Trans.*

3. Irving Kolodin, in the *New York Saturday Review* of 1 April 1967, called the series of three Lieder recitals "the Dietrich Fischer-Dieskau week" and praised the baritone's "inbred eloquence and artistic distinction." *Trans.*

4. Fischer-Dieskau himself, speaking on these themes, had said once that creative artists can never worry about "politics" or "living conditions." They can only be concerned with themselves and the work that they are called upon to do—a comment that was peculiarly appropriate to events in his own life just at this particular time, as we shall see. *Trans.*

5. Fischer-Dieskau, Dietrich. 1988. *Nachklang*. Stuttgart: DVA. 217.

6. From a letter to Hans Werner Henze, dated 10 January 1969.

7. John Russell, at that time an arts reviewer for the London *Sunday Times*, then for the *New York Sunday Times* in a letter to Dietrich Fischer-Dieskau, dated 8 October 1966. (He has also written on Fischer-Dieskau as a painter. See Whitton, K. S. 1981. *Dietrich Fischer-Dieskau: Mastersinger*. London: Wolff. 280. *Trans.*)

8. From a letter to Daniel Barenboim, dated 8 January 1987.

9. From a letter to Günter Baum, dated 21 January 1971.

10. From a letter to Heinz Friedrich, dated 27 April 1974.

11. From a letter to Wolfgang Sawallisch, dated 8 August 1969.

12. From a letter to Walter Schmieding, dated 20 January 1971.

13. Fischer-Dieskau has not visited as many of the towns of Great Britain as he has other countries'. Apart from the very early recital in Newcastle and his visits to Benjamin Britten's Aldeburgh, most of his appearances have been in London or at the Edinburgh Festival. Not all the venues there have been to his liking either—the "rather primitive" King's Theater, in Edinburgh, where he sang in *The Marriage of Figaro* in 1975, for example—but he always expresses his fondness for the Scottish capital, and this is reflected in many of his own paintings of Edinburgh, now hanging in his house in Berg near Munich's Lake Starnberg. *Trans.*

14. *Die Zeit* of 12 April 1968.

15. Kurt Heinz in the *Mannheimer Morgen* of 9 April 1968.

16. Helmut Schmidt-Garre in *N. Z. Neue Zeitschrift für Musik*, Mainz, No. 5/68.

17. From a letter to Elske Weissenborn, dated 7 September 1968.

18. At the end of his review of this 114th Anniversary Concert in the *Philadelphia Bulletin* of 24 January 1971, Max de Schauensee wrote that *Les Préludes* of Liszt "eventually heralded a supper of tournedos au coznac [sic] and coupe Alaska at the neighboring Bellevue." *Trans.*

19. After the concert, the German Ambassador, Jesco von Puttkamer, had a reception for Fischer-Dieskau and his wife Kristina in the Tel-Aviv Hilton, with over two hundred guests. *Trans.*

20. Fischer-Dieskau, Dietrich. 1988. *Nachklang*. Stuttgart: DVA. 284–85.

21. From a letter to Martin Fischer-Dieskau, dated 2 April 1979.

22. *Die Tücke des Objekts* (the cussedness of the inanimate object) is a common German phrase, popularized by the philosopher F. T. Vischer (1807–1887). *Trans.*

23. Moore's "official" retirement had been signaled by a wonderful farewell concert in London's Royal Festival Hall, organized by Walter Legge, the husband of the soprano

Elisabeth Schwarzkopf (who was later created a Dame of the British Empire by Queen Elizabeth II). Legge brought Fischer-Dieskau, Victoria de los Angeles, and Elisabeth Schwarzkopf together (after much bother) on 20 February 1967 to perform, in Gerald Moore's honor, a program of solo items, duets, and trios. Fischer-Dieskau sang a solo program of Schubert Lieder, and the concert finished with Gerald Moore's own piano version of his "signature tune": Schubert's *An die Musik* (To Music). The concert was recorded on two LPs.

24. Fischer-Dieskau, Dietrich. 1988. *Nachklang*. Stuttgart: DVA. 276–77. (Volumes I and II of the Schubert Lieder contained 408 songs. Volume III contained the three song-cycles *Winterreise, Die schöne Müllerin,* and *Schwanengesang,* thus giving a grand total of 466 Lieder. *Trans.*)

25. Fischer-Dieskau, Dietrich. 1988. *Nachklang*. Stuttgart: DVA. 189.

26. Harold C. Schonberg's comment on Fischer-Dieskau's Brahms recital in Carnegie Hall in the *New York Times* might stand for many: "As always with him, it was not so much a question of voice *qua* voice as it was the way the voice was used" (25 January 1973). *Trans.*

27. From a letter to Wieland Wagner dated 17 May 1966; cf. Haltrecht, Montague. 1975. *The Quiet Showman*. London: Collins.

28. Fischer-Dieskau, Dietrich. 1988. *Nachklang*. Stuttgart: DVA. 263.

29. Norbert Miller in the *Süddeutsche Zeitung* of 16 March 1976.

30. H. H. Stuckenschmidt in the *Frankfurter Allgemeine Zeitung* of 15 March 1976.

31. From a letter from Professor Hans Mayer, dated 9 July 1979.

32. From a letter to Wolfgang Sawallisch, dated 7 February 1970.

33. To Alan Blyth of the London *Times*; cf Whitton, Kenneth S. 1981. *Dietrich Fischer-Dieskau: Mastersinger*. London: Wolff. 144.

34. The introduction of the twenty-five-year-old Spanish tenor Placido Domingo in the role of Walther von Stolzing might have been a surprise for some, although Fischer-Dieskau reminded a friend that the Italian tenor Beniamino Gigli had recorded the aria "Nun sei bedankt, mein lieber Schwan" (Thanks Be to You, Dear Swan) from *Lohengrin. Trans.*

35. From a letter to a questioner dated 28 August 1985.

36. From a letter to Heinz Friedrich dated 26 November 1978. (He could have been thinking here of the director who made him sing Amfortas in *Parsifal* while lying on his back. *Trans.*)

37. From a letter to Jacques Roth dated 6 March 1982.

38. From a letter to Heinz Friedrich dated 8 June 1975.

39. Teresa Stratas (originally Anastasia Stratakis) (b. 1938), Canadian soprano. Friedrich Cerha (b. 1926), Austrian conductor. *Trans.*

40. From a letter from Antal Dorati dated 18 January 1985.

41. Reimann, Aribert. 1984. *Lear. Weg einer neuen Oper* (Lear: The Way to a New Opera), ed. Klaus Schultz. Munich: DTV.

42. Aribert Reimann in the RIAS Berlin radio broadcast of 28 May 1985.

43. From a letter from Ernst Křenek (1900–1991) dated 30 January 1974. Křenek's work for Dietrich Fischer-Dieskau (*Spätlese*) (Late Harvest) to his own poems had its premiere in Munich on 23 July 1974. Fischer-Dieskau was accompanied by the composer.

44. In an interview given to the Munich newspaper *TZ* on 23 July 1977, Julia Varady admitted to looking forward to receiving her German passport, since she would now have been residing in Germany for the necessary ten years. Even a marriage to Dietrich Fischer-Dieskau could not hurry that procedure! *Trans.*

45. In the *Frankfurter Allgemeine Zeitung* of 11 November 1978.

46. From a letter from Siegfried Matthus dated 18 December 1980.

47. Fischer-Dieskau, Dietrich. 1988. *Nachklang*. Stuttgart: DVA. 171.

48. Prawer, S. S. 1964. *The Penguin Book of Lieder*. London: Penguin. 17. *Trans.*

49. From a letter to Daniel Barenboim dated 22 December 1981.

Return to the World of Lieder

1. He was accompanied by Gerald Moore with whom he had just recorded five 78 rpm records on 7 October 1951, including "Ständchen" (Serenade) and "Du bist die Ruh" (Thou Art Repose), "Am Meer" (By the Sea), and "Der Doppelgänger" (The Double), all by Schubert; then "Erlkönig" (Schubert) and "Die beiden Grenadiere" (The Two Grenadiers) (Schumann); "Nacht und Träume" (Night and Dreams) (Schubert), and "Mondnacht" (A Moonlight Night) (Schumann) (these were all twelve-inch records, as was the complete *Die schöne Müllerin*); and, finally, on one ten-inch 78 rpm record "Das Fischermädchen" (The Fisher-girl) and "Die Stadt" (The Town), also by Schubert. All have now become collectors' items. These were the earliest records and made Fischer-Dieskau's reputation throughout the world in the 1950s, at a time when record-making was just beginning to become the mass industry that it is now—and when long-playing records were developing from dream into reality. *Trans.*

2. Mary Leighton wrote of that tour in *Musical America* with some foresight: "Mr. Fischer-Dieskau's voice was remarkably sonorous. He impressed me as a singer of the first magnitude." This was a review of his first concert, Bach's *Kreuzstab* cantata and Brahms's *German Requiem*, in Cincinnati on 15 April 1955. *Trans.*

3. It was in the Salle Pleyel in 1970 that a French critic, Maurice Fleuret, heard Fischer-Dieskau and wrote on 23 February in the *Nouvel Observateur* about "le miracle Fischer-Dieskau"; he let his pen fall as he was writing, for "la musique selon Fischer-Dieskau est tellement plus éloquent que tout ce qu'on peut en dire") (for Fischer-Dieskau's music is much more eloquent than anything that one can write about it). *Trans.*

4. Karl Schumann in the *Süddeutsche Zeitung* of 12 July 1983.

5. Hartmut Höll's wife is the brilliant Japanese soprano Mitsuko Shirai, whom he has accompanied on many recordings of Lieder. *Trans.*

6. Karl Heinz Ludwig Funk in the *Frankfurter Rundschau* of 3 October 1985.

7. Sybille Mahlke in the *Tagesspiegel* of 9 February 1986.

8. From a letter from Hans Erich Riebensahm dated 11 July 1982.

9. From a letter to Heinz Friedrich dated 10 November 1975.

10. Karl Schumann in the *Süddeutsche Zeitung* of 5 February 1986.

"For a Singer, the Fusion of Words and Music Is a Joy for Life"

1. An English translation, *The Fischer-Dieskau Book of Lieder*, by George Bird and Richard Stokes, in a much larger, hardcover format, was published by the Victor Gollancz Press and Pan Books Ltd. in 1976 and has proved itself just as popular. *Trans.*
2. cf. Beethoven's beautiful, confessional miniature of 1822, "Ich liebe dich" (I Love You), to the poem of C. F. Weisse (1726–1804). *Trans.*

"On the Trail of Schubert's Lieder"

1. An English translation by Professor Kenneth S. Whitton was published in the UK as *Schubert: A Biographical Study of His Songs.* London: Cassell, 1976, and in the US as *Schubert's Songs.* New York: Knopf, 1977. *Trans.*
2. The twenty-nine LPs had been greeted with enormous and unanimous critical acclaim, and gained, almost immediately, five prestigious awards. *Trans.*
3. Fischer-Dieskau, D. 1971. *Auf den Spuren der Schubert-Lieder.* Wiesbaden: Brockhaus. 15.
4. Fischer-Dieskau, D. 1971. *Auf den Spuren der Schubert-Lieder.* Wiesbaden: Brockhaus. 213f.
5. In a BBC3 interview with the British Schubert specialist Graham Johnson broadcast on 23 December 1995, Fischer-Dieskau revealed that he was working on a new book on Schubert that would go into much more detail (published in 1996 by DVA, Stuttgart). *Trans.*

"Life Without Music Is Just a Mistake, a Drudgery, an Exile!"

1. Fischer-Dieskau, Dietrich. 1988. *Nachklang.* Stuttgart: DVA. 306. cf. Fischer-Dieskau, Dietrich. 1974. *Wagner und Nietzsche: der Mystagoge und sein Abtrünniger.* Stuttgart: Deutsche Verlags-Anstalt. Translated into English by Joachim Neugroschel as *Wagner and Nietzsche*, US: Seabury Press, Inc., 1976; London: Sidgwick and Jackson, 1978.
2. Fischer-Dieskau, Dietrich. 1988. *Nachklang.* Stuttgart: DVA. 306.
3. Fischer-Dieskau, Dietrich. 1974. *Wagner und Nietzsche: der Mystagoge und sein Abtrünniger.* Stuttgart: Deutsche Verlags-Anstalt. 182.

"To Crown the Head of a True Poet with a Wreath of Music"

1. Fischer-Dieskau, Dietrich. 1981. *Robert Schumann, Wort und Musik. Das Vokalwerk.* Stuttgart: DVA. Translated into English by Reinhard G. Pauly as *Robert Schumann. Words and Music: The Vocal Compositions.* Portland, Oregon: Amadeus Press, 1988.
2. Fischer-Dieskau, Dietrich. 1981. *Robert Schumann, Wort und Musik. Das Vokalwerk.* Stuttgart: DVA. 73.

3. Fischer-Dieskau, Dietrich. 1981. *Robert Schumann, Wort und Musik. Das Vokalwerk.* Stuttgart: DVA. 8.
4. Fischer-Dieskau, Dietrich. 1981. *Robert Schumann, Wort und Musik. Das Vokalwerk.* Stuttgart: DVA. 14.
5. From a letter to a reader dated 9 January1982.

"He Gave Poetry Music and Music Words"

1. Fischer-Dieskau, Dietrich. 1985. *Töne sprechen, Worte klingen: Zur Geschichte und Interpretation des Gesangs* (Music Speaks, Words Resound. On the History and Interpretation of Vocal Music). Stuttgart / München: DVA / Piper.
2. Fischer-Dieskau, Dietrich. 1985. *Töne sprechen, Worte klingen: Zur Geschichte und Interpretation des Gesangs.* Stuttgart / München: DVA / Piper. 184.
3. Fischer-Dieskau, Dietrich. 1985. *Töne sprechen, Worte klingen: Zur Geschichte und Interpretation des Gesangs.* Stuttgart / München: DVA / Piper. 111–112.
4. Fischer-Dieskau, Dietrich. 1985. *Töne sprechen, Worte klingen: Zur Geschichte und Interpretation des Gesangs.* Stuttgart / München: DVA / Piper. 75.
5. Fischer-Dieskau, Dietrich. 1985. *Töne sprechen, Worte klingen: Zur Geschichte und Interpretation des Gesangs.* Stuttgart / München: DVA / Piper. 381.
6. Fischer-Dieskau, Dietrich. 1985. *Töne sprechen, Worte klingen: Zur Geschichte und Interpretation des Gesangs.* Stuttgart / München: DVA / Piper. 386.
7. Fischer-Dieskau, Dietrich. 1985. *Töne sprechen, Worte klingen: Zur Geschichte und Interpretation des Gesangs.* Stuttgart / München: DVA / Piper. 431–432.
8. Fischer-Dieskau, Dietrich. 1985. *Töne sprechen, Worte klingen: Zur Geschichte und Interpretation des Gesangs.* Stuttgart / München: DVA / Piper. 461.
9. Fischer-Dieskau, Dietrich. 1985. *Töne sprechen, Worte klingen: Zur Geschichte und Interpretation des Gesangs.* Stuttgart / München: DVA / Piper. 464.
10. Fischer-Dieskau, Dietrich. 1985. *Töne sprechen, Worte klingen: Zur Geschichte und Interpretation des Gesangs.* Stuttgart / München: DVA / Piper. 472.

"My Heart Feels Every Echo"

1. Fischer-Dieskau, Dietrich. 1988. *Nachklang.* Stuttgart: DVA. 9. English trans. Ruth Hein, *Echoes of a Lifetime.* London: Macmillan, 1989. (All translations of material in this biography are K. S. Whitton's, however, and refer to the original works. *Trans.*)
2. From a letter from the conductor Thomas Baldner, Bloomington, Indiana, USA, dated 2 January 1989.

"If Music Be the Food of Love"

1. Fischer-Dieskau, Dietrich. 1990. *Wenn Musik der Liebe Nahrung ist: Künstler-Schicksale im 19. Jahrhundert* (If Music Be the Food of Love: Artistic Destinies in the Nineteenth Century). Stuttgart: DVA.

2. Fischer-Dieskau, Dietrich. 1990. *Wenn Musik der Liebe Nahrung ist: Künstler-Schicksale im 19. Jahrhundert.* Stuttgart: DVA. 152.
3. Fischer-Dieskau, Dietrich. 1990. *Wenn Musik der Liebe Nahrung ist: Künstler-Schicksale im 19. Jahrhundert.* Stuttgart: DVA. 161.
4. Fischer-Dieskau, Dietrich. 1990. *Wenn Musik der Liebe Nahrung ist: Künstler-Schicksale im 19. Jahrhundert.* Stuttgart: DVA. 334.

"Because Not All My Blossoming Dreams Ripened?"

1. Fischer-Dieskau, Dietrich. 1992. *Weil nicht alle Blütenträume reiften: Johann Friedrich Reichardt: Hofkapellmeister dreier Preussenkönige* (Because Not All My Blossoming Dreams Ripened? Johann Friedrich Reichardt, Court Music Master to Three Prussian Kings). Stuttgart: DVA.
2. See the chapter "Background and Early Life" for Fischer-Dieskau's own connections with Giebichenstein. *Trans.*

"From Afar, the Plaint of the Faun"

1. Fischer-Dieskau, Dietrich. 1993. *Fern die Klage des Fauns. Claude Debussy und seine Welt* (From Afar the Plaint of the Faun. Claude Debussy and His World). Stuttgart: DVA. [The title (La plainte, au loin, du faune) is the translation of the title of Paul Dukas's contribution to the *Tombeau de Debussy* (1920). *Trans.*]
2. Fischer-Dieskau, Dietrich. 1993. *Fern die Klage des Fauns. Claude Debussy und seine Welt.* Stuttgart: DVA. 382.
3. Fischer-Dieskau, Dietrich. 1993. *Fern die Klage des Fauns. Claude Debussy und seine Welt.* Stuttgart: DVA. 164.

"A Resounding Play of Colors"

1. Fischer-Dieskau, Dietrich. 1988. *Nachklang.* Stuttgart: DVA. 302.
2. *Dietrich Fischer-Dieskau: Bilder aus drei Jahrzehnten* (Dietrich Fischer-Dieskau: Pictures from Three Decades). The catalog, printed by Erhard Jung of Berlin, has an introduction by Dietrich Fischer-Dieskau, pp. 7–8, and a short essay by Hans Neubauer, "Die Suche nach dem Selbst" (Search for the Ego), pp. 11–15. The quotations come from pages, 7, 13, and 7, respectively. There are forty-five reproductions. *Trans.*
3. From a letter from Siegfried Matthus, dated 8 January 1981.

"There Are Two Sorts of Blessings in Breathing"

1. Grubb, Suvi Raj. 1986. *Music-makers on Record.* London: Hamish Hamilton. 142.
2. Grubb, Suvi Raj. 1986. *Music-makers on Record.* London: Hamish Hamilton. 140.

3. Linda Winer in the *Chicago Tribune* of 28 April 1972 called his performance of Mozart arias with the Chicago Symphony orchestra under Georg Solti "an encounter with greatness." *Trans.*

4. Erich Trunz edited the *Hamburger Ausgabe* of Goethe's poems, here cited from Vol. 2, p. 13 of the 1982 edition. *Trans.*

5. Fischer-Dieskau, Dietrich. 1988. *Nachklang*. Stuttgart: DVA. 135ff.

6. Grubb, Suvi Raj. 1986. *Music-makers on Record*. London: Hamish Hamilton. 140–141.

7. From a lecture held in 1993 in the series *Berlin Lectures*.

8. "On Wilhelm Furtwängler." In the *Frankfurter Zeitung*, 18 October 1973.

9. Grubb, Suvi Raj. 1986. *Music-makers on Record*. London: Hamish Hamilton. 141.

10. Whitton, Kenneth.S. 1981. *Dietrich Fischer-Dieskau: Mastersinger*. London: Wolff. 276.

11. Fischer-Dieskau, Dietrich. 1988. *Nachklang*. Stuttgart: DVA. 136.

12. Peter Gradenwitz was reporting for the *Frankfurter Allgemeine Zeitung* from Tel Aviv. His article appeared on 1 March 1974.

13. Karl Schumann in the *Süddeutsche Zeitung* of 6 May 1976.

"Dear Friend, All Theory Is Gray!"

1. Aribert Reimann in the broadcast from RIAS Berlin on 28 May 1985.

2. Fischer-Dieskau, Dietrich. 1988. *Nachklang*. Stuttgart: DVA. 237.

3. Fischer-Dieskau, Dietrich. 1988. *Nachklang*. Stuttgart: DVA. 203.

4. From a letter to Reinhard Löw dated 8 July 1977.

5. Fischer-Dieskau, Dietrich. 1985. *Töne sprechen, Worte klingen: Zur Geschichte und Interpretation des Gesangs*. Stuttgart / München: DVA / Piper. 443, 458.

6. Andreas Richter in the *Stuttgarter Zeitung* of 11 January 1993.

7. After his retirement in 1992, *The Gramophone*, Britain's premier publication for music, honored Dietrich Fischer-Dieskau with the Award for Lifetime Achievement. At the end of the interview with Brian Newhouse, he was asked for "the last word." He said, "The last word? I would be honored if they said: 'He was a musician.' That's all I want" (November 1993). But the musician Dietrich Fischer-Dieskau has never ceased to perform. His itinerary for 1996 lists nearly thirty appearances, either in Lesungen (readings of the correspondence of celebrated musicians), or as Sprecher (orator) in works like Richard Strauss's setting of Tennyson's *Enoch Arden*, or as conductor of works such as Mahler's *Lied von der Erde* or Brahms's *German Requiem*.

Chronology

This chronological survey denotes signposts of the biography and, above all, of Fischer-Dieskau's career as a musician. The many tours of Lieder recitals through German towns, through Europe, the United States, and Japan, as well as his operatic performances, are illustrated by only a few examples.

1925   May 28. Dietrich Fischer-Dieskau is born in Berlin. His father, Dr. Albert Fischer (1865–1937) (since 1934, Albert Fischer-Dieskau) was a classical scholar, founder, and headmaster of the secondary school in Zehlendorf, Berlin. He wrote works for the stage and was a composer. His mother, Theodora Klingelhöffer (1884–1966), was a trained teacher; after her husband's death, she taught English and French.

1930   Began school in the primary school in Lichterfelde (Berlin).

1934   First piano lessons.

1937   Albert Fischer-Dieskau dies.

1941   Begins voice study with Georg A. Walter.

1942   Continues vocal studies with Hermann Weissenborn at the Hochschule für Musik (Academy of Music), Berlin. First public recital in the Community Hall, Zehlendorf: Schubert's *Winterreise* (interrupted by air-raid alarm).

1943   Abitur (graduation certificate). Meets the cellist Irmgard Poppen. Called up for the Wehrmacht (German Army).

1945   5 May. POW with the Americans in North Italy. First recitals in the camp.

1947   Released from POW camp. Sojourn with the Poppen family in Freiburg in Breisgau (southern Germany).
        First concerts, e.g. Brahms's *German Requiem* in Badenweiler.
        Studies again with Hermann Weissenborn in Berlin. First broadcast in RIAS, Berlin: *Winterreise*.

1948   Public Lieder recitals.
        Engaged by Heinz Tietjen for the Städtische Oper (Municipal Opera), Berlin.
        Debut as Marquis of Posa in Verdi's *Don Carlos* conducted by Ferenc Fricsay.

1949   Marries Irmgard Poppen.

First appearance in Schoenberg's *Gurre-Lieder* in Heidelberg. J. S. Bach's *St. John Passion* with Irmgard Poppen, cello continuo.

First gramophone recording for DGG, Brahms's *Four Serious Songs*.

Schubert's *Die schöne Müllerin* in the Titania-Palast, Berlin.

First performance as Wolfram von Eschenbach in Wagner's *Tannhäuser*, Städtische Oper, Berlin, conducted by Leopold Ludwig.

Guest contracts with the Vienna State Opera and Bavarian State Opera, Munich.

1950   First meeting with Wilhelm Furtwängler in Salzburg. Hindemith's *Requiem* in the Great Hall of Berlin Radio. *Dover Beach* by Samuel Barber in Titania-Palast, Berlin.

Kunstpreis (Art Prize) of Berlin.

1951   Mathias, first son, born.

Brahms's *German Requiem* in Vienna, conducted by Wilhelm Furtwängler.

First concert in London: Delius's *A Mass of Life*, conducted by Sir Thomas Beecham.

First appearance at the Bavarian State Opera as Wolfram in Wagner's *Tannhäuser*.

Debut at the Salzburg Festival: *Songs of a Wayfarer*, Gustav Mahler, conducted by Wilhelm Furtwängler.

First recordings with Gerald Moore, EMI Studios, London.

First Count Almaviva in Mozart's *Marriage of Figaro* at the Städtische Oper, Berlin.

1952   Debut at Edinburgh Festival.

Kurwenal in Furtwängler's recording of Wagner's *Tristan and Isolde* with Kirsten Flagstad and Ludwig Suthaus.

First John the Baptist (Jochanaan) in Richard Strauss's *Salome* at the Städtische Oper, Berlin, conducted by Ferenc Fricsay.

Sings Morone in a Cologne recording of Hans Pfitzner's *Palestrina*, conducted by Richard Kraus.

1953   First *Don Giovanni* in Mozart's opera at the Städtische Oper, Berlin, conducted by Karl Böhm.

1954   Martin, second son, born.

Debut at the Bavarian Festival as Wolfram in Wieland Wagner's production of *Tannhäuser*, conductor Joseph Keilberth, then as the Herald in Wagner's *Lohengrin*, conducted by Eugen Jochum.

First Italian Lieder tour: Florence, Rome, Perugia, Milan, Turin.

1955   First Doktor Faust in Busoni's opera in the production by Wolf Völker and Caspar Neher, at the Städtische Oper, Berlin, conducted by Richard Kraus.

Tour of the USA and Canada: Ohio, St. Paul, Toronto, Montreal, Ottawa, Washington, New York.

1956   First Count Almaviva in the Salzburg production by Oscar Fritz Schuh.
        Tour of the USA.
        Recording of Hans Werner Henze's *Five Neapolitan Songs* with the Berlin Philharmonic, conducted by Richard Kraus.

1957   First Falstaff in Verdi's opera in the production by Carl Ebert at the Städtische Opera, Berlin.
        Orpheus in a concert performance of Gluck's *Orpheus and Eurydice* in Berlin, conducted by Ferenc Fricsay.
        Guest appearance as Renato in Verdi's *A Masked Ball* at the Hamburg State Opera, after the previous premiere with Wolfgang Sawallisch in Berlin.

1958   First Mandryka in Richard Strauss's *Arabella* with Lisa della Casa, at the Salzburg Festival.
        First Duke Bluebeard in a Salzburg concert performance of Béla Bartók's *Duke Bluebeard's Castle*, with Hertha Töpper, conducted by Ferenc Fricsay.
        Tour of USA and Canada.

1959   First Mathis in Hindemith's *Mathis der Maler* (Mathis the Painter), at the Städtische Oper, Berlin, conducted by Richard Kraus.
        Lieder recitals in Brussels, London, Edinburgh, Copenhagen, Stockholm, Geneva, Lucerne, Paris, Milan, Zurich. Tour of Germany.

1960   First Wozzeck in Alban Berg's opera at the Städtische Oper, Berlin, conducted by Richard Kraus.
        Recording of Wagner's *The Flying Dutchman*, conducted by Franz Konwitschny.

1961   First Onegin in Tchaikovsky's *Eugen Onegin* at the Vienna State Opera, conducted by Lovro von Matačič.
        Premiere of Hans Werner Henze's *Elegie für junge Liebende* (Elegy for Young Lovers), Fischer-Dieskau as Gregor Mittenhofer, conducted by Heinrich Bender in Schwetzingen.
        Opening of the Deutsche Oper (German Opera), Berlin, with Mozart's *Don Giovanni*. Fischer-Dieskau in the title role, conducted by Ferenc Fricsay.

1962   Recording of Verdi's *Rigoletto*. Fischer-Dieskau as Rigoletto, with the Berlin Philharmonic conducted by Horst Stein.
        Premiere of Benjamin Britten's *War Requiem* with Peter Pears and Heather Harper in Coventry Cathedral.

1963   First tour of Japan with *Fidelio* (Fischer-Dieskau as the Minister) and *The Marriage of Figaro* (Count Almaviva) in the Nissei Theater, Tokyo. (Guest performance of the Deutsche Oper with Karl Böhm as conductor.)

Lieder recitals (Schubert and Schumann) in Kyoto.

Opening of the renovated National Theater, Munich, with *Die Frau ohne Schatten* (The Woman Without a Shadow) by Richard Strauss. Fischer-Dieskau as Barak; conductor, Joseph Keilberth.

Verdi's *Macbeth* and *Falstaff*, as well as Gottfried von Einem's *Dantons Tod* (The Death of Danton) in Berlin.

Manuel, his third son, is born. His wife Irmgard dies.

1964   Premiere of Karl Amadeus Hartmann's *Gesangsszene* (Song Scene), conducted by Dean Dixon.

Recording of *Rigoletto* on the stage of La Scala, Milan, conducted by Rafael Kubelik.

1965   Premiere of Benjamin Britten's *Songs and Proverbs of William Blake* at the Aldeburgh Festival, Suffolk, UK.

Lieder recitals with Sviatoslav Richter.

First guest appearance at Covent Garden as Mandryka in Richard Strauss's *Arabella*, conducted by Georg Solti.

Married Ruth Leuwerik.

Macbeth and *Don Carlos* (Posa) in Berlin.

Mandryka in *Arabella* and Hindemith's *Cardillac* (title role) in Munich, and *Macbeth* in Salzburg.

1966   *Falstaff* (Verdi) in Vienna. Directed by Luchino Visconti, conducted by Leonard Bernstein.

German premiere of Sir Michael Tippett's *The Vision of St. Augustine.*

Japan tour with the Deutsche Oper Berlin: *La Traviata* (as Germont) and *Falstaff*, conducted by Lorin Maazel. *Elegie für junge Liebende* (Henze), conducted by Hans Werner Henze.

Lieder recitals in Tokyo and Osaka.

1967   *Falstaff* at Covent Garden, conducted by Edward Downes.

Gerald Moore's Farewell Concert in London with Victoria de los Angeles and Elisabeth Schwarzkopf.

Lieder recitals in New York and Washington.

1968   Wotan in Wagner's *Rheingold* at the Salzburg Festival, conducted by Herbert von Karajan.

Lieder recitals in New York with Leonard Bernstein.

Dress rehearsal and premiere of Hans Werner Henze's *Das Floss der Medusa* (The Raft of the Frigate Méduse) in Hamburg.

1969   Doktor Faust in Busoni's opera, concert performance in Munich, conducted by Ferdinand Leitner.
First Lieder recitals with Daniel Barenboim in London.
US tour: Santa Barbara, Los Angeles, California; Tempe, Arizona.

1970   Recording of all Schubert Lieder for the male voice, with Gerald Moore (1970–1971).
Japan tour with *Falstaff*, conducted by Lorin Maazel.
Lieder recitals in Tokyo, Fukuoka, Sapporo, Nagoya.
London: Recital of Lieder by Webern and Beethoven with Daniel Barenboim (piano), Pinchas Zukerman (violin), Jacqueline DuPré (cello).
Hamburg: John the Baptist (Jochanaan) in Richard Strauss's *Salome* with Gwyneth Jones, conducted by Karl Böhm.

1971   First visit to Israel: *Lieder eines fahrenden Gesellen* (Mahler).
Premiere of Aribert Reimann's *Zyklus* (Cycle) in Nuremberg.
New program: Lieder of the Twentieth Century with Aribert Reimann in Munich, Salzburg, Paris, and London.
Auf den Spuren der Schubert-Lieder published.

1972   Alfonso in Mozart's *Così fan tutte* in Salzburg, conducted by Karl Böhm.
Schumann "Scenes from *Faust*" in Aldeburgh, conducted by Benjamin Britten.

1973   First recordings as a conductor with the New Philharmonic Orchestra in London: Schubert's Symphonies No. 5 and 8.
Premiere: Gottfried von Einem's *Rosa mystica* in Vienna, conducted by Karl Böhm.
Lieder recitals in Warsaw, Prague, and Budapest, with Sviatoslav Richter.
Further concerts as conductor with the Camerata Academica, Salzburg, the Scottish National Orchestra, and the English Chamber Orchestra (Haydn, Schubert, Schumann).
First meeting with Julia Varady at the rehearsals for Puccini's *Il tabarro* in Munich.

1974   First appearance as a conductor in the USA with the Los Angeles Philharmonic, and concert tour with the Israel Philharmonic Orchestra.
Premiere: Aribert Reimann's *Wolkenloses Christfest*, Ernst Křenek's *Spätlese* (Late Harvest), with the composer at the piano.
Tio Lucas (the miller) in Hugo Wolf's *Der Corregidor* (The Magistrate) at the Deutsche Oper Berlin, conducted by Gerd Albrecht.

1975   Tour as conductor with the Bamberg Symphony (Mendelssohn, Chopin, Schumann). Soloist: Jorge Bolet.
Premiere: Gottfried von Einem's *An die Nachgeborenen* (To Those Who Come After) in New York, conducted by Carlo Maria Giulini.

1976   First Hans Sachs in Wagner's *Die Meistersinger* at the Deutsche Oper Berlin, conducted by Eugen Jochum, directed by Peter Beauvais.
Penderecki *Magnificat*, conducted by the composer.

1977   Richard Strauss's *Arabella* (with Julia Varady for the first time as Arabella) in the National Theater, Munich.
Marries Julia Varady.
Recitals in Moscow and Leningrad (now St. Petersburg) with Sviatoslav Richter.

1978   Premieres: Witold Lutoslawski, *Les espaces du sommeil* (The Spaces of Sleep) in Berlin; Aribert Reimann, *Lear* (with Julia Varady as Cordelia) National Theater, Munich, conducted by Gerd Albrecht.

1979   Berlioz, *La damnation de Faust* (role of Mephisto) at the Salzburg Festival, conducted by Seiji Ozawa.
Wagner's *Die Meistersinger* (for the first time with Julia Varady as Eva) in Munich and Berlin.

1980   Premieres: Ernst Křenek, *The Dissembler* in Berlin, conducted by L. Zagrosek; Aribert Reimann, *Lear-Fragments* in Berlin, conducted by Gerd Albrecht.
First exhibitions of his paintings in Bamberg.

1981   Recordings for the film of *Elektra* after Richard Strauss's opera, in Vienna. Last collaboration with Karl Böhm.
Premiere: Siegfried Matthus, *Porträt des Holofernes* (Portrait of Holofernes) in Leipzig, conducted by Kurt Masur.
Robert Schumann: Das Vokalwerk published.

1982   Verdi's *Aida* (role of Amonasro) with Julia Varady as Aida and Luciano Pavarotti as Radames.
Premieres: Aribert Reimann, *Requiem* in Kiel; Reinhard Schwarz-Schilling, *Die Botschaft* (The Gospel) in Berlin, conducted by R. Bader.

1983   Begins teaching as Professor of Vocal Music at the *Hochschule der Künste* (Academy of the Fine Arts) in Berlin.
Takes over master class for song.
First Lieder recitals with Hartmut Höll as accompanist.
No more operatic performances.
Tour of Japan with exhibition of his paintings: five Japanese towns visited.
Further exhibitions in Munich, Berlin, Feldkirch (Schubertiade).

1984   Premiere: Wolfgang Rihm, *Umsungen* (Re-sung).
        The number of Lieder recitals (with, *inter alia*, Alfred Brendel,
        Hartmut Höll, Aribert Reimann, Wolfgang Sawallisch as accompa-
        nists) rises to thirty-six this year, not counting orchestral concerts,
        oratorios, and concert performances of operas.

1985   *Töne sprechen, Worte klingen* (Music Speaks, Words Resound) pub-
        lished.
        Concert performance (in title role) of Olivier Messiaen's *Saint
        François d'Assise* in Salzburg.
        Premiere: Peter Ruzicka, *Der die Gesänge zerschlug* (The Man Who
        Demolished Songs) in Berlin.
        New Lieder program: Lieder of Alban Berg and Schoenberg.

1986   New Lieder program: Cycles by Britten, Reimann, Fortner, accom-
        panied by Aribert Reimann.
        Frank Martin's *Golgotha* (role of Christ) in Salzburg.

1987   Premiere: Ysang Yun, Fifth Symphony in Berlin, conducted by
        Hans Zender.
        New Lieder program: Hanns Eisler, *Hollywood Tagebuch*
        (Hollywood Diary), accompanied by Aribert Reimann.
        Nachklang: Ansichten und Erinnerungen (Echoes: Views and
        Reminiscences) published.

1988   Premiere: Siegfried Matthus, *Nachtlieder* (Night Songs) with the
        Brandis Quartet in Berlin.
        Concert with students of his master class.

1989   Concert performance of Wagner's *Parsifal* (role of Amfortas) in
        Munich, conducted by Daniel Barenboim.
        Shostakovich: *Suite* in the Kunsthaus (House of Art), Lucerne, con-
        ducted by Vladimir Ashkenazy.
        Premiere: Aribert Reimann, *Shine and Dark*, recorded in Berlin,
        accompanied by the composer.

1990   *Wenn Musik der Liebe Nahrung ist* (If Music Be the Food of Love),
        biography of Pauline Viardot and her circle, published.

1991   First public performance of Aribert Reimann's *Shine and Dark* in
        the Tonhalle, Zurich.

1992   Public reading of correspondence between Richard Strauss and
        Hugo von Hofmannsthal with Gerd Westphal in the Hebbel
        Theater, Berlin.
        Public master course with students of his singing class in the
        Bavarian Academy of Fine Arts in Munich.
        Last Lieder recitals in Berlin, Paris, Düsseldorf, Garmisch-
        Partenkirchen, London, Feldkirch, Munich, Ludwigsburg, Salzburg,
        Leipzig, and Stuttgart.

Once again, Schubert and Brahms (*German Requiem*) in Tokyo.

Last public appearances as a singer: 13 December 1992, Shostakovich, *Michelangelo-Suite* with Hartmut Höll in Stuttgart; 17 December 1992, Mahler, *Lieder eines fahrenden Gesellen* in Berlin, conducted by Vladimir Ashkenazy; 31 December 1992, Mozart, *Marriage of Figaro* (as Almaviva), Finale, Act I, *Così fan tutte* (as Alfonso), excerpts; and Verdi, *Falstaff*, final monologue and fugue "Tutto nel mondo è burla" (All Life Is a Comedy).

Retires from singing.

Weil nicht alle Blütenträume reiften published.

1993 Dietrich Fischer-Dieskau ends his career as a singer.

"Hölderlin-Morning" with students of his master class.

Readings of correspondence between Strauss and Hofmannsthal.

Busoni's *Augustin*, double fugue, played four-handed with Daniel Barenboim in Berlin.

Enoch Arden (Tennyson), melodrama set by Richard Strauss with Gerhard Oppitz as accompanist in the Philharmonie, Cologne.

Fern die Klage des Fauns. Claude Debussy und seine Welt published.

Since Increased activity as conductor, reciter, author, and teacher of
1994 master classes for young singers.

Dietrich Fischer-Dieskau's
Compact Discs

The asterisk * indicates the conductor or the accompanist.

Bach	B Minor Mass, *Richter, DG
Bach	*St. John Passion*, *Rilling, CBS
Bach	*St. Matthew Passion*, *Furtwängler, Monumento Musica
Bach	*St. Matthew Passion* (Bass arias), *Richter, DG
Bach	*St. Matthew Passion* (Jesus), *Richter, DG
Bach	*St. Matthew Passion*, *Klemperer, EMI
Bach	*St. Matthew Passion*, *Karajan, DG
Bach	Christmas Oratorio, *Thomas, EMI
Bach	75 Cantatas, *Richter, DG
Bach	Cantata arias, *Forster, EMI
Bach	Cantatas 158, 212, 211, *Forster, EMI
Bach	Cantatas 211, 212, *Marriner, Philips
Bach	Cantata 140 and *Magnificat*, DG
Barber	*Dover Beach*, *Juilliard, Sony
Bartók	*Duke Bluebeard's Castle*, *Fricsay, DG
Bartók	*Duke Bluebeard's Castle*, *Sawallisch, DG
Beethoven	*Fidelio*, *Fricsay, DG
Beethoven	*Fidelio*, *Bernstein, DG
Beethoven	Lieder, and six Gellert Lieder, *An die ferne Geliebte*, *Moore, Orfeo
Beethoven	Lieder, *Höll, EMI
Belle Epoque, Lieder	Gounod, Saint-Saëns, Bizet, Chabrier, Massenet, Fauré, d'Indy, Chausson, Pierné, Hahn, *Höll, Teldec
Berg	*Lulu*, *Böhm, DG
Berg	*Wozzeck*, *Böhm DG
Berg	Four Lieder, Op. 2, *Reimann, DG
Berg	Jugendlieder (Early Songs), *Reimann, EMI
Berlioz	*Harold in Italy*, Suk, Czech Philharmonic, cond. Dietrich Fischer-Dieskau, Supraphon

Brahms	Fourth Symphony, Czech Philharmonic, cond. Dietrich Fischer-Dieskau, Supraphon
Brahms	*Die schöne Magelone,* *S. Richter, AS-Disc
Brahms	*Die schöne Magelone,* *Moore, EMI
Brahms	*Die schöne Magelone,* S. Richter, EMI
Brahms	German Folk Songs, with Schwarzkopf, *Moore, EMI
Brahms	*A German Requiem,* *Kempe, EMI
Brahms	*Four Serious Songs,* Lieder, *Moore, Orfeo
Brahms	*Four Serious Songs,* Lieder, *Demus, DG
Brahms	*A German Requiem,* *Klemperer, EMI
Brahms	*A German Requiem,* *Barenboim, DG
Brahms	*Liebesliederwalzer* (Love-song Waltzes), *Engel, Sawallisch, DG
Brahms	Lieder, *Höll, Bayer
Brahms	Complete Lieder for male voice, *Sawallisch, Moore, Barenboim, EMI
Brahms	Complete Lieder, with Norman, *Barenboim, DG
Brahms	Complete Lieder, *Barenboim, DG
Brahms	*Liebesliederwalzer,* *Engel, Sawallisch, DG
Britten	*Songs and Proverbs of William Blake,* *Britten, Decca
Britten	*War Requiem,* *Britten, Decca
Britten	*Cantata misericordium,* *Britten, Decca
Busoni	*Doktor Faust,* *Leitner, DG
Busoni	Four Goethe-Lieder, *Moore, The Classical Society
Cimarosa	*Il matrimonio segreto* (The Secret Marriage), *Barenboim, DG
Debussy	*L'enfant prodigue* (The Prodigal Child), *Bertini, Orfeo
Debussy	Chansons et mélodies, *Höll, Claves
Debussy	*Pelléas et Mélisande,* *Kubelik, Orfeo
Dvořák	*Biblische Lieder* (Biblical Songs), *Demus, DG
Eichendorff	Lieder to his poems by Mendelssohn, Schumann, Pfitzner, Walter, Schwarz, Schilling, and Wolf, *Sawallisch, Orfeo
Eisler	*Hollywood Tagebuch* (Hollywood Diary), *Reimann, Teldec
Fauré	*Requiem,* *Barenboim, EMI
Fauré	*Requiem,* *Cluytens, EMI
Gluck	*Iphigenie on Tauris,* *Gardelli, Orfeo
Gluck	*Iphgenie in Aulis,* *Eichhorn, Eurodisc
Handel	*Saul,* *Harnoncourt, Teldec
Hartmann	*Gesangsszene* (Song Scene), *Kubelik, Wergo

Haydn	Cello Concerto in C Major (Boettcher), *Camerata Academica Salzburg, cond. Dietrich Fischer-Dieskau, Orfeo
Haydn	Symphony No. 104 in D Major, Camerata Academica, cond. Dietrich Fischer-Dieskau, Orfeo
Haydn	*The Seasons*, *Marriner, Philips
Haydn	*The Creation*, *Marriner, Philips
Haydn	*The Creation*, *Karajan, DG
Henze	Scenes from *Elegie für junge Liebende* (Elegy for Young Lovers), *Henze, DG
Henze	*Das Floss der Medusa* (The Raft of the Frigate Méduse), *Henze, DG
Hindemith	*Cardillac*, *Keilberth, DG
Hindemith	*Mathis der Maler* (Mathis the Painter), *Kubelik, DG
Hindemith	Scenes from *Mathis der Maler*, *Ludwig, DG
Hindemith	*Requiem*, *Sawallisch, Orfeo
Hindemith	Lieder, *Reimann, Orfeo
Humperdinck	*Hansel and Gretel*, *Eichhorn, Eurodisc
Liszt	Complete Lieder for male voice, *Barenboim, DG
Liszt	Choral Lieder, *Gronostay, Globe
Loewe	Lieder and ballads, *Demus, DG
Loewe	Lieder and ballads, *Höll, Teldec
Lutoslawski	*Les espaces du sommeil* (Spaces of Sleep), *Lutoslawski, Philips
Mahler	*Das Lied von der Erde* (Song of the Earth), *Bernstein, Decca
Mahler	*Das Lied von der Erde*, *Kletzki, EMI
Mahler	*Lieder eines fahrenden Gesellen* (Songs of a Wayfarer), Lieder on Rückert poems, *Kindertotenlieder* (Songs on the Death of Children), *Böhm, DG
Mahler	Four Rückert-Lieder and other Lieder, *Bernstein, PPL
Mahler	Lieder and *Songs of a Wayfarer*, Lieder from *Des Knaben Wunderhorn* (The Youth's Magic Horn), Four Rückert Lieder, *Bernstein, CBS
Mahler	*The Youth's Magic Horn*, with Schwarzkopf, *Szell, EMI
Mahler	*Songs of a Wayfarer, The Youth's Magic Horn*, *Barenboim, Sony
Mahler	Symphony No. 8 ("Symphony of a Thousand"), *Kubelik, DG
Mahler	*Songs of a Wayfarer*, *Furtwängler, Priceless

Mahler	*Songs of a Wayfarer,* *Furtwängler; *Songs on the Death of Children,* *Kempe; Five Rückert Lieder, *Barenboim, EMI
Martin	Three fragments from *The Tempest,* *Ansermet, Cascavelle
Mendelssohn	*Elijah,* Frühbeck de Burgos, EMI
Mendelssohn	*St. Paul,* *Frühbeck de Burgos, EMI
Mendelssohn	Lieder, *Sawallisch, EMI
Mendelssohn	Lieder not in the above collection, *Höll, Claves
Gerald Moore Tribute	Two Lieder by Schubert, two by Schumann, five by Mendelssohn, two by Haydn, *Moore, EMI
Mozart	*The Magic Flute,* *Böhm, DG
Mozart	*The Magic Flute* (Speaker), *Solti, Decca
Mozart	*The Magic Flute,* *Fricsay, DGG
Mozart	*Requiem,* *Barenboim, EMI
Mozart	*Don Giovanni,* *Böhm, DG
Mozart	*Don Giovanni,* *Fricsay, DG
Mozart	*Marriage of Figaro,* *Böhm, DG
Mozart	*Marriage of Figaro* (live), *Böhm, GDS
Mozart	*Marriage of Figaro,* *Maazel, Movimento Musica
Mozart	*Marriage of Figaro,* *Barenboim, EMI
Mozart	*Marriage of Figaro,* *Fricsay, DG
Mozart	Scenes from *Figaro* (in German), *Leitner, DG
Mozart	Coronation Mass and Vespers, *Jochum, EMI
Mozart	Six Notturni, *Leister, Orfeo
Offenbach	*Tales of Hoffmann,* *Wallberg, EMI
Orff	*Carmina burana,* *Jochum, DG
Puccini	*Tosca,* *Maazel, Decca
Puccini	Scenes from *La Bohème* (in German), *Erede, DG
Pfitzner	*Palestrina,* *Kubelik, DG
Pfitzner	Lieder, *Engel, Reimann, Reutter, EMI
Pfitzner	Lieder, *Höll, Orfeo
Ravel	Chansons et mélodies, *Höll, Orfeo
Reger	Songs with orchestra, *Albrecht, Orfeo
Reichardt	Selected songs, *Graf, Orfeo
Reimann	*Unrevealed,* *Cherubini Quartet, Orfeo
Reimann	*Shine and Dark,* *Reimann, Orfeo
Reimann	Three poems by Michelangelo, *Reimann, Teldec
Rheinberger	*The Star of Bethlehem,* *Heger, EMI
Rihm	*Umsungen* (Resung), *Bour, Harmonia Mundi
Romanticism, Lieder of	(with several instruments) Berlioz, Hermann, Reissinger, Kraussold, Donizetti, Wolf, etc., *Klöcker, Orfeo

Rossini	*William Tell,* *Rossi, Clacque
Rossini	*Petite Messe solennelle* (Little Solemn Mass), *Sawallisch, Ariola Eurodisc
Ruzicka	*Der die Gesänge zerschlug* (He Who Demolished Songs), *Bour, Harmonia Mundi
Salzburg	Lieder recitals, scenes from operas, orchestral concerts, *Moore, Richter, Sawallisch, Mehta, Furtwängler, Orfeo (Salzburg)
Schoeck	*Unter Sternen* (Under Stars), *Höll, Claves
Schoeck	*Das stille Leuchten* (Quiet Gleam), *Höll, Claves
Schoeck	*Lebendig begraben* (Buried Alive), *Rieger, Claves
Schoeck	*Das holde Bescheiden* (Divine Modesty), *Shirai, Höll, Claves
Schoenberg	Lieder, *Reimann, EMI
Schoenberg	Lieder, *Reimann, DG
Schubert	German Mass, *Salve regina,* Psalms 23/92, *Hymn to the Holy Spirit,* *Sawallisch, EMI
Schubert	Mass in A-flat Major, Mass in C Major, *Sawallisch, EMI
Schubert	*Die schöne Müllerin,* *Moore, EMI
Schubert	*Die schöne Müllerin,* *Moore, DG
Schubert	*Schwanengesang* (Swan Song), *Moore, EMI
Schubert	*Schwanengesang,* *Brendel, Philips
Schubert	*Schwanengesang,* *Billing, Melodram
Schubert	Lieder recital tours, *Richter, DG
Schubert	Lieder, *Brendel, Philips
Schubert	All Lieder for male voice, *Moore, DG
Schubert	Lieder, *Moore, Orfeo
Schubert	Lieder, *Moore/Engel, EMI
Schubert	*Winterreise* (Winter's Journey), *Moore, EMI
Schubert	*Winterreise,* *Moore, DG
Schubert	*Winterreise,* *Brendel, Philips
Schubert	*Winterreise,* *Billing
Schubert	*Winterreise,* *Klust, Melodram
Schubert	*Winterreise,* *Reutter, Verona
Schubert	*Winterreise,* *Barenboim, DG
Schubert	*Winterreise,* *Perahia, Sony
Schubert	Lieder recital in Salzburg, *S. Richter, Orfeo
Schumann	Lieder to poems by Eichendorff and Kerner, *Moore, Orfeo
Schumann	*Liederkreis* (Song Cycle), Op. 39, *Dichterliebe* (A Poet's Love), Op. 48, *Brendel, Philips

Schumann	*Dichterliebe, Liederkreis,* Op. 39, and Lieder from *Myrten* (Myrtles), *Eschenbach, DG
Schumann	*Requiem,* Op. 148, *Requiem for Mignon,* Op. 98b, *Klee, EMI
Schumann	*Scenes from Faust,* *Klee, EMI
Schumann	*Scenes from Faust,* *Britten, Decca
Schumann	*Scenes from Faust,* *Boulez, Harmonics
Shostakovich	Suite on poems by Michelangelo, *Reimann, Teldec
Shostakovich	Symphony No. 14, *Haitink, Decca
Spohr	*Jessonda,* *Albrecht, Orfeo
Spohr	Lieder, *Höll, Orfeo
Stephan	*Liebeszauber* (Love's Magic), *Zender, Schwann
Strauss, J.	*Die Fledermaus* (The Bat), *Boskovsky, EMI
Strauss, J.	*Der Zigeunerbaron* (The Gypsy Baron), *Boskovsky, EMI
Strauss, R.	*Capriccio* (Olivier), *Sawallisch, EMI
Strauss, R.	*Capriccio* (Count), *Böhm, DG
Strauss, R.	*Elektra,* *Böhm, DG
Strauss, R.	*Der Rosenkavalier,* *Böhm, DG
Strauss, R.	*Arabella,* *Keilberth, DG
Strauss, R.	*Arabella,* *Sawallisch, Orfeo
Strauss, R.	*Intermezzo,* *Sawallisch, EMI
Strauss, R.	*Ariadne on Naxos,* *Masur, Philips
Strauss, R.	*Salome,* *Böhm, DG
Strauss, R.	Lieder, *Sawallisch, DG
Strauss, R.	All Lieder for male voice, *Moore, EMI
Verdi	*Don Carlos,* *Solti, Decca
Verdi	*Rigoletto,* *Kubelik, DG
Verdi	*Falstaff,* *Bernstein, CBS
Verdi	*Macbeth,* *Sawallisch, Frequenz
Verdi	*Macbeth,* *Gardelli, Decca
Verdi	Scenes from *La Traviata* (in German), *Bartoletti, DG
Verdi	*La Traviata,* *Maazel, Decca
Wagner	Scenes from *The Flying Dutchman,* *Konwitschny, EMI
Wagner	*Tannhäuser,* *Konwitschny, EMI
Wagner	*Tannhäuser,* *Keilberth, Melodram
Wagner	Scenes from *Tannhäuser,* *Gerdes, DG
Wagner	*Lohengrin* (Herald), *Jochum, Classica
Wagner	*Lohengrin* (Herald), *Solti, Decca
Wagner	*Lohengrin* (Telramund), *Kempe, EMI
Wagner	*Tristan and Isolde,* *Furtwängler, EMI
Wagner	*Tristan and Isolde,* *C. Kleiber, DG

Wagner	*Parsifal*, *Knappertsbusch, Classica
Wagner	*Parsifal*, *Solti, Decca
Wagner	*Die Meistersinger*, *Jochum, DG
Wagner	*Das Rheingold*, *Karajan, DG
Wagner	*Götterdämmerung* (Twilight of the Gods), *Solti, Decca
Weber	Selected Lieder, *Höll, Claves
Wolf	Early Lieder, *Höll, Claves
Wolf	*Der Corregidor* (The Magistrate), *Albrecht, Schwann
Wolf	*Spanish Song Book*, *Moore, DG
Wolf	*Italian Song Book*, *Moore, EMI
Wolf	*Italian Song Book*, *Werba, Orfeo
Wolf	Lieder to poems by Mörike, *Moore, Orfeo
Wolf	All Mörike Lieder, *Moore, EMI
Wolf	Orchestral Lieder, *Soltesz, Orfeo
Wolf	Lieder to poems by Mörike and Goethe, *Barenboim, DG
Wolf	All Lieder for the male voice, *Barenboim, DG
Zelter	Lieder, *Reimann, Orfeo
Zemlinsky	Lyrical Symphony, *Maazel, DG

Selected Books by
Dietrich Fischer-Dieskau

Fischer-Dieskau, D. 1971. *Auf den Spuren der Schubert-Lieder*. Wiesbaden: Brockhaus. Translated into English by Kenneth S. Whitton in the UK as *Schubert: A Biographical Study of His Songs*. London: Cassell, 1976, and in the US as *Schubert's Songs: A Biographical Study*. New York: Knopf, 1977.

Fischer-Dieskau, Dietrich. 1974. *Wagner und Nietzsche: der Mystagoge und sein Abtrünniger*. Stuttgart: Deutsche Verlags-Anstalt (DVA). Translated into English by Joachim Neugroschel as *Wagner and Nietzsche*. US: Seabury Press, Inc., 1976; London: Sidgwick and Jackson, 1978.

1976. *The Fischer-Dieskau Book of Lieder: The Original Texts of Over 750 Songs*. New York: Limelight Editions.

Fischer-Dieskau, Dietrich. 1981. *Robert Schumann, Wort und Musik. Das Vokalwerk*. Stuttgart: DVA. Translated into English by Reinhard G. Pauly as *Robert Schumann. Words and Music: The Vocal Compositions*. Portland, Oregon: Amadeus Press, 1988.

Fischer-Dieskau, Dietrich. 1985. *Töne sprechen, Worte klingen: Zur Geschichte und Interpretation des Gesangs* (Music Speaks, Words Resound: On the History and Interpretation of Vocal Music). Stuttgart / München: DVA / Piper.

Fischer-Dieskau, Dietrich. 1988. *Nachklang*. Stuttgart: Deutsche Verlags-Anstalt (DVA). English trans. Ruth Hein, *Echoes of a Lifetime*. London: Macmillan, 1989. English trans., first paperback ed. *Reverberations: The Memoirs of Dietrich Fischer-Dieskau*. New York: Fromm International, 1989.

Fischer-Dieskau, Dietrich. 1990. *Wenn Musik der Liebe Nahrung ist: Kunstlerschicksale im 19. Jahrhundert* (If Music Be the Food of Love:

Artistic Destinies in the Nineteenth Century). Stuttgart: Deutsche Verlags-Anstalt (DVA).

Fischer-Dieskau, Dietrich. 1992. *Weil nicht alle Blütenträume reiften: Johann Friedrich Reichardt: Hofkapellmeister dreier Preussenkönige* (Because Not All My Blossoming Dreams Ripened? Johann Friedrich Reichardt, Court Music Master to Three Prussian Kings). Stuttgart: Deutsche Verlags-Anstalt (DVA).

Fischer-Dieskau, Dietrich. 1993. *Fern die Klage des Fauns. Claude Debussy und seine Welt* (From Afar the Plaint of the Faun. Claude Debussy and His World). Stuttgart: Deutsche Verlags-Anstalt (DVA).

Fischer-Dieskau, Dietrich. 1996. *Schubert und seine Lieder.* Stuttgart: Deutsche Verlags-Anstalt (DVA).

Sources of Photographs

Ilse Buhs, pages 51, 54, 90 (right), 91 (left), 132, 146 (left), 147 (left)
Photo Ellinger, page 129
Foto Fayer, page 139
Gewandhaus, Leipzig, page 181
Anne Kirchbach, page 180 (right)
Heinz Köster, page 147 (right)
Krapich Photo, page 189
Dr. F. Laubenthal, page 9
Siegfried Lauterwasser, page 201
Peter Mathis, pages 298, 299
Klaus Rudolph, page 270
Oda Sternberg, pages 178, 180 (left)
Felicitas Timpe, page 208
Sabine Toepffer, pages 90 (left), 91 (right), 149, 160, 163, 164
Nikolaus Walter, pages 117, 229, 251, 261
Hans Wunschel, pages 31, 40

All other illustrations were supplied by Dietrich Fischer-Diskau and by Deutsche Verlags-Anstalt, Stuttgart.

Index of Names